Distance, Theatre, and the Public Voice, 1750–1850

Distance, Theatre, and the Public Voice, 1750–1850

Melynda Nuss

DISTANCE, THEATRE, AND THE PUBLIC VOICE, 1750–1850
Copyright © Melynda Nuss, 2012

All rights reserved.

First published in 2012 by PALGRAVE MACMILLAN® in the United States—a division of St. Martin's Press LLC, 175 Fifth Avenue, New York, NY 10010.

Where this book is distributed in the UK, Europe and the rest of the world, this is by Palgrave Macmillan, a division of Macmillan Publishers Limited, registered in England, company number 785998, of Houndmills, Basingstoke, Hampshire RG21 6XS.

Palgrave Macmillan is the global academic imprint of the above companies and has companies and representatives throughout the world.

Palgrave® and Macmillan® are registered trademarks in the United States, the United Kingdom, Europe and other countries.

ISBN: 978-1-137-29140-0

Library of Congress Cataloging-in-Publication Data is available from the Library of Congress.

A catalogue record of the book is available from the British Library.

Design by Scribe Inc.

First edition: December 2012

10 9 8 7 6 5 4 3 2 1

Transferred to Digital Printing in 2013

For Jane Moody

Contents

Acknowledgments		ix
Introduction: Impossible Theatres: Distance, Theatre, and the Romantic Voice		1
1	Pantomime: Killing the Drama in Order to Save It	13
2	Spaces with Meaning: Crossing from Stage to Closet in Byron and Inchbald	33
3	Man Seeing: Wordsworth and the Theatrical Voice	59
4	"The Great Master of Ideal Mimicry": Shelley's Struggle with the Actor	119
5	Creative Spectacle: Hunt, Hazlitt, De Quincey	151
Conclusion: Reaching a Mass Audience Face to Face		171
Notes		177
Works Cited		183
Index		193

Acknowledgments

I have been lucky to come into the study of Romantic drama just late enough to find the fields well-tilled but early enough to take advantage of the sense of camraderie among the scholars who broke the ground. I cannot begin to express how much I have benefited from the helpful comments of scholars like Catherine Burroughs, Frederick Burwick, Jeffrey N. Cox, Thomas Crochunis, Michael Gamer, Greg Kucich, Jonathan Mulrooney, Daniel O'Quinn, Marjean Purinton, Charles Rzepka, and especially the late Jane Moody. I realize that it is unusual to dedicate a first book to a fellow scholar, but this group has been so close that at times it has felt like a scholarly family. Jane's early death has been a shock to all of us. I hope this book is the first of many that will show that her work lives on.

I was also lucky to begin this project working with Kurt Heinzelman at the University of Texas at Austin. Everyone knows that Kurt is a gentleman, a scholar, and a poet, but only a few of us are fortunate to know what rare skills he has as a dissertation advisor. He offered help when I needed help and left me alone when I needed to be left alone. With this book I pay him a debt that I have owed for many years. I also owe thanks to the late Thomas McFarland, whose lectures at Princeton University put me in a trance that has lasted almost thirty years, and to Mark Kipperman, whose insight and intelligence inspired me to study literature as a profession.

Some portions of this book have appeared in earlier versions elsewhere. The discussion of Marino Faliero in Chapter 2 began its life as "'The Gory Head Rolls Down the Giants' Steps!': The Return of the Physical in Byron's Marino Faliero," in *European Romantic Review* 12.2 (Spring 2001), and all of Chapter 5 appeared as "Creative Spectacle: Hunt, Hazlitt, De Quincey" in *European Romantic Review* 21.2 (2010). These sections are used with the kind permission of the *European Romantic Review* and Taylor and Francis, http://www.tandfonline.com. The section on *The Borderers* in Chapter 3 appeared as "'Look in My Face': The Dramatic Ethics of The Borderers" in *Studies in Romanticism* 41.4 (Winter 2004), and is used with their permission. I am grateful for the insightful comments of the editors and readers at those journals. Thanks also go to the staff at Palgrave and Scribe, Inc. for making the road to production smooth, and to Rory Lalwen and the Westminster City Archives for the cover image.

For glasses of wine and fine conversation, I'm indebted to Romanticists Elisa Beshero Bondar and Samantha Webb; closer to home I've depended on my colleagues at the University of Texas Pan American, especially David Anshen and Caroline Miles. My close friends have helped me even from afar, especially Julie Garbus, David Gold, and Felicia Steele. Special thanks go to Chris RB Fay, who gives me a dose of humanity whenever I need it.

Love goes to my mom and dad, my brothers, all my nieces and nephews, and to my grandmother, who waited 101 years to see this book.

And finally, I must acknowledge José Skinner, who brings me a new world every morning.

Introduction

Impossible Theatres

Distance, Theatre, and the Romantic Voice

In 1795, the Haymarket Theatre began its season with a light-hearted song that sums up a choice faced by late eighteenth- and early nineteenth-century performers:

> When people appear
> Quite unable to hear,
> 'Tis undoubtedly needless to talk; ...
> 'Twere better they began
> On the new invented plan,
> And with Telegraphs transmitted us the plot: ...
> But our House here's so small
> That we've no need to bawl,
> And the summer will rapidly pass,
> So we hope you'll think fit
> To hear the Actors a bit,
> Till the Elephants and Bulls come from grass:
> Then let Shakespeare and Jonson go hang, go hang!
> Let your Otways and Drydens go drown!
> Given [sic] them Elephants and White bulls enough,
> And they'll take in all the town,
>   Brave boys![1]

The song makes a boast that theatregoers of the late eighteenth and early nineteenth centuries would have been quite familiar with: the Haymarket, unlike its competition at Drury Lane and Covent Garden, had kept its theatre small. The audience is close enough to the actors to hear their voices and see their faces—"without the aid of glasses or grimaces," as another waggish prologue put it.[2] But more than simply advertising the technical advantages of a small theatre, the Haymarket invokes an entire theatrical culture that is in the process of being lost. The atmosphere is conversational. The actors and audience "talk" rather than "bawling," passing as pleasant a summer afternoon at the Haymarket (presumably) as the elephants and white bulls do in their grass.[3] The experience harks back to a simpler time, associated with the great names of English theatre: Shakespeares and Jonsons, Otways and Drydens. Patrons at the "little theatre" could be assured that not only were they watching high-culture entertainment, but they were watching it in an intimate setting, face to face, just the way that their ancestors did.

But far from presenting the alternative as horrifying, as so many rants concerning the larger theatres were wont to do, the Haymarket makes distance sound exciting. True, the prologue rehearses a common trope: the larger houses make theatre a less human experience. Telegraphs transmit the plots; elephants and white bulls replace the actors. But the animals and machines have the modern advantage of size and speed. The larger theatres are a "new invented plan," using the latest technology—the "telegraph" doubtless referred to Claude Chappe's system of semaphore towers, which was developed in 1794. And the elephants and white bulls represent strength domesticated—exotic animals tamely coming in from grass. Most of all, the song makes it clear that the "new invented plan" is here to stay. Audiences might enjoy the Little Theatre in the Haymarket for the summer, but when winter comes and the bulls and elephants have enjoyed their grass, audiences will naturally cycle into the new relationship, effortlessly moving from the close-up entertainment of the old to the more distant theatres of the new.

I tell this story to introduce one of my central contentions: distance mattered to authors in the Romantic period. It obviously mattered to theatrical authors, whose success depended on whether audiences could see or hear their works. But looking beyond the theatre, we can see a concern with distance even in the most canonical works. Wordsworth sees Tintern Abbey from a secluded spot on an adjoining hillside; Coleridge establishes a bond with his friends while imprisoned in a lime-tree bower; Elizabeth in *Pride and Prejudice* feels closest to Mr. Darcy when she sees Pemberley from afar. Porphyro in "Eve of St. Agnes" voyeuristically observes Madeline from her closet, only to find that she is just as far away when he sits at her bedside. The Romantic period is full of silent watchers and distant prospects, of strange and hallucinatory intimacies achieved over time and space. Telegraphs, the wags at the Haymarket might say, might be the best explanation for the way the Romantic soul connects to its object, or the Romantic writer to her reader.

Why distance? In this book, I argue that the debate over distance in the Romantic period—in both theatre and print—was a way for writers to work out the difficulties of connecting with a new mass audience. As authors moved from a world where it was possible to envision literature as a comfortable coterie into a more modern world of mass culture, debates over distance in the theatre became a way to rethink the changing relationship between authors and their audiences. Authors could imagine a bucolic world of pleasant conversation, where actors and audiences were so close that they could hear each other's voices and see each other's faces, or a technologically advanced world where mass audiences could be reached from a distance by telegraph and the English could enjoy exotic pleasures like elephants and white bulls. Through the wonders of print and the magic of new theatrical techniques, they might even imagine that they could give their audiences both. In the tumult of change, they might fear that they could give them neither.

Theatre, then, comes to symbolize a whole complex of social relations for authors in the late eighteenth and early nineteenth centuries. As Betsy Bolton has shown, theater became a way to talk about shaping Britain's different classes into a nation. If pit, boxes, and galleries could shape themselves into a harmonious audience, perhaps Britain, too, could work as a harmonious whole. Jane Moody has shown how the "legitimacy" of the theatre played a powerful role in questioning the "legitimacy" of class, social structures, and governments. It is not surprising, then, that theatre became a screen on which late eighteenth- and early nineteenth-century authors projected the difficulties and contractions of reaching a mass culture. The distance between actor and audience came to represent not only the loss of a theatrical experience but the growing distance between author and reader. The fear of a loss of interaction between audience members signals a larger fear of a lack of interaction in the growing culture of spectacle. Theatre gets blamed for mass culture's dangers, failures, and dislocations, but it is also the form that authors used to think through new ways of relating to a fragmenting and expanding public. In dramas both stage and closet, in theatrical criticism, and in theatrical situations imagined in print, authors experimented with different ways of connecting with readers separated in space and time—readers too distant to be reached even with telegraphs. In the process, they imagined impossible theatres—theatres that preserved old notions of theatrical and coterie intimacy while gaining the reach of mass distribution.

"Impossible," for me, also signals the range of creative solutions that authors found to the problem of distance. While authors used the stage to visualize the relationship between author and audience, their experimentation went far beyond the stage itself and into more and more "theatres" constructed on stage and in print. While distance might seem fairly fixed, even within the confines of the physical theatre authors and actors found ways to play with their distance from the audience. Romantic dramas are full of illusions and shifts of perspective that adjust the relationship between actors and audience, sometimes even within a single scene. Indeed, this "impossibility" might be one reason why so many Romantic dramas seem so congenitally "unstageable," even though many were evidently intended for the stage.

But the theatre is not the only—or even the primary—place that authors used as a way of experimenting with the relationships between writer and reader. Dramatic monologues, scenes of spectatorship, closet dramas, and dramas staged in novels and poetry are all ways of experimenting with stages that might not exist. Even a single work might experiment with several different theatrical situations, flitting from one impossible theatre to another. Indeed, we might see the entire debate over *whether* to use the theatre as a way of rethinking the relationship between actor and audience. Romantic authors' love/hate relationship with the stage shows both the theatre's power as a way of thinking about the relationship between authors and their audiences and authors' profound dissatisfaction with it as a solution.

The fact that authors could move so easily from the physicality of the theatre to the abstraction of the printed page shows an unusual closeness between theatre and public writing. By now, we are luckily past the days where critics could declare that Romanticism is inherently "undramatic," where simply to talk about the drama required an excuse or an explanation of terms. But we have yet to realize exactly how close the written and theatrical worlds actually were. We already know that most of the writers we know as "Romantic" wrote dramas—Wordsworth intended one of his first professional projects for the stage, Coleridge had a popular hit with *Remorse*, Scott began his career translating German drama and twice tried to get his own plays staged in London, and John Keats spoke of all his writing as apprentice work that could someday "nerve me up to the writing of a few fine Plays." We know, courtesy of Jonathan Mulrooney, that Keats modeled his poetic persona on the actor Edmund Kean, and from Emily Hodgson Anderson that women writers like Eliza Haywood, Frances Burney, Elizabeth Inchbald and Maria Edgeworth used their stage personas to express identities and emotions that otherwise would have been difficult to express.

But theatre did not merely serve print authors as a model or an alternative form of expression. The close interchange between theatre and print is possible because both writing and theatre were undergoing similar cultural stresses. In print, as literacy grew and the demand for print expanded, authors faced the challenge of adjusting to a larger and more diffuse audience. The Romantic period was, according to Bertrand Bronson, the time that authors gradually begin to "write to an indefinite body of readers, personally undifferentiated and unknown,"[4] an age, as Jon Klancher has said, where "perhaps ... the last time ... it was still possible to conceive the writer's relation to an audience in terms of personal compact."[5] As Klancher notes, Romantic authors addressed an audience fragmented by class and increasingly unknown: "The small, deliberative, strategic world of early nineteenth-century reading and writing still allowed for Wordsworth to imagine the reading of a poem as a personal exchange of 'power' between writer and reader, for Shelley to imagine rather intensely the 'five or six readers' of *Prometheus Unbound*, or for Coleridge to scan the audience of his plays and to recognize those who had also attended his lectures."[6] Authors would try to recover the feeling of personal contact through coterie and avant-garde groups, through writing communities like the *Blackwoods* circle, and through real and imaginary interchanges between correspondents in various journals and reviews.[7] In many of these efforts there was a feeling of recuperation—a feeling that old ways of relating could be revived, or that the new ways offered freedoms that more than compensated. But the way that literature reached its audience—and the audience itself—had changed.

Theatre was undergoing many of the same stresses. Although theatre had been a traditional part of British life for centuries, the late eighteenth and early nineteenth centuries saw an expansion and diversification of the audience almost as large as that which was occurring in print. London, the center of theatrical activity, was bursting at the seams. Between 1700 and 1800 its population increased from

575,000 to almost 900,000; on top of that, as the center of trade and commerce, many people who did not consider themselves Londoners lived in the city temporarily or passed through it. The two "major" houses, Drury Lane and Covent Garden, which by law enjoyed a monopoly on five-act spoken comedies and tragedies, were rebuilt and remodeled several times to accommodate the growing demand. In 1660, Christopher Wren's original Drury Lane held 650 persons; in 1794, the remodeled theatre held more than 3,600.[8] Summer theatres were authorized at the Haymarket and Sadler's Wells to accommodate some of the additional demand, and "illegitimate theatres" that offered entertainments that skirted the edges of the law—Astley's, the Surrey, the Coburg, the Adelphi, the Olympic—grew up in and around the city.[9] The late eighteenth century saw a flood of theatre openings in the provinces—Richmond, Bath, and Tunbridge Wells. When we add the regular public performances at inns and fairs, theatricals in private households, and streets filled with animal exhibits, rare shows, and performances of all kinds, there was scarcely a segment of British culture that theatre did not reach.

Theatre's expansion provided an interesting mirror through which to view the changes taking place in both print and theatre. First there was the simple fact that the theatre was an older, more prestigious medium that could give public importance to arguments that had their roots in novels, journals, and chapbooks. Sanctioned by royal patent in the reign of Charles II, carrying the great names of Shakespeare, Garrick, Betterton, Sheridan, and Otway, theatre was undoubtedly part of British public culture. For champions of the ancients, the theatre was the home of Aeschylus, Sophocles, and Aristotle. For writers looking for a British literary tradition, theatre was the home of Marlowe, Jonson, and Shakespeare. Authors with concerns about the expansion of print might find a more receptive audience if they phrased those complaints in terms of complaints about the theatre.

Furthermore, theatre's familiarity and physicality gave writers a concrete means to express developments in print, which they did not yet have a language for discussing. Without an easy language for talking about audience groups, space gave writers an easy way to equate psychic distance with physical distance. The physical changes in the theatre provided a way of making less visible distances between print authors and their multiple and scattered audiences concrete. There was already a tradition of equating the relations between social groups with their proximity in the theatre. Pit, boxes, and galleries were considered democratic when they intermingled; antagonism in the theatres signaled stress between the social orders. It was only a short jump to think of the physical distance between actors and audiences as a metaphor for the difficulty reaching new audiences.

The theatre also provided a compelling metaphor for authors' fears about playing to a mass audience: the loss of the human face and voice. In 1666, the forestage area at the newly remodeled Drury Lane theatre jutted at least 20 feet into the auditorium, so that, as Colley Cibber put it, "the Voice was then more in the Centre of the House."[10] There was little separation between actor and audience. Actors generally came outside the proscenium arch and toward the audience to deliver their lines. Patrons of all ages sat on the stage; the backstage area was open to young gentlemen of fashion who, by hereditary right, made their way backstage and sometimes even onstage to flirt with the actresses. Sets and costumes were rudimentary, props were all but unheard of; in terms of costuming, the actors looked more or less like the audience. By the beginning of the Romantic period, however, the major theatre houses had begun to change. The area in front of the proscenium arch gradually shrunk back from 20 feet at Drury Lane in 1674, to 15 feet in 1774, to 10 feet in 1818, so that finally, by 1843, an advertisement for the Haymarket could speak of "the useless portion of the Stage in front of the Curtain" that had been enclosed for orchestra stalls.[11] Garrick evicted the backstage beaux in 1747 and got rid of the onstage seating in 1762. Theatre designers began to think of the proscenium arch as a gilded picture frame. While actors familiar with the old style would occasionally come forward to deliver their lines, stage directions began to call for the action to move behind the proscenium, and for actors to interact with each other rather than with the audience. As theatre historian Allardyce Nicoll put it, the major theatres had evolved into "a structure composed of two basic parts, one reserved for the audience and the other for the actors, two virtually separate worlds divided almost literally by an iron curtain."[12]

What was lost was a sense of social interaction between actor and audience. Sir Walter Scott called for a smaller playhouse where "we can hear our old friends with comfort."[13] Leigh Hunt, in one of his numerous pleas for a smaller theatre, mourns "our pleasure at sitting [at the theatre] and coming as it were into social contact with the dramatis personae."[14] Even the most joking commentary stressed the audience's inability to see the actors' "real faces" and hear their real voices. Samuel Arnold's welcoming address for the (smaller) Opera House in the Strand in 1816 jeered,

> Pray, how d'ye like our House? Is't snug and easy?
> Upon our life we've done our best to please ye!
> You all can *hear* and *see*, I hope—Yes—all!
> Those are rare virtues of a House that's small!
> For such, are *Actors* ever bound to pray,
> Where you can see the *stage* and *hear* the *Play*.
> Where you with ease can mark our real faces.
> Without the aid of glasses or grimaces!
> And each inflection of the voice is heard,
> Your ears preserved, and our poor lungs are spared![15]

Just as in the Haymarket prologue quoted earlier, the human interaction has been converted into an interaction produced and enabled by machines. The "real faces," the natural inflection of the voice, and even the audience's poor ears and lungs have been replaced by technological aids: "glasses and grimaces." F. G. Tomlins, in his 1840 *Brief View of the English Drama*, repeats the technological analogy: spectators "cannot see the countenances of the performers without the aid of a pocket telescope."[16]

Amid these fears of technological intrusion, it is easy to hear something like the Romantic voice emerging. John Philip Kemble's memoirs recount a moment when a patron in the farthest gallery cried out "We can't hear," and Kemble responded "I will *raise* my voice, and the GALLERIES shall *hear* me. (Great tumult.)"[17] Theatre historian W. J. Lawrence remembers, "For the old-fashioned proscenium arch was substituted a gilded picture frame, remote from the footlights, over which the actors were forbidden to step. Grumblings both loud and deep were heard among the players over their various deprivations, and finally old Dowton, pluckier than the rest, broke into open rebellion. 'Don't tell me of frames and pictures!' he exclaimed, with choler. 'If I can't be heard by the audience in the frame, I'll walk out of it.' And out he came."[18] In this scenario the voice wins out over its technical circumstances. Just like Wordsworth asserting his voice over the din of "gross and violent stimulants," or Byron imposing his own hero over the rabble that cloy the gazettes with cant, the poet/actor breaks through the communicative frame, commanding universal attention and acclaim.

But asserting oneself over the crowd was not the only pose that the theatre offered to the Romantic author. Just as the "legitimate" theatre was only one type of theatre among many in Romantic-era England, the actor speaking to a distant crowd was only one way to think about the author's role. Late eighteenth-century and early nineteenth-century England was full of theatrical models to riff on and to imitate. Street shows, performances at inns and fairs, theatricals in private homes, panoramas, dioramas, magic lantern shows, tiny theatres that held only a few hundred, giant stages reinforced to hold horse charges or giant tanks of water, direct addresses by actors and spectacular scenery designed to transport viewers to wonders overseas: all of these formed a part of England's theatrical repertory. Even the theatres of the recent past were present through the memories of actors and the genre of theatrical memoirs. Authors who wanted to imagine a more intimate setting could look to shows in private rooms or theatricals in private houses; authors looking for a chaotic public might imagine the crowds at Bartholomew Fair. Authors wanting a conversational atmosphere might look to smaller houses like the Haymarket or the Opera House in the Strand, or recall Colly Cibber's nostalgic remarks about a time when the "voice was then in the center of the house"; authors in love with the grand might evoke spectacular sets and costumes, horse charges, and recreations of world historical events.

Most interestingly, though, Romantic authors often took the freedom of print and the evolution of new theatrical techniques as an invitation to weave together different theatrical models. Oscillating between closeness and distance, public and private—even stage and page—authors wove together a persona that tried to bridge the intimacy of the old theatre with the reach of the new. We can see strange fusions of theatres everywhere. Joanna Baillie's famous passage from her introduction to *Plays on the Passions*, for example, begins by imagining real theatrical situations—public executions, the sacrifice of prisoners of war—but quickly shifts from an actual theatre to an impossible one: "lift[ing] up the roof of [a prisoner's] dungeon, like the *Diable boiteux,* and look upon a criminal the night before he suffers, in his still hours of privacy."[19] Baillie bridges the public force of an execution with the privacy of solitary contemplation to create a new kind of theatre—one possible only in the imagination.

Baillie's situation is not an uncommon one. Romantic authors are famous for avoiding the stage, but it would be more accurate to say that they circled around the stage, using it and testing it, trying to find its possibilities and its limits. In its own way, this book is its own series of tests. What follows here is a series of case studies exploring how authors experimented with theatre across a variety of genres and media. In a variety of genres, and with a variety of authors, I want to sketch some of the possibilities that theatre offered authors and some of the fears and hesitations that it engendered. How did authors manipulate distance and perspective? What did they gain from using the theatre, and what did they fear?

Each chapter, then, traces the way that authors used theatre to think about relationships between actor and audience in a different medium. The book begins in the theatre, where even the popular drama had to adjust to changing audience conditions. Chapter 1, "Pantomime: Killing the Drama in Order to Save It," examines the way that the pantomime tried to take advantage of larger audiences and larger spaces while maintaining the intimacy that had made it an audience favorite. But even though much of the rhetoric surrounding the theatre preached that one type of drama had to "die" for a new theatre to arise, the pantomime actually made its fortune by combining sections that simulated the intimate audience relationships of the smaller theatres with sections that took advantage of the larger theatres' ability to produce grand spectacles. Rather than "killing" the old drama, the pantomime drew audiences by combining the old and the new.

Such combinations of old and new were not always as successful, however, and even when they were they created a good deal of anxiety. Which form would be most effective at reaching an audience? Would making the wrong choice damage the message? Chapter 2, "Spaces with Meaning," revisits Romantic authors' vacillation between stage drama and closet drama and finds that much of authors' dithering between stage and page is actually a manifestation of their uncertainty about which medium would forge the most intimate connection with the audience. The chapter looks at two authors familiar with the stage, Elizabeth Inchbald and Lord Byron, who, at crucial points when their political impact was most important, turned away from their usual media. Inchbald, a stage dramatist, wrote her only closet drama; Byron, usually a closet dramatist, wrote dramas suited for the stage. Looking at these dramas reveals authors thinking through the political impact of the concrete: cultures of familial closeness and spectacular leadership, comforts of homes and enclosed spaces, and possibilities of open public spaces. Above all, Byron and Inchbald look to define a new sort of "public" space, either in the stage or in the closet.

This public space is important even for authors who abandon theatre altogether and write almost entirely for print. Chapter 3, "Man Seeing," argues that William Wordsworth's quintessentially "Romantic" poetic perspective originates in his early experience with theatre. In one of his first works, *The Borderers*, which was originally intended for performance at Covent Garden, Wordsworth experimented with an ethics of viewing from a distance, and even after the play was rejected, Wordsworth continued experimenting with different theatrical situations, both in openly dramatic pieces like "The Thorn" and Book VII of *The Prelude* and in works where theatre is less obvious, like "The Solitary Reaper," "The Discharged Soldier," "Tintern Abbey," and the sonnet "Composed on Westminster Bridge." Through his experiments with theatre, Wordsworth learns to position himself as both actor and spectator to create a unique and all-encompassing public voice.

But Romantic experiments with stagecraft were not all positive. In Chapter 4, "The Great Master of Ideal Mimicry," I argue that Shelley longed for a poetic voice that could incorporate the multiple arts that make up the drama. Unable to find an art form like a drama "employed language, action, music, painting, the dance, and religious institution to produce a common effect in the representation of the highest idealisms of passion and of power" (518), Shelley masochistically tears his poetic figures apart, both to demonstrate their incompleteness and to yearn for a mythical figure that might incorporate multiple bodies and multiple voices into one.

The book's final chapter, "Creative Spectacle," presents an alternative to a traditional Wordsworthian view that would condemn entertainments meant for the eye alone. Leigh Hunt, William Hazlitt, and Thomas De Quincey, writing for an upwardly mobile middle class, used the sublime to think about the way that theatre's materiality could bring its audience together. For these critics, theatre's concreteness and its communal setting could not only bind its audience together as a nation but encourage compassion and creativity. Leigh Hunt's light sympathy, De Quincey's ecstatic union with his fellows, and Hazlitt's quotidian creativity all find a way to rebuild individuals and communities using properly designed theatrical experiences. Far from being fearsome, distance becomes creative.

These five chapters provide a glimpse into the ways that thinkers in the late eighteenth and early nineteenth centuries used the theatre to think through the social relations created by a new mass culture. Both inside and outside of the actual theatrical space, theatre provided a field for experimentation for authors who sought a more human relationship between authors and their audiences.

I

Pantomime

Killing the Drama in Order to Save It

There Princess, stay till thy gay Knight has power to relieve thee—
Nor ever hope to be Sir Arthur's wife
Till he who loves thee best attempt thy life

Harlequin and Humpo

By 1812, when Thomas Dibdin penned *Harlequin and Humpo*, both Dibdin and his audience would have been quite familiar with the argument that the pantomime was killing the serious drama. An anonymous letter to *The Thespian* magazine in 1793 proposed "that licentious Comedy and Pantomime buffonery should be entirely banished from [the theatre], and nothing introduced but what has real moral effect";[1] Leigh Hunt, in his application to Parliament for a third theatre, argued that "Mother Geese and Blue Beards," "Italian Operas," and the "vulgar medley of Mr. ELLISTON's Circus" were squeezing out space for "good English plays."[2] Pantomime reputedly carried the finances of the major theatrical houses, but it carried them at the cost of driving "legitimate" drama, and especially classic works like Shakespeare, into the closet.

It is easy, then, to see Dibdin's own ambivalence in the pantomime's final scene. The hero's final challenge is to shoot the woman he loves best—killing the heroine in order to save her. The situation is oddly parallel to Dibdin's own. Brought up in the great tradition of London theatre—his godfather was David Garrick—and trained in the minors and the provinces, Dibdin might well have felt that in taking a career arranging pantomimes, he was betraying the theatre he loved. But of course, this being pantomime, the ending is happy. The hero shoots only a false princess—a bad fairy in disguise—and her death enables the hero and heroine to live happily ever after. The princess seems to die, but she is truly more alive than ever.

Harlequin and Humpo tells an interesting parable about genre in the Romantic period. As Frederic Jameson reminds us, genre serves as a proving ground for the dominant anxieties and ideals of an age.[3] If, as William St. Clair has suggested, scholars should look for Romanticism's "spirit of the age" in works that were widely read (or in this case viewed) rather than in works deemed "representative,"[4] one could do worse than to look at the pantomime as a flashpoint for Romantic culture. Aristocrats and artisans, merchants, servants, and serious critics all flocked to the annual ritual;[5] its antics were discussed in both the high press and the low. True, the pantomime never occupied the high-culture niche reserved for tragedy, but it was seen, appreciated, and praised by audiences and critics from all classes and political stripes. In a fragmented literary culture, it was one of the few types of entertainment that everyone saw.

What we see in the pantomime, however, is a genre tremendously anxious about its changing relationship to the mass audience. Forced to balance between high culture and low culture, between an ancient past and a modern future, the pantomime was the genre that most successfully experimented with distance and perspective. It had the uncanny knack of being all things to all people. In the early eighteenth century, writers stressed the pantomime's materiality, its sensual immediacy, and its "liveness," "the fact that performers and spectators are in such close physical proximity as to interact with each other" (O'Brien, *Harlequin Britain* xviii–xix). But by the late eighteenth century, pantomime was one of the few genres that did not seem to suffer from the expansion of the houses. *The Times* observed in 1830, "However prevalent may be the feeling that the size of the large theatres prevents the intellectual enjoyment of tragedy and comedy, their spacious area and magnificent decorations are in themselves a superb sight, and they ... are almost indispensable to the effect of pantomimes ... Pantomime, therefore, labours under great disadvantage in a small theatre."[6] Pantomime, then, goes from being the signal genre of the small houses to being the signal genre of the large. But more than simply adapting to the changing times, the pantomime actually helped its audience adapt to new forms of spectatorship. It took the audience through their own series of "harlequin changes"—De Quincey's term[7]—by moving them from place to place, dwarfing them through gigantism and gigantizing them through miniature, exposing them to optical illusions and deviations from physical reality through pantomime tricks, bringing them close and pushing them away, so that by the end of the show, the audience was not sure whether the spectacle they had observed was intimate or distant.

Harlequin in Motion

Perhaps no genre has come to symbolize performance in the Romantic period as much as the pantomime. Comedies and tragedies might be read in the closet; melodrama and burlesque were just coming into their own. But pantomime was exclusively a stage genre. Even today, John O'Brien notes with frustration, documentation is scarce.[8] There are descriptions from theatregoers, reviews from newspapers and magazines, pictures of performers in costume, and a few scattered libretti and popular songs. But the detailed scripts that we have for other forms of drama are nonexistent; it is clear that what happened in performance far exceeds any record that we have of it. The pantomime remains, as Marilyn Gaull has observed, the residue of an oral and performed culture, the last remains of an endlessly adaptable culture of underground popular theatre.

The pantomime, of course, had a foot in the old and a foot in the new from the very beginning. Adapted from the Italian *commedia dell'arte*, scholars have traced the roots of its allegorical characters to the Atellan farces in Rome, to medieval street minstrels and medicine shows, and perhaps even to Asiatic mimes.[9] But improvisation on the old characters made them constantly new. As the pantomime traveled across Europe, it mixed the allegorical with the contemporary. As Marilyn Gaull would have it, it enacts "festivals beyond memory" (208); as David Mayer says, it "easily and confidently documented the everyday trivia of its milieu" (8).

But for observers in the Romantic period, the thing that made pantomime such a subtle negotiator between high culture and low culture was not its status as ancient and modern, but its focus on movement itself. "The three general pleasures of a Pantomime," writes Leigh Hunt, "are its bustle, its variety, and its sudden changes."[10] Thomas De Quincey could think of no better metaphor for his own shifting style than the pantomime: "a maze of inversions, evolutions and harlequin changes."[11] *The Times* described the pantomime in 1821 as part of a grand chase: "*Columbine* flies away from her jaundiced admirer with all due rapidity, and *Harlequin* follows her fantastic flight with all the agility which love can be supposed to add to a light pair of heels. *Pantaloon* and *Clown*, as in pantomimic duty bound, immediately pursue them; but, unfortunately for themselves, display more haste than good speed in their mode of pursuit" (Mayer 30). Hunt concurs: "The stage is never empty or still; either Pantaloon is hobbling about, or somebody is falling flat, or somebody else is receiving an ingenious thump on the face, or the Clown is jolting himself with jaunty dislocations, or Columbine is skimming across like a frightened pigeon, or Harlequin is quivering hither and thither, or gliding out of a window, or slapping something into a metamorphosis" (Hunt 144). Establishment and radical agree: the very essence of pantomime is its rapid motion.

It is this sense of constant motion, I would argue, that made it possible for pantomime to "move" its audience from world to world, creating new perspectives and new audience relations. As Jane Moody puts it, the "dizzying, awe-inspiring world of Romantic travel—from the towering magnificence of the Alps to the icy landscapes of the North Pole—found its first, enchanted mass audience."[12] Pantomimes transported their viewers to India, China, Europe, and the Middle East; titles like *Kelaun and Guzzarat; or, Harlequin in Asia* (Royalty 1807), *Whang-Fong; or, The Clown of China* (Sadler's Wells 1812), *The Brachman; or, The Oriental Harlequin* (Sadler's Wells 1813), *Harlequin Harper; or, a Jump from Japan* (Drury Lane 1813), *The Valley of Diamonds; or, Harlequin Sinbad* (Drury Lane 1814), *Harlequin and Fortunio; or, Shing-Moo and Thun-Ton* (Covent Garden 1815), *Harlequin Gulliver; or The Flying Island* (Covent Garden 1817), *Monkey Island; or, Harlequin and the Loadstone Rock* (Lyceum, 1824) and even *Harlequin Highflyer; or, Off She Goes* (Sadler's Wells 1808) promised far-flung journeys, both real and imagined. *Harlequin Rasselas; or, The Happy Valley* (Sans Pareil 1815) took Harlequin, Columbine, and their companions on a trip through Egypt, France, and England. For *Davy Jones* (Drury Lane 1829), Drury Lane paid Clarkson Stanfield £300 for a diorama showing the sights along the carriage road of the newly opened Simplon Pass; *Harlequin and Fortunio; or, Shing-Moo and Thun-Ton* (Covent Garden 1815) led its viewers on a chase from a "Chinese Port" to three successive views of the prince regent's new Brighton Pavilion.

At a time when the unities of time, place, and action were still being debated by luminaries like Stendhal and A. W. Schlegel,[13] these movements must have seemed much more of a literal "transport" than they seem today. Although by the Regency era, most critics rejected the three unities, and discussions about the unity of place occasionally surfaced to illustrate an audience's tolerance for illusion. Even in the middle of the eighteenth century, Cristoph Friedrich Nicolai could wonder whether changes in scene might remind the spectator that "the theatrical palaces and gardens are nothing but painted canvas" (Burwick 85). And while, in 1828, Schlegel could laud the audience's ability to change from scene to scene as proof of their imaginative flexibility, he still considered the unity of place a useful tool to help the audience maintain the illusion of verisimilitude. By openly flouting the unity of place, the pantomime showcased its format as a modern theatre, where the audience maintained a distance from the illusion. But at the same time, its open theatricality exposed the artificiality of the changes in perspective. The audience was brought close as part of the joke at the same time they were distanced in wonder. Like the shift from frame story to harlequinade, the pantomime's travelogue not only shifted the audience from one place to another but also allowed them to simultaneously experience the pleasures of both closeness and distance. It could be transported to China but at the same time always be aware that it was in one place all the time.

But pantomime's movement is not only within the realm of the literal. By its very nature, the bipartite structure of the Regency pantomime moved its audience from one theatrical world to another. The pantomime would begin with a frame story taken from fairy tale, folklore, or popular culture, only to find the characters of the frame changed into their allegorical counterparts of Harlequin, Columbine, Pantaloon, Lover, and Clown. Tellingly, these stories were much more separate in the late eighteenth and early nineteenth centuries than they were in the early part of the eighteenth century. In *Harlequin Dr. Faustus* (Drury Lane 1723), the pantomime tricks are a well-integrated part of the story: after Harlequin Dr. Faustus signs his contract with Mephistopheles, he uses his magic powers to play all sorts of pantomime tricks before being carried to damnation. There was never any need for change of character: the frame was magical, and the allegory fit right in. In the late eighteenth and early nineteenth centuries, however, the stories were much more random, connected only by a chase. In *Harlequin and the Swans; or, The Bath of Beauty* (Covent Garden 1813), the mythological story of Prince Rinaldo, who disguises himself to meet his princess when she renews her youth at the Bath of Beauty, gives way to comic songs about the Napoleonic War and a banquet at "[St.] Winifred's Banqueting Hall"; *Harlequin and the Red Dwarf, or, The Adamant Rock* (Covent Garden 1812) shifts from the magic adamant rock to an English street scene and back to the Magic Green Bird's fairy palace.

Thus as the relationship between actor and audience changed, the pantomime led its viewers through two different sorts of theatrical worlds. The fairy-tale opening, with its exotic settings, elaborate processions, and actors in papier-mâché "big heads" represented both the best and the worst of the new, more distant theatres: grand spectacles, fabulous depictions of faraway places, and actors made outsize by their papier-mâché "big heads." The opening of Dibdin's 1813 pantomime *Harlequin Harper; or, a Jump from Japan*, for example, featured no fewer than five grand processions, exotic representations of the "Water Palace of Bud-so, Governor of Xo-ko-ko," a "Splendid Japanese Banquet Gallery," "The Terrific Temple of Tai-co," a magic harp, and a storm at sea; *Harlequin and Padmanaba* (Covent Garden 1811) not only introduced an elephant to Covent Garden but also offered such scenes as "The Sultan's Palace," "The Sultan's Kitchen," the "Gardens of the Seraglio," and, in the splendid last scene, "A Persian Palace." While the harlequinade section embedded within the fairy-tale story also relied on spectacular tricks and stage machinery, its settings were often much more local. Harlequin and his pursuers made their way through rural cottages and villages or city shops and entertainments. Jane Moody has even characterized Joseph Grimaldi's clown character as an "urban anarchist" (209), running through a world of shops, placards, and billboards that would have been quite familiar to the urban audience of the pantomime. Actual London scenes would materialize—Moody mentions the transformation of Ward's medicine shop to Jarvis's coffin shop in *Peter Wilkins, or, The Flying World* performed at the Wells in 1800 (218–19)—and by 1808, after including the Cornhill Lottery Office in *Thirty Thousand, or, Harlequin's Lottery* (Sadler's Wells 1808), Dibdin was besieged by local tradesmen who wanted to have their own shops included in the pantomime. London fads like coach driving (*Fashion's Fools* 1809), dandyism (*Harlequin and Fancy* 1815), and military fashion (*Harlequin and the Red Dwarf* 1812), and even everyday events like an audience leaving a theatre in a rainstorm and fighting over umbrellas (*Harlequin and Little Red Riding Hood* 1828) all appeared in the harlequinade section of the pantomime and heightened the effect of an exotic, theatrical world giving way to the foibles of ordinary London.

Furthermore, critics generally saw the harlequinade portion of the pantomime, not the fairy-tale story, as the section where the audience could identify with the characters. *The Times* wrote in December of 1823 that if Grimaldi's clown "only drew a cork, it was the commentary upon the face of one of our acquaintance" (Mayer 47). "The Clown is a delightful fellow to tickle our self-love with," writes Leigh Hunt. "[W]e feel a lofty advantage over him, so he occasionally aspires to our level by a sort of glimmering cunning and jocoseness, of which he thinks so prodigiously himself as to give us a still more delightful notion of our superiority" (141). When the French army retreated from Russia in the winter of 1813, George Cruikshank caricatured the near-capture of Napoleon by identifying the emperor with the nimble Harlequin: "The Narrow escape, or Boney's Grand Leap *a la Grimaldi!!* No sooner had Napoleon alighted and entered a miserable house for refreshment, than a party of Cossacks rushed in after him. Never was Miss Platoff so near Matrimony!! Had not the Emperor been very alert at Vaulting, and leapt through the Window with the nimbleness of an Harlequin, while his faithful followers were fighting for his life, there would, probably, have been an end at once to that Grand Bubble, the French Empire" (Mayer 14). The pantomime, then, took its audience to exotic places only to return them to a local world made fantastic, and from that local world made fantastic, it led them back into the theatre. Through its two-part structure, the pantomime not only taught its audience how to transition from their local worlds into the distant and exotic world that could be created by more elaborate staging techniques, it actually taught them that the seemingly distant and exotic world could dissolve at any moment into the world they know every day. The grand personages of the frame narrative, for all their pretensions and exotic settings, are "really" the allegorical Harlequin and Columbine, Pantaloon, Lover, and Clown. Even Bonaparte, as fearsome as he is, is a pantomime character underneath.

The pantomime also enacted shifts in perspective by taking its audience from the gigantic to the miniature, making them either impossibly large or impossibly small compared to the spectacles onstage. Again, its very titles—*Harlequin and the Red Dwarf* (1812), *Jack the Giant Killer* (1809), *Jack and the Beanstalk; or, Harlequin and the Ogre* (1819), *Harlequin and Mother Bunch; or, the Yellow Dwarf* (1821), *Harlequin and the Ogress; or, the Sleeping Beauty of the Wood* (1822), *Harlequin and the Dragon of Wantley; or, More of More Hall* (1824), and *The Man in the Moon; or, Harlequin Dog-Star*

(1826)—often point to figures outsize and out of perspective. *Jack the Giant Killer* provides a take on the Jack-and-the-Beanstalk story (Mayer 91); *Harlequin Gulliver* leads its hero through Lilliput and Brobdignag. Pantomimes frequently made fun of their characters' deformities, like the Emperor Longoheadiano and Empress Rondabellyiana in 1812's *Harlequin and the Red Dwarf* (Covent Garden 1812). The papier-mâché "big heads," the grand spectacles, and giant props like the "very large folio edition of Shakespeare," which was brought onstage in 1811's *The White Cat* and then replaced with an equally large mock elephant, gave the pantomime a feeling of being larger than life (Mayer 40). Charles Dickens tells the story of a backstage visit from the Duke of York, George III's brother, who offered Grimaldi snuff "from the largest snuff box Grimaldi had ever beheld" (Mayer 10). The entourage was delighted when Grimaldi not only took snuff from the box but used it in the pantomime as well.

But in the midst of all this largeness, the pantomime was also a genre of miniature. *The Times* identified the pantomime's method as "*reductio ad absurdum!*" (Mayer 50), and at least part of its task seemed to be to belittle greatness. Thackeray used the miniaturism of the pantomime to describe the German court's "monstrousness" and "prodigious littleness":

> What a strange court! What a queer privacy of manners and morals do we look into! Shall we regard it as preachers and moralists and cry Woe, against the open vice and selfishness and corruption; or look at it as we do at the king in the pantomime, with his pantomime wife and pantomime courtiers, whose big heads he knocks together, whom he pokes with his pantomime sceptre, whom he orders into prison under the guard of his pantomime beefeaters, as he sits down to dine at his pantomime pudding? It is grave, it is sad; it is theme most curious for moral and political speculation; it is monstrous, grotesque, laughable, with its prodigious littleness, etiquette, ceremonials, sham moralities; it is as serious as a sermon, and as absurd and outrageous as Punch's puppet-show. (Mayer 14–15)

At times, the pantomime would mix the gigantic and the miniature, crazily shifting proportions so that things unlike in life could interact onstage. In *Harlequin's Vision; or, The Feast of the Statue* (Drury Lane 1817) (a take on Mozart's *Don Giovanni*), the equestrian statue, toppling to crush the Don Giovanni Harlequin, falls into a large bowl of macaroni (Mayer 62). In *Harlequin and Asmodeus* (1810), the Clown drops a lobster into a kettle and pulls out a red-coated soldier; in *Harlequin and the Red Dwarf* (1812), the Clown pops a little fellow representing Napoleon into the mouth of a giant bear. In *London; or, Harlequin and Time* (Sadler's Wells 1813), the clown tells a nonsensical story about a thief who swallows a monument that he has stolen in order to avoid detection by the watchman. Once he is caught, the man is found to have stolen an entire collection of London sights (Moody 220). As Jane Moody puts it, it was a genre "in which palaces and temples turned into huts and cottages, men and women into wheelbarrows and joint-stools, and colonnades into beds of tulips" (211).

The audience, then, was taken in illusion from place to place, made large and then made small. Like the pantomime's fascination with travel, its fascination with the gigantic and the miniature also serves to dislocate the audience by pulling them closer and pushing them farther away. Like Gulliver, who sees Lilliputian society from a distance and Brobdignagian society too close, the change from large to small brings the pantomime audience, in its imagination, first close to the spectacle and then farther away.

The pantomime's play with the gigantic and miniature is also a play with nature and art. As Susan Stewart observes in *On Longing*, both the gigantic and the miniature are ways of extending bodily scale into the world of abstraction. The miniature reveals a closed, secret, interior life, a world distant in space or time, a place where time stops, a world of perfect order, proportion, and balance. The gigantic, its perfect opposite, makes closure impossible. It can only be experienced in broad stretches of time—history, travel—or in the transcendent. It represents the body's relationship to forces outside of itself, too large for it to control. The miniature is a created thing—a dollhouse, a book—and often a thing created precisely to give its viewers a sense of "owning" the world—returning, in pleasure, to a time that has been lost, an island separated from reality. Like the "fourth wall" of the stage, or the book in a stranger's hands, the miniature is always something seen from a distance. The gigantic, by contrast, is a creature of appetite, of consumption, of production, of labor. It is our relationship to the landscape, to history, to the sublime. In mixing the two, then, the pantomime brings in commentary on a broader outside world while at the same time making it a plaything for its audience. The pantomime takes the gigantic forces of the turn of the century—revolution, history, industrialization, the fast-paced urban world—and makes them into a toy that the audience can play with.

And in fact, the pantomime played with the idea of illusion throughout. While the frame story depended on the mechanics of illusion—magnificent sets, processions, the magic appearance of the benevolent and malevolent agents—the harlequinade section always made sure the audience was in on the trick. In *Broad Grins; or, Harlequin Mag and Harlequin Tag* (Olympic 1815) Harlequin attempts to leap through a mirror, but falls and breaks it, then rises to complain that leaps are to be done by a substitute (Mayer 85). Spectators at *Harlequin and Little Red Riding Hood* (Covent Garden 1828) were treated to the spectacle of an audience leaving a theatre in a rainstorm. The contest for places in coaches turned into a pitched battle fought with umbrellas and ended with a dandy, his clothing disheveled, sitting in the dirt (Mayer 183). Harlequinades are full of image makers, camera obscura men, and raree-shows. The frame story gives the audience the pleasures of illusion; the harlequinade punctures it.

Thus the pantomime gave its audience their show and then warned them that they were seeing it, skipping, as Jane Moody says, "with lightning irony between the deceptiveness and seductiveness of metropolitan illusion" (222). Like the camera obscura man who opens the harlequinade portion of Covent Garden's *Harlequin and the Red Dwarf* (1812), it promises to turn the world upside down:

> Come, Ladies and Gentlemen, don't be asleep
> In the wonderful Camera Obscura come peep
> 'Twill show you the whim of this bustle and strife,
> It will, sure as Death, and as nat'ral as life
> I, like modern philosophers, manage my mark,
> So you always see best when you're most in the dark;
> Don't grumble, tho' nothing but shadow you see,
> Since substance has long ceas'd the fashion to be
> And I'm sure you'd each pay double price to be peeper
> Could I shew you the shadow of things growing cheaper.

Here, the audience both is the joke and is in on the joke. For the camera obscura man promises only illusion—"shadows" sold at a price to "Ladies and Gentlemen" who are in the dark and half asleep. But he inserts just enough knowingness to make the audience feel that they are the privileged parties in this illusion. They can see through the camera obscura man, and with him the "modern philosophers" and an economic system that would be better if things were cheaper. The camera obscura man, like the pantomime itself, manages to be both huckster and confederate, a "showman" who makes the audience part of the show.

Harlequin and Humpo

So far I have been depicting the pantomime that, like its heroes, effortlessly performs a delicate balancing act. But that view leaves out the difficulty of the struggle that individual pantomime authors had negotiating that balance each year. London's two "legitimate" houses, Drury Lane and Covent Garden, had a reputation for quality to uphold even as they tried to compete with other entertainments; London's "minor" theatres had to keep their reputation for small size and intimacy even as they wooed audiences with ever more spectacular effects.

For the rest of the article, then, I would like to focus on a single author at a single moment: Thomas Dibdin's *Harlequin and Humpo*, first performed at Drury Lane as the Christmas pantomime for 1812. I should note at the outset that this is one of the few pantomimes for which there is a good quality and widely available text, courtesy of Jeffrey N. Cox and Michael Gamer's *Broadview Anthology of Romantic Drama*, and confess that in choosing a widely available text rather than an obscure one I hope to make it easier for fellow scholars to work the popular drama into the classroom. Even without this advantage, though, *Harlequin and Humpo* comes at a particularly significant moment of change for both its author and the theatre that performed it. Thomas Dibdin had dedicated his life to performance, starting at the age of four, when he was selected to play Cupid to Mrs. Siddon's Venus at a Shakespeare Jubilee at Drury Lane. In his teens he left his apprenticeship to join the Dover Circuit. He spent most of his early years in the minor theatres, performing at Sadler's Wells, managing the Surrey Theatre, and writing pantomimes, melodramas, and adaptations for a host of minor houses. By the age of 21 he could "sing 'Poor Jack,' paint scenes, play the fiddle, write a farce, get up a pantomime, attempt Sir Francis, Gripe, Apollo in 'Midas,' Mungo in the 'Padlock,' Darby in the 'Poor Soldier,' Captain Valentine in the 'Farmer,' and Polonius in 'Hamlet'; not to mention all dialects, as the Irishman in 'Rosina,' or any thing else, with French and German characters."[14] Although he did write some pantomimes for Covent Garden, his big break into the legitimate theatre came in 1812, when he was hired as the prompter and writer of pantomimes at the rebuilt Drury Lane.

It was quite an entry. The opening of the new Drury was the grand event of 1812. London had been waiting for the new theatre since the old one burned in 1809. Newspaper accounts cite inadequate police presence and crowd control. The Committee of Management had announced a prize for the best opening address to commemorate the occasion and received 112 entries; they rejected all of them, causing consternation among the rejected authors and the press. A volume of the rejected addresses was published; the committee eventually commissioned Lord Byron to write the opening address. The comedian John Bannister wrote in his memoirs, "No such confusion of tongues had accompanied the erection of any building since the tower of Babel."[15]

Notwithstanding all the publicity—or perhaps because of it—the new Drury Lane saw itself as part of the grand tradition of English theatre. Byron's opening address referred to "Siddons' thrilling art," Garrick's "last adieu," and the "Immortal names, emblazon'd on our line": "Heirs to their labours, like all high-born heirs, / Vain in of *our* ancestry as they of *theirs*" (31, 35, 46–47, 51). Pantomime was conspicuously not mentioned; in fact, Byron puts in a little dig at the pantomime audience: "If e'er frivolity has let to fame, / and made us blush that you forbore to blame; / If e'er the sinking stage could condescend, / To soothe the sickly taste it dare not mend" (56–59).

But if this Drury was to "emulate the last" (27), audiences needed to be reconciled to the larger size of the new theatre. The new Drury Lane held 3,120 patrons, an increase of more than 1,000 over the most recent Drury Lane's 2,000.[16] Stage boxes were almost 54 feet from the stage. Its architect, Benjamin Wyatt, had made "the Size or Capacity of the Theatre," along with the "pecuniary return to be made to those whose Property might be embarked in the Concern" a primary consideration (Leacroft 166). Wyatt's theatre operated as a picture frame: "the Proscenium," he wrote, "must be considered as forming part of the Spectatory, and not a part of the Scene . . . it is a line of separation between the two, and is to the Scene what the frame of a Picture is to the Picture itself" (Leacroft 167). Actors, audiences, and critics all complained about the ability to see and hear; James Boaden, in his *Memoirs of the Life of John Philip Kemble*, complained, "The great secret, in front of the spectator, is to give the actor his relative importance—here, he was lost in an immense space, and the scenery that should have born [sic] his performance, and given locality to the character, was a diminutive picture, hung behind him at a distance" (1.566). Dibdin's task, then, when it came time to write the first pantomime for the glorious new house, was to create the old intimacy while taking full effect of the opportunities for spectacle that its size provided. Thus *Harlequin and Humpo* is nothing if not magnificent. As with Dibdin's pantomime *Harlequin Harper; or, a Jump from Japan* (Drury Lane 1813), produced a year later, *Harlequin and Humpo*[17] has an elaborate four-scene opening, with a procession of dwarves, a "Palace of Black Marble enriched with Gold Entablatures and Massy Architecture" (208), a grand dance by the princess's attendants, a "romantick Pass, near a ruin'd Tower" (212), the "Grand Pavilion of the Dwarf King," the "Cave of Night," and suitably grand entrances for the benevolent and malevolent agents, one of whom appears with thunder, the other in "a most brilliant cloud containing a Sun" (211). The harlequinade section, if more local, is no less elaborate, with a bower, a coachmaker's shop in London, a "Romantick Forst Scene," a Dutch clockmaker's shop filled with animated figures, a country public house, a seaport town, a plumber's shop, a city street full of elaborate signs (which play their own part in the play), scenes seen through a telescope, and a village with a raree-show.

But the play itself shows Dibdin somewhat insecure about the power of a spectacular theatre, cut off from the audience and the world outside. The princess in the frame story is imprisoned in a world of candlelight, unable to see the daylight before she reaches the age of 18. Her massy, windowless palace—a figure, perhaps, for the grandiose new theatre—is also her prison. Within the palace, the princess leads a grand life, indulged by her father and beloved by her lover, surrounded by waiting women, dancing troupes, and amusements. It is no wonder that the princess tells Sir Arthur "The son of Humpo comes—yet sooner than with him / The day I'll share, I'll here remain with thee—/ And love by lamplight—Lamplight did I say? / I would not fear e'en in the dark to stay" (210). But as comfortable as the darkened theatre is, the princess must escape her confinement and reconcile herself to the world. She is threatened, tellingly, only with miniaturization: her father requires her to marry the prince of the dwarves, rather than her own right-sized companion. In her own castle, she is a princess, but the "kingdoms" that her father says her intended bridegroom offers to her are miniature kingdoms—thus the reason why dwarves are such a threat in the Regency pantomime. A genre that had been, if not grand, at least life-sized, is threatened with miniaturization. Large in its own world, to the world outside, all its kings and princesses, trickster harlequins, and clever clowns are only playthings, afterpieces in a world of five-act tragedies. Thus in *Harlequin and Humpo*, and in so many other pantomimes, the lavish dwarf is a figure of ridicule—a tiny crew dressed in all the finery of royalty, ignoring all its smallness and pretending to marry princesses. A toy pretending to greatness is always ridiculous. *The Times* writes of the "procession of little figures, with immense faces and turbans, weighed down with finery" (Cox and Gamer 384). Even Dibdin, in his own memoirs, makes fun of "three hundred humpy men from the neighbourhood of the Temple" who had "determined to oppose the piece." "I had no apprehension," he says, "of those whose backs were so awfully *up*" (Cox and Gamer 389). Thus "exposed" to the light, the princess is threatened with becoming not just transformed, but insignificant.

Even the harlequinade, traditionally the realm of acrobatics and visual trickery, seems leery of the grand spectacle. Though the harlequinade is traditionally the place where magic brings the frame story and the harlequinade together—where Harlequin's transformation of objects prefigures the transformation of the helpless lovers into the courageous and agile Harlequin and Columbine, and where that transformation prefigures the transformation of frame story to harlequinade, exotic spectacle to urban reality and back—Harlequin's bat is short on magic. The harlequinade section only has three transformations: in scene 6, Harlequin transforms a coach into a balloon; in scene 10, he strikes a wall, which then turns over to produce a collection of ballads; and in scene 8, he changes a telescope into a gun, which goes off and shoots Clown. In fact, there is little magic at all in *Harlequin and Humpo*. Most of the actions in the harlequinade can be explained by natural means. Harlequin and Columbine flee in a coach when their pursuers are distracted; Pantaloon, Lover, and Clown mistake Harlequin and Columbine for clock figures or leaden dolls; Harlequin dresses as an old woman, then substitutes the real old woman in his place after he has antagonized Clown. The acts of magic are few and small. When Columbine longs for apples in scene 10, Harlequin holds up his sword and apples fly off the tree onto the point of it; in scene 11, Harlequin and Clown each disappear from a sack when Pantaloon and Lover are about to beat them. Like so many gothics of the period, *Harlequin and Humpo* seems to take pains to disenchant itself, even including explanations of the tricks in the printed text (though those were not necessarily given to the audience). If the princess is to be saved and the blocking forces defeated, it will not be through supernatural means.

What *Harlequin and Humpo* substitutes for transformation is distraction and good acting—the very "magic," one might say, of theatre. Harlequin and Columbine evade Pantaloon, Lover, and Clown when the Pursuers are so distracted by a moving carriage that they do not see that Harlequin and Columbine are in an identical one. Clown is so busy climbing a tree (and his comrades so busy watching him) that they do not see Harlequin jump to the next one. They are fascinated by figures in a clock shop, hypnotized by a clock pendulum, sidetracked by Clown's injuries, both real and pretended. As an urban audience, they are unable to sustain attention, fascinated by the sheer multiplicity of creative imitation around them. Harlequin and Columbine, on the other hand, are consummate mimics. They pose as clock figures at a Dutch clockmaker's shop and leaden dolls at a plumber's. Theirs is the art of illusion—of producing effects so realistic that they surprise, amaze, and—yes—fool the audience. And aside from the fact that the shows slow their pursuit of Harlequin and Columbine, Pantaloon, Lover, and Clown love such shows. In scene 8, the pursuers stand mesmerized by animated clock figures, even though Harlequin uses those figures to play tricks on them. In scene 13, Clown steals a telescope from the opticians and the three pursuers look through it; in scene 14, the last scene of the harlequinade, Clown is distracted by a raree-show, tries to steal the show, and is eventually enclosed in the show box. Clown even tries to build his own figure out of a barrel, a plum pudding, grapes, a pair of spectacles, and a gun.

And in fact, competition between the classes—both for resources and for creativity—is one of the major themes in *Harlequin and Humpo*. John O'Brien has observed that the pantomimes of the early eighteenth century have a democratic impulse, but by *Harlequin and Humpo* that impulse has increased to the degree that the "lower" comic characters threaten to take over the social functions of the "higher" fairy-tale characters. In the frame story, the duenna exposes the princess to the light because she wants to become Humpino's bride herself—"No great revenge neither to give him a wife like me, methinks" (211). She goes so far as to masquerade as the princess in her wedding gown before she is discovered, and, like one of the characters in the harlequinade to follow, "[s]he bullies some, cuffs others, and kicks up a dust in the Palace" (213) when forced to give up her prize. And in the harlequinade section of *Harlequin and Humpo*, as in so many late eighteenth-century and early nineteenth-century pantomimes, Harlequin and Clown compete for center stage. Harlequin pretends to drive off in a carriage; Clown is caught in the motion of the wheel and turns cartwheels around the stage. Harlequin hides in a tree; Clown gets sympathy for falling out of the tree. Harlequin poses as a clock figure; Clown steals a clock. Harlequin escapes from a sack when he is imprisoned and about to be beaten; Clown escapes from a sack when he is imprisoned and is about to be beaten. In a game of "anything you can do, I can do better," Harlequin and Clown follow each other around the stage, both free agents pursued (in various ways) by Pantaloon and Lover.

And even though Dibdin tries valiantly to keep the magic continuity between the frame story and the harlequinade, it does not quite work. In *Harlequin and Humpo*, as in many other pantomimes of the period, Harlequin comes to represent distance and spectacle, even within the more intimate format. Instead of bringing the two stories together, making the passage through the harlequinade a necessary step for the frame-story lovers and conceding that even illusion needs to benefit from a dose of reality in order to remain relevant, in *Harlequin and Humpo* Harlequin becomes more separate, cut off from the action, a stranger in the harlequinade just as Clown would become a stranger in the frame story. He is a frame-story hero in a harlequinade world. Dibdin tries to counteract this trend by having *Harlequin and Humpo* break the frame to a degree unusual even for pantomime. This Harlequin interacts quite a bit with his onstage audience, not through magic or trickery, but through simple camaraderie. He hides in the coachmaker's shop, rather than in the enclosed coach, in scene 6; he hides in a clockmaker's shop in scene 8 and in a plumber's shop in scene 12; and he runs through all the shops in scene 13. He hobnobs with the landlord of the country public house and an apple woman in scene 10 and dances with sailors in the seaport town in scene 11 and with the raree-show man, the hurdygurdy woman, and the entire crowd gathered to watch them in scene 14. And in the sections where Harlequin plays a part, he breaks character frequently. When Harlequin poses as a clock figure, he reaches out to move the hands on the clock; when Harlequin poses as a leaden doll, he starts a fight by tickling the plumber's ear with his sword, and even from his frozen pose during the fight he hits the pursuers with several smart slaps. This is not an agile Harlequin, standing outside the ordinary world to work his magic. We see him doing ordinary things—having dinner, dancing. This, Dibdin seems to be saying, is a Harlequin who can use the techniques of illusion but break them to reach out into the real world. This is a Harlequin who interacts.

And Dibdin probably did feel the competition. Illegitimate theatres, as Jane Moody has shown, were beating the majors in both intimacy and spectacle. Their small houses, which made it easy to see and hear, provided a sense of contact that made even the silliest shows worthwhile. Drury Lane had grandeur on its side: its cultural status as a major house, the size and technical grandeur of its new theatre building, and the publicity surrounding the new reconstruction were formidable advantages. But because the minor theatres were forced by law to put on shows that relied on gesture rather than the spoken word, they were also far ahead in spectacle. When Dibdin came to Drury Lane—indeed, one might say when the managing committee asked Dibdin to come to Drury Lane—they must have thought that he would be the one who would be able to bring the energy and intimacy of the minors into their grand major house.

What they got instead, however, is Dibdin's killing the theatre in order to save it. In fact, he kills it twice. By bringing the techniques of the minor houses into the major, Dibdin, like his hero Sir Arthur, gives his beloved theatre only a slight wound, "necessary to her disenchantment" (213). Both Dibden and Sir Arthur must have taken courage from the fairy Aquila's assurance that if his beloved's life "has been sought by him who loves her" (213), the magic power of the pantomime can heal everything. But although Dibdin's pantomime story has the requisite happy ending, it is complex enough to make one wonder if the ending might be a bit forced. Twice Sir Arthur must seem to aim falsely in order to aim true; once shooting the princess while aiming at the evil fairy, once shooting the evil fairy while aiming at the princess. The shootings separate the frame story from the harlequinade, as if the theatre could not pass from one to the other without undergoing some type of death.

Thus the nervous Dibdin gives his audience a good deal of direction, just in case love is not enough. The pantomime begins with a direct address to the audience by the king's fool, Punfunnidos—an address that ironically reveals that the audience (contrary to the foolish Punfunnidos's expectations) already knows everything that Punfunnidos is about to tell them. The fool tells the audience to prepare for "illumination" in the form of Prince Humpino's magnificent procession, but warns them that in order to see the procession, the audience will have to hide—to "vanish" in comparison to the lavish parade before them. It is as if the audience needs to be prepared for the kind of spectacle that they will see, and prepared in the kind of intimate way that they might have grown accustomed to in the older theatre and at the minors.

Dibdin also does a good deal of covert direction during the harlequinade section. While it is not unusual for pantomimes to showcase contemporary technologies of illusion—indeed, technologies in general—*Harlequin and Humpo* brings in a slew of shape-shifting technologies, especially toward the end of the harlequinade, as if Dibdin were desperately trying to adjust the piece in order to achieve the ending he was looking for. Clown steals a telescope at an optician's shop through which he, Pantaloon, and Lover each sees his imagined future—Lover a pair of horns and the word "Matrimony," Pantaloon a vision of the happy Harlequin and Columbine, and Clown the gallows. It is as if the technology of illusion, even one that distances its perceivers from the action, allows them to see a more distant truth. But a few tricks later, Harlequin and Clown vault through the lenses of a pair of spectacles—the sign of the optician's shop—suggesting their mastery over different technologies of seeing. Whatever the case, these scenes suggest that illusion is dangerous. In the telescope scene, Harlequin changes the telescope to a gun, which goes off and shoots Clown. In the scene with the spectacles, the spectacles fall on Pantaloon, trapping him under the bridge for the nose. Spectacle may have the power to show the truth—and to help Harlequin escape—but it can also kill.

But perhaps the most telling show is at the end of the harlequinade, where Harlequin and Columbine rent a raree-show. Interestingly, they do not watch the show; they only use it to misdirect their pursuers. It is Clown who is fascinated and stays to watch it, and eventually tries to steal it. For his trouble, Harlequin encloses Clown in the box, trapping him within the show. The clown is carried off by the real raree-show man and hurdygurdy woman, roaring, and eventually gets into a fight where the hurdygurdy woman smashes her instrument over his head.

Thus, at the end of the harlequinade section, it is Clown who is trapped inside the show, a creature only of theatre, while Harlequin and Columbine cleverly use the illusion to escape. But in the actual show, things turn out differently. There it seems to be Harlequin, not Clown, who is frozen, a creature of illusion, unable to move out of the show and into the real world. Harlequin, usually so agile, is often inanimate and frozen. Dibdin often has him pose as an inanimate object—a clockwork figure, a leaden doll—or take on another identity. He does not project personality because he never has a personality of his own to project. As a figure from another, more heroic world, he must either stand out from the urban scene by transforming it, as he does in pantomimes with more magic, or simply blend into the background.

Clown, on the other hand, while indisputably part of the urban world, always stands out. He steals food, stuffs himself, feigns illness and is overmedicated, sings ballads and comic songs, falls from trees, gets beaten and escapes from being beaten. The figure of urban anarchy so takes over the harlequinade that the frame story and its heroic chase are almost forgotten. When Clown steals a telescope and all the pursuers look through it, Clown stands in front of the lens so that all they can see is Clown.

Indeed, this is the criticism of *Harlequin and Humpo* that appeared in *The Times*:

> The enchantments of the Princess were libels upon magic; harlequin lost the power of his sword, and to all its slaps and circlings, the scenery remained inexorable. Chaos came again;—solid walls walked up and down the stage in the deepest distress,—whole houses went astray.—pistols and cannons missed fire with "malice prepense,"—an antique fountain, spouting volumes of water, pushed its presence into a watchmaker's shop in Cheapside, and staid there with apparent satisfaction. A plumber's shop dancing away, was interrupted in the height of its gaiety by a roar from all parts of the theatre, and the whole leaden assemblage of birds and beasts carried off in the arms of the stage servants. (Cox and Gamer 384)

Deprived of his magic, Harlequin is consumed by the grand scenery, just one more spectacle among many. Walls, houses, cannons and pistols, antique fountains, and a plumber's shop have more life than the Harlequin of *Harlequin and Humpo*, who "feel[ing] the influence of the roar . . . calmly exchanged somersets and springs for the gentler amusement of climbing" (Cox and Gamer 384). What impressed the reviewer from *The Times* is not grand spectacle, but human contact. The "thing intended for a Bear" that did a clumsy dance with "the most deplorable of Monkies" becomes charming when it "pulled off a piece of its cuticle, slipped the fur from one side of his face, and shewed, that if it was not entirely a man, it was at least but moderately a bear" (384). (Even so, the thing was "at length hissed off.") And *The Times* reserves its highest praise for one boy "dressed in some savage character":

> His slight figure was fitted for activity; but his activity surpassed all that we have ever seen of human distortion. He gave an extraordinary idea of the

powers that lie concealed in the human frame. Practice has brought this boy to such command of his limbs, that to walk on his hands, or his head, or his back, or his feet, seems almost equal to him. He ran rapidly around the stage on his hands and feet, with his belly upwards; he bounded from shoulder to shoulder; he sprung from lying flat upon the ground with a frightful suppleness of a serpent. (Cox and Gamer 384)

The contrast between human and scenery, intimacy and spectacle, could not be more finely drawn. Although Dibdin gave his audience a spectacle that took full advantage of the capacities of the new theatre, and even imported a species of realism into the harlequinade by foregoing the traditional magic of transformation, the reviewer from *The Times* longs for a theatre more human and more intimate, one that showcases the skills of performers rather than the skills of stage managers: "The fabric and contignation of our bodies is wonderful . . . No other animal possesses so fine, so intimate, and so applicable a union of agility and strength" (Cox and Gamer 384).

Thus in *Harlequin and Humpo*, the spectacular theatre might be, like the princess, not quite ready to go out into the light of day. No matter how much Dibdin plays with perspective or makes his Harlequin break the illusion, the balance between intimacy and spectacle was bound to be off. *The Times* and the *European Magazine* missed the intimacy with the performers—"So far as scenery can recommend a Piece, that of the present harlequinade deserves much commendation," wrote the *European Magazine*, "but the tricks are dull, and afford little that is new" (Cox and Gamer 385). *Bell's Weekly Messenger*, on the other hand, found that although some parts of the scenery were deficient, it found the failure of the pantomime to be "the fault of the actors" (Cox and Gamer 385). Does the piece need to showcase the actors or the spectacles that surround them? Thus, by the end of the harlequinade section in *Harlequin and Humpo*, Harlequin, frustrated, throws down his sword. It changes to a bow and arrow—an instrument for shooting things from a distance. The close-up Harlequin must change to a spectacular Harlequin in order to operate in the larger theatres.

But while this solution might seem provisional and inadequate to the reviewers and perhaps even to Dibdin himself, even the attempt at mixing the old theatre and the new still satisfied the audience. "To say the truth," wrote *Bell's Weekly Messenger*, "the Pantomime entertained us, and therefore, perhaps, we are bound to speak well of it" (Cox and Gamer 385). After initial bad reviews, the pantomime ran a spectacular 48 nights.

2

Spaces with Meaning

Crossing from Stage to Closet in Byron and Inchbald

It has been one of the hallmarks of the recent interest in Romantic drama to insist that closet drama is more than just failed stage drama. But the stench of failure is difficult to shake. Writers who wrote for either stage or closet seemed haunted by the idea that they had made the wrong choice. "But *Juan* was my Moscow," Byron writes, "and *Faliero* / My Leipsic, and my Mont Saint Jean seems *Cain*."[1] For all her success in publication, Joanna Baillie could not see her project as complete until her plays were staged: "The Series of Plays was originally published in the hope that some of the pieces it contains, although first given to the Public from the press, might in time make their way to the stage, and there be received and supported with some degree of public favour."[2] Wordsworth, by contrast, after flirting with the stage, would only consider the closet success: "It is impossible that *The Borderers* should succeed in representation."[3] And Byron, in his "Preface" to *Marino Faliero*, sees failure in either alternative: "The sneering reader, and the loud critic, and the tart review, are scattered and distant calamities; but the trampling of an intelligent or of an ignorant audience on a production which, be it good or bad, has been a mental labour to the writer, is a palpable and immediate grievance" (306). Of course, there is no good reason why either the closet or the stage should excite fears of failure in the Romantic period. As Thomas Crochunis has pointed out, the Romantic period was something of a golden age where writers of drama could, and often did, publish their work "either before, after, or instead of performance."[4] Closet dramas, as Alan Richardson has shown, were respected for their forays into the mind. Reviewers praised Joanna Baillie's "complete ... knowledge of the springs of human action" and "familiarity with every emotion of the heart" based on the print version of her *Plays on the Passions* and called her evocative of England's "old and excellent dramatic writers."[5] But stage production was not a prize to be scorned either. An author with a hit onstage could look forward not only to public fame and financial success, but perhaps to a reputation as England's new great national dramatist, the heir to Shakespeare, Jonson, and Otway. John Keats at the height of his powers would tell John Taylor that all of his writing was just apprentice work that might "nerve me up to the writing of a few fine Plays."[6]

But while Baillie might have approached this dramatic climate with "passionate ambivalence," where "both publication and theatrical production were venues that offered her something of what she desired,"[7] more often authors' nervous shifting from stage to closet and back indicates discontent. Charles Lamb, the very poster boy of Romantic antitheatricality, kept returning to the stage despite his pronouncement that the tragedies of Shakespeare were unfit for stage representation.[8] Wordsworth and Coleridge swung from denouncing the theatre to writing plays. Joanna Baillie wrote for the closet but longed for the stage (or perhaps wrote for the stage but was put in the closet). Percy Shelley penned *The Cenci* for the stage and *Prometheus Unbound* for the closet in a single year. Lord Byron's intentions for his "mental theatre" were sufficiently unclear that critics even to this day debate whether Byron really wanted them staged.[9] All this restless movement shows authors unsure about what staging their plays (or exhibiting them in the closet) might mean. Whichever choice they made—stage or closet—seemed wrong. Closet authors longed for the stage; stage authors ran to the closet.

To highlight the choices that writers faced in choosing the stage or the closet, I would like to look at two authors who went against type when their political principles were most at stake: Lord Byron and Elizabeth Inchbald. At first they might seem like an unlikely pair: an actress who wrote her way into respectability beside a lord who wrote his way out of it, a professional writer and actress who crafted her dramas to suit the practical demands of the theatre[10] set against the noble poet who coined the term "mental theatre" and swore that he "had no view to the stage."[11] But the two share much in common. Both were intimately familiar with the practical running of the theatre. Inchbald was known for her canny manipulation of managers, her mastery of stage effects, and her ability to size up an audience.[12] Byron, while less experienced, had acted in school declamation contests and private theatricals, had served on the managing board of Drury Lane Theatre, and had had his own experience with theatrical politics in the fracas over his opening address for the new Drury Lane. Both were also experienced in publicity: Inchbald enjoyed a reputation as a beauty—a reputation that both made her acting career and subjected her to harassment by actors and managers— and Byron's rakish reputation and souvenir portraits came at the cost of tremendous insecurity, exercise, and crash dieting. Both also were familiar with the body and its frailties: Inchbald's acting career depended on her overcoming her stutter; Byron's heroism, on his overcoming his club foot.

Most importantly, however, both shared a devotion to radical politics—Inchbald through her involvement in the Godwin/ Holcroft circle, Byron through his involvement in the revolutions in Greece and Italy. Both used their works to promote their political views. But when each turned to write their most serious political plays, they went outside the main genre they had worked in. Inchbald, the stage dramatist, wrote her only closet drama *The Massacre*; Byron, the closet dramatist, wrote his two most stageable plays, *Marino Faliero, Doge of Venice* and *Sardanapalus*.[13]

As might be expected, these three dramas show their writers confusedly shifting from stage to closet and back in choosing the form that would make the most effective political impact. But in the process, their works tell us a good deal about the concerns about both print and drama that led them to look for new hybrid genres that could give them the advantages of both. They cannily assessed the force of seeing something in its concrete, material reality but realized that an audience might ignore even those phenomena that are literally right before their eyes. They realized the spectacle's power to turn human bodies into objects, but they also recognized the power those objects had on their observers. They praise the theatre's concreteness and monumentality—the power of "true words" (in Byron's term) to become "things"—but they are unsure if those "things" can outweigh the power of words. They yearn for the immediacy of an audience's instinctive reaction, but at the same time, they appeal to the audience's liberal sentiments and their power of reason.

These closet dramas do not offer an easy solution to the question of whether "stage" or "closet" is the best forum for political action. Indeed, they try their best to be both and neither. They dodge, they hedge, they experiment. In the end, they create dramas that are not fully at home in either the stage or the closet.

Flying from the Stage: Inchbald's *The Massacre*

As Daniel O'Quinn has pointed out, Elizabeth Inchbald's *The Massacre* is a curiosity in almost every sense of the word: the only closet drama written by a stage dramatist; the only tragedy for a writer who made her name with comedies and farces. But until recently, critics have treated it as just that: an anomaly. Inchbald may have taken a brief hiatus from the stage for reasons of censorship—Terence Hoagwood and Paula Backscheider have pointed out that a violent play about "the unhappy state of a neighbouring nation"[14] written at the beginning of the Terror would have been politically unpalatable to both censors and audiences. Or, as O'Quinn has suggested, Inchbald may have made a strategic decision not to publish the play in order to intervene in the private deliberations of the Godwin/Holcroft circle. But on the whole, *The Massacre* stands as a theatrical oddity—a brief foray into the closet for a playwright committed to the stage.

But if we look at *The Massacre* not as an oddity but as part of the entire sweep of Inchbald's career, the picture looks quite different. The author of ten successful comedies and farces while she played as an actress, Inchbald had retired from the stage in 1789 and published her first novel *A Simple Story* in 1791. Although Inchbald would later go on to write some of her best and most successful comedies after *The Massacre*, including *Every One Has His Fault* (1793), *Wives as They Were; Maids as They Are* (1797), *Lovers' Vows* (1798), and *To Marry, or Not to Marry* (1805), from the perspective of 1792, as political troubles mounted and her print career took off, Inchbald may have begun rethinking her allegiance to the stage.

Why would Inchbald have wanted to leave the stage? As Catherine Burroughs and Marjean Purinton ("Women's Sovereignty") have argued, both the closet and the stage offered women a chance to explore the "theatricality" of their everyday life, almost making women's domestic spaces into a species of experimental theatre. The theatre also offered a unique sort of public visibility: Judith Pascoe and Betsy Bolton have both argued that actresses provided a model for women writers through their association with heightened emotion and ornament; indeed, Bolton has argued that the female dramatist became, during this period, the coequal of the male demagogue.

But as Pascoe and Bolton both realize, the theatre's power is also its limitation. Women were empowered to act in a variety of socially sanctioned roles—grieving mother, hopeful ingénue, conniving spinster. But the woman who broke out of the theatre's closely prescribed casting list risked losing both her power and her reputation.

As matters stood in 1792, the type of power—and the type of restriction—with which Inchbald would certainly have been most familiar was the theatre's physicality. In fact, women's close association with the theatre derived in part from women's association with the physical. Creatures of the body rather than the mind, women were ideally suited for a forum that privileged space, body, and costume over the more abstract notions of philosophy and motivation. As Charles Lamb famously wrote in his essay "On the Tragedies of Shakespeare," performance "embod[ies] and realiz[es] conceptions which had hitherto assumed no distinct shape," "materialis[ing] and bring[ing] down a fine vision to the standard of flesh and blood." In going from the imagination to the theatre's physicality, "we have let go a dream, in quest of an unattainable substance."[15] And Inchbald, as Paula Backscheider points out, was a particularly physical playwright. As a writer of farces and afterpieces, she was enmeshed in what Backscheider has called "gimmicks, improbabilities . . . bustle, mistakes, and contrivances" (xix). Humor comes from mistaken identity, improbable characters hiding behind screens or in adjoining rooms or closets, costumes exchanged, traded, or snipped. Inchbald's plays are full of hand-holdings and embraces—for men and for women—tableaux, poses, entrances, exits, and displays. It is as if the women's role managing domestic costumes, spaces, and emotions was perfectly tailored to the farce writer's craft. If the male playwright's role is in the "mental theatre," the female playwright's role is decidedly in the physical.

When Inchbald wanted to make a political gesture, then, she might well have felt that physicality was confining, and have wanted to turn to print to enter into the male, "mental" world. But at the same time, the physical world was her home—limited, perhaps, but safe. In *The Massacre*, Inchbald dramatizes the situation by using the conventions of sentimental farce.[16] The drama begins in a comfortable domestic situation, where a woman's greatest fear is a man's overstaying his promise by a few hours. Closeness—the intense personal contact of the home—is the currency of this domestic space. Mme. Tricastin exclaims, "What misers are we all of our real pleasures! I condemn avarice; and yet, was gold half so precious to me as the society of my dear Eusebe Tricastin, I should be most avaricious! . . . and think the loss of him, for one day only, beyond the appointed time of his return, a robbery on my happiness not to be forgiven" (1.1). And Mme. Tricastin is not the only one in this domestic world who privileges physical closeness. Old Tricastin the father-in-law is shocked that his daughter-in-law is "sorry to see [him]" (1.1); Conrad and Amadee go to meet Eusebe's coach, and when it does not arrive they go out of town to wait for it. When Old Tricastin leads the family in prayer in act 2, they all hold hands, then sink into a theatrical tableau where Eusebe and Madame Tricastin kneel before the father. Even in devastation, physical closeness seems paramount. Old Tricastin proclaims that "in whatever country, if I meet my child, I shall not call it banishment" (2.1). When Conrad speaks of the devastation in Paris, he speaks in terms of sundering physical bonds: "children torn from the breast of their mothers, husbands from the arms of their wives, and aged parents from their agonizing families" (1.1). And when Eusebe speaks of defending his wife's family he remembers "thy mother—thy uncles—thy sisters—and all of those, who clung fast round me" (1.1).

Inchbald's metaphor of Mme. Tricastin as a "miser," however, deftly suggests two things about personal presence. First, it quietly asserts, in the middle of a closet drama, that print is "doubtful currency" compared to the domestic and theatrical commonplace of bodily experience. Later in the play when Eusebe Tricastin plans to flee with nothing but paper money, Old Tricastin tells him—in so many words—that "paper is doubtful currency" (2.1). Trunks of jewels may be showy and cumbersome, but they are authentic in a way that the easier currency of paper can never be. Indeed, this is probably why the characters compete for their "shows"—and their control of the public space—throughout the play. Old Tricastin begs to speak to the mob—"a kind word has sometimes done, with most ferocious enemies, more than a thousand swords" (2.1); Dugas tells his followers, "Don't give way to your vengeance here—but there, in the midst of all our fellow-citizens, the example will be more terrible" (2.1). And in the same way, men attempt to control presence in private spaces as well. Old Tricastin tries to segregate Conrad in a private room so that his news doesn't upset Mme. Tricastin; Eusebe tries to shield Mme. Tricastin's person, not by arming her, but by placing her in a private room. Presence is a valuable commodity and must be hoarded and stored if it cannot be used in a way that enhances its value.

But Mme. Tricastin's characterization of herself as a "miser" also points to a second, more important defect of personal presence—its power is limited to the immediate and personal. When Mme. Tricastin wishes to "see [her husband] once again—and living" (1.1), he immediately appears with the literalness of a farce, suggesting that personal presence is far too easy (and far too private) a way to make an impact. Just like the female playwright, Mme. Tricastin is allowed the close bonds that hold the family together—the roles of wife, mother, and child—but denied political power. Mme. Tricastin cannot even broach her husband's absence to defend her own family in the capital. And her own reach is correspondingly limited. While her husband plays a shaping role in political events, she is denied that role. In fact it may be Mme. Tricastin's "miserly" tone that sets the claustrophobic feel of the entire play. The first two acts take place entirely inside the house of Eusebe Tricastin, and during that time both Old Tricastin and Madame Tricastin move toward being enclosed in even smaller spaces. And while Old Tricastin hopes for a more psychological form of closeness, the family's "clinging" mostly takes the form of banding together in limited spaces, excluding the outside world with gates and bars.

But if the private world is imprisoning, the public one might be ineffectual. When Old Tricastin goes to make his stirring address to the crowd, the leading scouts again mistake him—in a farcical gesture—for his son. When Dugas attempts to drag his captives to a public trial, the judge has his own agenda and his own hand-picked audience. If Inchbald's final gesture of dragging the murdered bodies before the crowd produces a response that seems to be anticlimactic—while Eusebe Tricastin is consumed with grief, the other characters go on about their business of doing justice as if nothing out of the ordinary has occurred—the audience has been amply prepared by the series of audience failures that mounts throughout the play.

But this series of audience failures is quite disturbing if we hold onto the idea that Inchbald wrote *The Massacre* to make a political gesture. If, as O'Quinn argues, Inchbald wrote the drama to make a private impact on members of the Godwin circle, she would have been perfectly happy with Mme. Tricastin's private point within her domestic field. But everything we know of the circumstances surrounding the play points to Inchbald's desire to expand her sphere of influence to a larger field. Even Inchbald's proclamation to Godwin that "there appears an inconsistency in my having said to you,

'I have no view to any public good in this piece,' and afterwards alluding to its preventing future massacres: to this I reply that it was your hinting to me that it may do harm which gave me the first idea that the play might do good"[17] indicates that at some point in the composition process Inchbald conceived the idea of working good on a larger audience, and perhaps even preventing future massacres in the process.

But how? O'Quinn notes a contradiction between Inchbald's two statements about audience affect in the play's "Advertisement": on one hand, like Walpole's tragedy *The Mysterious Mother*, "the subject matter is so horrid, that I thought it would shock, rather than give satisfaction, to an audience," but at the same time, she "found it so truly tragic in the essential springs of *terror* and *pity*, that I could not resist the impulse of adapting it to the scene" (353). The tragedy, in other words, is so horrid that it would provoke an improper reaction—shock—in the audience, but it is also so truly tragic that it would provoke the proper reaction of terror and pity. This trope of doubt about the audience's possible reaction runs through the play. When Thevenin and Clevard see Eusebe, Old Tricastin, and the household paraded through the street on the way to court, they ask the proper tragic questions—"But this he has strength of mind to bear, no doubt, with dignity?" (3.1)—and have the proper tragic response—"this city cannot boast a more virtuous man" (3.1). But the rabble, tellingly, do not. Even at the most sentimental point in this tiny play-within-a-play, when, Thevenin reports, Old Tricastin "turns towards his son ... then I can see his countenance change, the tears gush to his eyes, and stream down his furrowed cheeks," the audience reaction is quite the opposite of what it ought to be: "the rabble triumph!" (3.1).

And it may not be only the rabble that Inchbald is worried about. As Thevenin and Clevard conclude their brief scene, Clevard says "I'll join them, and be a spectator of all that passes," and Thevenin responds, "I would as soon be—a sufferer" (3.1). And indeed, Eusebe Tricastin's experience in Paris suggests that it is difficult for spectators to draw the line between actor and spectator when it comes to violent spectacles. Though Eusebe styles himself a "spectator" of the massacre, as he tells the tale he finds himself unable to separate himself from the events he relates: "But am I with [my family]? really with them? My ideas are confused.—Poor helpless victims of ferocious vengeance, pale, convulsed with terror, and writhing under the ruffian's knife, pursue and surround me.—Am I, am I with my living family?" (1.1).

First mistaken for one of the murderers then fancying himself one of their writhing victims, the spectacle makes Eusebe anything but himself. Quite literally, his "senses" leave him; the overstimulus changes his vision so that he can see nothing but disjointed images, and the spectacle so changes his perception that he no longer knows who he is or what his role might be in the events that he witnesses.

The political consequences of this bad spectatorship, Inchbald suggests, are profound. First, Eusebe forgets both himself and the family he loves in his desire for revenge. Indeed, we might almost say that the spectacle makes him into a singular observer rather than a member of a family—"At the sight, single as I was, I would have attempted vengeance" (1.1). But whether from the singleness or the simple force of the spectacle, the events Eusebe witnessed in Paris seem to have instilled an emotional desire for revenge that resists all reason. Even in act 2, after his wife and father have called him back to his familial duties and the family has planned their flight, Eusebe returns to his schemes of vengeance at the slightest provocation. Spectacle has made Eusebe into an emotional rather than a rational actor. Indeed, given the number of sentimental spectacles onstage, we might even speculate that it is too much time at the theatre, rather than simple sexism, that makes him dead set against giving his wife a weapon to defend herself. Menancourt, at least, has no such scruples, and no other man speaks out against giving Mme. Tricastin a weapon. It is only Eusebe, with chivalric ideals well-suited to the theatre, who plans his own heroic last stand.

But this is not the worst of it, Inchbald implies. The worst is Eusebe's first reaction to the spectacles of Paris, which is to forget—"Oh, that I could forget them all—banish the whole for ever from my memory!—That all who were spectators could do the same, and human nature never be scandalized by the report!" (1.1). And though Eusebe immediately follows up the wish with a denial—"But that's impossible" (1.1)—forgetting is exactly what the crowd does when presented with the body of Mme. Tricastin. Eusebe, while moved to action by the Parisian spectacles, "stands like a statue of horror at the sight" (3.2); he reaches for Rochelle's story of Mme. Tricastin's last moments as a way to "calm [his] despair" (3.2), but makes no gesture toward preserving justice or her memory. To the extent that the death causes any reaction, it is private; publicly, the matter seems to be best put aside. Conrad is philosophical: "But when was joy superlative?"

(3.2); Glandeve, practical: "take every care that the perpetrators of this barbarous outrage are secured" (3.2). The very spectacle that ought to produce horror—or, at the very least, terror and pity—is quickly forgotten amid the press of more serious political business.

Of course as O'Quinn and Nielsen point out, the gender of the body in question matters. Mme. Tricastin's untimely end only serves to secure the homosocial foundations of male liberty and to underscore that system's failure to protect the women under its care. Like the eighteenth-century anatomical wax models that Elisabeth Bronfen discusses in *Over Her Dead Body*, the dead bodies of Mme. Tricastin and her children give a beautiful figure to death in order to guard against its uncertainty and decay. Their deaths fetishistically stand in for the deaths of the massacred crowds of the Terror, guaranteeing both their well-preserved pastness and the power of the male gaze to regulate and control them. Their murdered bodies, as O'Quinn points out, serve as the bedrock of Glandeve's society based on Christian charity, a material ground for an abstract idea.

Except, of course, the bodies are not concrete. In *The Massacre*'s shimmer between page and stage, Inchbald is able to have her body and deny it, too. By staging *The Massacre* as a closet drama, "adapting it," as she says in the "Advertisement," "to the scene," she is able to obtain the force and closeness—the shock and horror—of exhibiting the murdered bodies onstage without (in Lamb's terms) "materialis[ing] and [bringing] down a fine vision to the standard of flesh and blood." For Inchbald, closet drama is about bringing the private world of domestic closeness into the public world of political discourse. She can keep the physical play of farce and the physical shock of horror—indeed, the physical memory of the dagger stained with the mother's blood—but take them out of the "house" and into the public realm of print culture.

Thus Inchbald's turn to narrative. For as much as Inchbald insists on the physical force of the body, it is in the end narrative that must "suffer" the body, in Old Tricastin's final words, "to have its effects" (3.2). Throughout the drama, narrative has been as much a staple of the performance as performance itself. Mme. Tricastin tells a story through her face, for as Old Tricastin says, "Tell!—is there cause for *telling* when a woman of sensibility loves or hates? when she feels hopes or fears, joy or sorrow? No—the passions dwell upon her every feature—none but the female hypocrite need fly to the tongue to express them" (1.1). But more often, stories come from the mouths of men, and in the more prosaic medium of words. Eusebe

Tricastin's description of the massacres in Paris transport not only him but also his family and eventually the audience into the scene; indeed, the scene is so realistic that Inchbald feels the need to put in a footnote to confirm that Eusebe's narrative not only seems but is historically accurate. Conrad's narrative of the events in Paris and Menancourt's story of the massacres in town move the plot along.

At the end, Mme. Tricastin takes advantage of the male form of storytelling by having a man tell her tale: she provides the body, but Rochelle gives the narrative background. It is telling to watch the effect of the tale: confronted with the body, Eusebe "stands like a statue of horror" (3.2) and considers the sight "greater anguish than human nature can support" (3.2). The tale allows him to take in the horror but still be able to move again; it classes his wife as a "dying saint" (3.2) and allows him to "calm [his] despair" (3.2). Thus the narrative moves Eusebe from being a passive spectator frozen by horror into being an active spectator instructed by pity and terror. And, as Old Tricastin observes, the narrative was not merely to "calm [Eusebe's] despair" but to "suffer it to have its effects" (3.2). A body, concrete and unforgettable when present, becomes abstract and forgettable when absent—shock, as Eusebe's earlier narrative shows, quickly becomes forgetfulness. It is the narrative that gives the body staying power and overcomes the inherent transience of theatre.

Even with Mme. Tricastin's narrative triumph at the end, however, *The Massacre* remains a story of a woman trapped in her own space, unable to defend herself, and exhibited against her will. If *The Massacre* was an attempt, however transient, to escape from the boundaries of that woman's space, the stage, one wonders how Inchbald must have looked back on *The Massacre* in her later career. For despite Mme. Tricastin's repeated requests to fly, she leaves her house only when borne out on a bier. Since the stage had spawned and nurtured her as a writer, Inchbald might well have felt like leaving was a form of death. Her words in prose might have a wider circulation and wider significance, but they would never have the animated life that they took when performed by actors—even by herself—onstage. Given her relationship with Godwin, she might also have felt the need for protection. It is telling that Inchbald sought Godwin's "protection"—or at least his advice about publication—for a play about a woman's being unprotected in her home space. Like Eusebe Tricastin, Godwin "protected" Inchbald by sequestering her—not in the woman's showy, emotional, or domestic space of the stage, but in a back room that ultimately provided no protection and in the secrecy of an unpublished manuscript. And indeed, though *The Massacre* remained "protected" in manuscript form until Inchbald's death, Godwin could not protect Inchbald in her next foray into the public world: *Every One Has His Fault* received severe criticism for its aesthetic and political transgressions, even though Inchbald seems to have taken Old Tricastin's tack of calm reasoning with her attackers. Ultimately, as Thomas Crochunis points out, Inchbald would make a career straddling stage and page, successful as a playwright, novelist, and critic. But in many ways her analysis in *The Massacre* was right on target: though she would seek men's assistance with narrative and publicity, in many ways, she would live and die in her home onstage.

Why True Words Aren't Things:
Marino Faliero and Sardanapalus

Why make "words" into "things"? It is a phrase Byron used often around 1819–1821.[18] In *Marino Faliero, Doge of Venice*, Byron has his Doge promise that "true words are things, / And dying men's are things which long outlive, / And oftentimes avenge them" (5.1.289–91) In *Don Juan* canto III, Byron says of his "eastern antijacobin" poet—a parody of Southey but perhaps also a way of expressing his own fears that his status as a commercial poet might render his work irrelevent—that

> words are things, and a small drop of ink,
> Falling like dew, upon a thought, produces
> That which makes thousands, perhaps millions, think. (*Don Juan* 3.793–95).

The Prophecy of Dante speaks of "the Spirit of the fervent days of Old,/ When words were things that came to pass, and thought / Flash'd o'er the future" (2.1–3). In *Childe Harold III*, Byron proclaims his faith:

> I do believe,
> Though I have found them not, that there may be
> Words which are things,—hopes which will not deceive,
> And virtues which are merciful, nor weave
> Snares for the failing. (1059–63)

L. E. Marshall has argued that Byron's prophecy engages with Horne Tooke's theory that words are indispensable facilitators of thought:

his desire to make "words" into "things" is a desire to call things by their proper names so that the world can be properly understood. But there is a fixity and concreteness in Byron's "things" that seems to be at odds with the simple proper meanings of words. Only one of Byron's four uses of the phrase actually deals with literal words—*Don Juan*'s "small drop of ink"—and even then words are boiled down to their concrete materiality. The rest of the examples, as Marshall recognizes, deal with "silent poets"—with words that go unsaid, or perhaps cannot be said. The desire for a "word" that is a "thing" is a desire for a medium more powerful than words—a medium more concrete, more permanent, more lasting.

But it is tantalizing to think of "words" becoming "things" in the medium of the drama, and especially in the only one of Byron's dramas to be performed—albeit much against his will—in his lifetime: *Marino Faliero, Doge of Venice*. The performed drama, after all, is the only form that does make a poet's "words" into "things": sets, costumes, actors. If Byron wanted his words to become "things," the stage was a natural place to turn. The theatre, as he says in his opening address for Drury Lane, is "the Drama's tower of pride" (2), a "pile . . ." "[r]ear'd where once rose the mightiest in our isle" (17–18). If, as Jerome Christensen has argued, Byron's dramas were his way "to indulge the fantasy that he might return to England during the ensuing chaos as the man on the horse who would command the rebellious masses and shape a new social and economic order" (265), or if, as Michael Simpson has speculated, Byron contemplated his closet dramas' eventual enactment, Byron could have thought of the theatre as a concrete way to make "words" into "things" in the realm of political possibility.

But for Byron, there was a worry in making "words" into "things." As Adam Potkay has pointed out, the late eighteenth and early nineteenth centuries were a time when the word "thing" was shifting in meaning, from its inclusive Old English sense of a "creature, object, property, cause, motive, reason, lawsuit, event, affair, act, deed, enterprise, condition, circumstance, contest, discussion, meeting, council, assembly, court of justice, point, respect, sake" (Potkay 393–94), to its more modern sense of a manufactured object or commodity. Old English, according to Potkay, "did not in general conceive of material objects in a delimited physical sense, separate from events, from the constitution and frame of that which is and comes to be, and from the transcendental conditions for knowing what little we can know of systems or stories that exceed our comprehension" (394).

In the eighteenth century, however, "thing" began to have its sense of the impersonal, objective, and material: Samuel Johnson defined "thing" as "[w]hatever is; not a person" (Potkay 394); in Blackstone's *Commentaries on the Laws of England*, it is a "being without life or consciousness; an inanimate object, as distinguished from a person or living creature" (Potkay 394).

Byron's engagement with the word-as-thing, then, is quite problematic. On one hand, "things" last when all other things (including the poet) are dead: the *Don Juan* poet's "small drop of ink" "[s]urvives himself, his tomb, and all that's his" (3.793, 800); Marino's words "are things which long outlive, / And oftentimes avenge [him]" (5.1.290–91). But on the other hand, separated from their maker, they become commodities, circulating promiscuously through the system. It is a problem that would have concerned Byron a good deal as his commodified image circulated around Europe in bootleg poems, portraits, and locks of hair. Words and things, words-made-things: Byron might well have wondered where the original "word" was in all of these "things," and how that "word" might relate to the original sayer of the word. And worse yet, what might be the political effect of these words-made-things? Would they last? And is there any effect to them in the present? Byron wrote to John Murray a few months before finishing *Marino Faliero*:

> We are on the verge of a *row* here—last night they have overwritten all the city walls—with "up with the Republic[""] and ["]death to the Pope &c.&c." [T]his would be nothing in London where the walls are privileged—and where when Somebody went to Chancellor Thurlow to tell him as an alarming sign that he had seen "Death to the king" on Hyde park wall—old Thurlow asked him if he had ever seen "C--t" chalked on the same place, to which the alarmist responding in the affirmative—Thurlow resumed "& so have I for these last 30 years and yet it never made my p--k stand. But here it is a different thing[;] they are not used to such fierce political inscriptions—and the police is all on the alert, and the Cardinal glares pale through all his purple.—" (*Letters* 7: 84)

What might be the effect of Byron's own fierce inscriptions? Do either words or things operate in a "privileged" space, exempt from public discourse? And might one have the power to move where the other does not?

This is precisely the problem in *Marino*, a play where, as Jerome Christensen has observed, "Romantic ambition labors in a theatre of baroque inconsequence" (264). As William Jewett has suggested, this is a play about the problem of forming individuals into groups—about the ways that power can create or deny connection, and about the ways that connection can create or deny power. But if communities are to be built, the mechanism does not seem to be through words. Despite the Doge's stunning affirmation that "[t]rue *words* are *things*" (5.1.289), the human voice means almost nothing. As Jerome Christensen has observed, Steno's scrawl means less than nothing—"patriarch, patrician, and plebe all deny that the scrawl has any consequences" (267). As Angiolina says, "The dying Roman said, "twas but a name: / It were indeed no more, if human breath / Could make or mar it" (2.1.58–61). The Doge's name is but a "word":— "nay, worse—a worthless by-word" (1.2.100),— and Philip Calendaro chafes at being ruled "with a word / As with a spell" (2.1.118).

But set in opposition to the word is the physical certainty of the material sign. The architecture of Venice is almost as like a character in this drama: —the "lofty walls / Of those tall piles and sea girt palaces" that calm and strengthen Lioni;, the "[t]all fane" that holds the bodies of the Doge's ancestors;, the great bell of St. Mark's, which holds the "last poor privilege they leave their prince" (3.2.248), the palace gates and the Giant's Staircase that form the scene of the Doge's execution.

Even human language is static and presentational—almost a physical object itself. We know very little about the characters in this play through their words—a fact that has led many critics to view Byron's characters as "puppets," with no life, no freedom, no individuated subjectivity.[19] If there is "character" in *Marino*, it manifests itself from the outside in rather than from the inside out. Very little information is exchanged through conversation: Angiolina might plead "let me not be shut out / From your distress" (2.1.214–15), but in a way all characters are equally "shut out," despite the verbal bombast. When they speak, the characters tend to declaim their feelings rather than interacting with each other. Nor does the word have any more power in social interaction. This is not a play of persuasion. Israel Bertuccio goes to recruit a Doge who has already been self-seduced; the Doge woos an Angiolina who has already been chosen and made her choice. No one ever changes because of what is said to them; conversation has no power to show, to persuade, to act as an instrument of knowledge and power. Even in the soliloquy, that most private of theatrical forms, we learn little about the characters' inner lives. Lioni's 110-line soliloquy tells us little about him other than that he is tired, and the Doge's soliloquies express little except his anger and his impotence. The ultimate power in Venice is not the word, but the hand that draws the blood. The blood on Israel Bertuccio's face signals his wrong more strongly than any word.

Given this truth, reading the physical is a necessity rather than a luxury in Byron's Venice. Everyone in Venice is a reader of the word made thing—Steno's scrawl, the marble of Venice, the Doge's robes, the Doge's marriage vows, even the Doge's execution and the execution of the other conspirators. Each wants to know which is the word made flesh and which is the word made merely word—whether Steno's scrawl is a grave insult or "the wind / Unto the rock" (5.1.421–22), whether Angiolina's marriage vows are written in stone or wax, whether the Doge's robes signify power or mere puppet play, what it means that, as Calendaro says, "these unmanly creeping things . . . rule us with a word / As with a spell" (3.1.118), whether the conspirators, when called, will back up their words with their bodies. And everyone is a reader of the body as well. The officers outside the Doge's chamber try to read the Doge's mood in his expression, Angiolina does the same in act 2, the Doge tries to read the sentence of the Forty in the judges' faces, Philip Calendaro tries to read Bertram's resoluteness through his bodily actions, Lioni tries to read Bertram's mission in his dress and in his expression. The real question in this play is Angiolina's: "Ah, why / Do you still keep apart, and walk alone, / And let such strong emotions stamp your brow, / As not betraying their full import, yet / Disclose too much?" (2.1.175–79). All are looking for the truth of the body, a truth that escapes the falseness and ineffectuality of words, a truth that immediately compels assent. The physical sign—the public symbol, the blood on the face—is the only sort of sign that has any power in Venice.

It is not just Byron's insistence on the unities, then, that gives these plays their claustrophobic feel. Both *Marino Faliero* and *Sardanapalus* begin with their heroes trapped—both literally within their palaces and figuratively within a network of public words and public things. The Doge is literally "cover'd o'er / With all the apparel of the state" (1.1.7–8); Sardanapalus, self-hidden, "ne'er looks / beyond his palace walls" (1.2.110). For Faliero, this claustrophobia is contrasted with an earlier day, when he sailed the Adriatic and fought at Zara: "Oh! but for even a day / Of my full youth, while yet my body served / My soul as serves the generous steed his lord, / I would have dash'd amongst them, asking few / In aid to overthrow these swoln patricians!" (1.2.274–78). And his present confinement is associated with all the "apparel of the state," and particularly the ducal crown, robes, and throne: "Haply had I been what the senate sought, / A thing of robes and trinkets" (3.2.309).

In fact, these "things"—the robe, crown, throne, and trinkets—seem to have made Marino a "thing" himself. "A chief in armour," he says, "is their Suzerain, / And not a thing in robes" (4.2.377–78); "better that / They ne'er had been, than drag me on to be / The thing these arch-oppressors fain would make me" (1.2.350–52); "I cannot quench a glorious life at once, / Nor dwindle to the thing I now must be" (3.1.106–7), "When I *am* nothing, let that which I *was* / Be still sometimes a name on thy sweet lips, / A shadow in thy fancy, of a thing / Which would not have thee mourn it" (2.2.509–12). In making his words "things," the Doge seems to have become their inhuman carrier, a "thing" among "things," powerful but solid.

What seems to provide an alternative to this world of "things," as Christensen has argued, is a Byronic digressiveness, one that is usually expressed in words. Steno the patrician, "[y]oung, gay, galliard and haughty" (1.1.21), is as free as Marino is captive—we might speculate that the reason Steno's sentence, one month of close arrest, is so galling to Marino is because it underscores Marino's own sentence to life within the palace walls. Patricians reserve two freedoms that Marino does not have. The first is the freedom to speak. Where Marino is condemned to mute physical symbolization—the robes, the throne, the ducal bonnet—patricians are free to use words, and to use them promiscuously. In fact, Steno's only appearance in the play is to take the liberty of apologizing to Angiolina and the Doge, a liberty that counts as a double liberty, since the Doge's crime has released him from his physical confinement. As Christensen suggests, Steno's mark is the very emblem of Byron's own digressive style: the freedom to say, the freedom to apologize, all mark the patrician's ability to do and say whatever he chooses. Where Marino is limited by the nature of his allotted material signs—his robe and crown and the final pealing of the bell of St. Mark's—Steno can say anything he wants.

The second freedom that a concrete "thing" like Marino is denied is the freedom of movement. Just as Steno has the power to digress in his conversation, Lioni, the play's other patrician, insists on his freedom to roam. Although Lioni is partially responsible for making the architecture of Venice the force that it is in this play—he contrasts the "tall piles and sea-girt palaces . . . like altars ranged along the broad canal" (4.1.76–79) with the more transient enchantments of the "delusion of the dizzy scene" indoors (4.1.62)—he refuses to be trapped by that architecture. When Bertram warns him to stay at home when the bell rings for the council, Lioni absolutely refuses, even if by leaving he risks his life. "Nor is there aught which shall impede me" (4.1.194): just as Steno speaks at will, Lioni goes at will. Where the Doge cannot leave the palace without leaving behind a part of himself, Lioni feels at home both outside and inside. Associated with the piles, he is free to choose which one will be his home.

What, then, is the political effect of the fluid and concrete? The Doge lays claim to the quasi-physical power of words-as-things— "dying men's [words] are things which long outlive, / And oftentimes avenge them" (5.1.290–91). But words are precisely what the Doge doesn't get. When the junta informs him that his place in the Hall of Doges will be covered with a black veil and an inscription, Marino responds, "Were it not better to record the facts, / So that the contemplator might approve, / Or at the least learn *whence* the crimes arose?" (5.1.509–11). That request is denied. But the Doge is left with something that might be more powerful: a simple thing, or, more accurately, a simple space. Christensen argues that the black veil is the perfect satire on censorship, a mark that marks the digressiveness and inconsequentiality of all authoritative utterance. But more than simply a sign, the veil marks a place where signification can happen. Just like the balcony of the red columns where Israel Bertuccio and Philip Calendero are hung, or the court of the ducal palace where Marino is both crowned and executed, or the plaza of St. Mark's where the conspirators plan to stage their revolution, the portrait space is a space where there should be meaning. Just like the resurrected Drury Lane, "[r]ear'd where once rose the mightist in our isle" (18), the portrait space creates a place where stories can take place, and where truth can be told. Even in leaving the space blank, the ruling junta tell a story.

And in fact, contrary to Christensen's assertion that *Marino* constitutes a satire on authoritative utterance by exposing its digressiveness, the very digressiveness of the junta's authoritative utterance proves to be its downfall: "This place is of Marino Faliero, / Decapitated for his crimes" (5.1.499–500). As the Doge points out, the junta eschews the explanatory power of narrative. But because they do not take control of the story, their intended signification, that Marino was a traitor to the state, has been lost. All that is left is a tantalizing space that tempts the poet to write. In fact, it is that very blank space that motivates Byron to write his drama: "The black veil which is painted over the place of Marino Faliero amongst the Doges, and the Giants' Staircase where he was crowned, and decrowned, and decapitated, struck forcibly upon my imagination; as did his fiery character and strange story" (195–96). While words might have freedom and power in the short term, Byron suggests, it is the *things* that remain, and the things that create poetry.

And there is another sense of the word "thing" that Byron plays with in *Marino*, one that offers the promise of a drama not imprisoned by its spectacle, not held inhuman by its distance. As Potkay explains, the English word "thing," at least up to the eighteenth century, preserves part of the sense of the Roman word *res*: its capacity to designate "a case, an affair, an event."[20] Where our current thinking about "things" remains concrete and material—subject, perhaps, to commodification and objectification—there is also a sense in which it is transient and ephemeral: a "happening," a sense that survives in our current phrases *the way things go* and *thinking about things*.[21] The dramatic performance, then, might be a "thing" not in the sense of being material, but in the sense of being ephemeral, one of the kind. The use of the word "happening" to describe a particular type of theatrical performance takes this term into the twentieth century: a theatre performance is a transient event in the world.

Thus it is fitting that Byron ends with a scene that is theatrical, ephemeral, and highly significant: the moment when a crowd of plebeians gathers around the gates of the Ducal palace to watch the Doge's execution. It is an extraordinary moment of seeing in a play that has emphasized reading as its dominant mode of gaining knowledge, and an extraordinarily clear call to action in a play that has constantly downplayed the significance of its public signs and symbols. The visceral experience of seeing the gory head roll down the Giants' Steps finally offers the promise of a sign that truly communicates its meaning. Moreover, it offers a sign that directly motivates action—as the crowd breaks through the gates, presumably with revolutionary intent. Sight leads to knowledge, knowledge leads to power, and power leads to action, all in one continuous, unbroken sequence.[22] There is never any doubt about whether the plebeians can see the inside through the outside—whether they can ever know, completely, by seeing the physical. The only doubt in the scene—"Are you sure he's dead?"—is quickly resolved by the brute physical fact of the gory head rolling down the Giants' Staircase. The force of the sign is such that the people are completely united in their interpretation: "Then they have murder'd him who would have freed us" (5.4.22); "He was a kind man to the commons ever"; "Wisely they did to keep their portals barr'd. / Would we had known the work they were preparing" (5.4.23–24). The truth of the sign unites the audience behind it. There is no need for conspiracies, no need for persuasion, no need for words. The true knowledge of the physical body unites the audience, gives it control over a situation that it has previously had no control over, and finally motivates it to exactly the sort of collective action that the Doge has been trying to put together for the entire play. "True words," as the Doge says, may be "things," but only an event produces action.

At the same time, as I have previously written, Byron must surely have been aware that had this scene actually been played onstage, the effect probably would have been comic rather than tragic.[23] Although Byron's stage directions do not make it clear whether an actual gory head is actually supposed to roll—or rather, bounce—down the Giant's Staircase, the sight of the physical object, so necessary for the physical power of the scene in the play, would almost certainly have been anticlimactic. Its staginess would only underscore its lack of truth; the power it has for its audience of plebeians onstage would only underscore the lack of power that it would have for its audience in the pit. Far from the "tramplings" of an "intelligent or of an ignorant audience," Byron may have been afraid of the lack of trampling—the sitting still, or perhaps even the laughter, that the physical sign would evoke.

Marino, then, is suspended between words, actions, and objects. Words are free but impotent; material objects permanent but imprisoning and inhuman. A world in which things "are" as they "are"—as in Marino's "I will be as I should be, or be nothing" (2.1.453)—is a world in which things cannot change. But a society where "unmanly creeping things" rule by "words" is just as bad. And while *Marino* holds out some promise that an event—that thing that holds the promise of the concrete coupled with the ephemerality of theatre—might be able to escape the traps of power set by words and things, even that solution is hedged about with irony. In the end, it is the space of signification that remains—the place for the portrait, the place of the execution. Spaces hold the power of words locked within the solidity of things, waiting to be released by an event. But if an event might not be effective, what then?

The question of whether words or things were the best way to gain power continued to preoccupy Byron. Even after he had falsely heard that *Marino Faliero* had been hissed offstage,[24] he was enticed by the theatre's ability to combine the power of narrative and the power of concrete objects. In *Sardanapalus*, finished about a year after *Marino*, Byron seems to be torn between a closer, more intimate theatrical world and a theatre with broader reach, a theatre that, not coincidentally, seems to require Sardanapalus's conversion away from the concrete and toward a myth that is more immaterial.

In *Sardanapalus*, Byron had evolved a more complex way of thinking about the interrelationship of words and things, one that recognizes the interdependence of words and things in creating power. Although it is tempting to place Sardanapalus, the play's mythmaking dandy, squarely in the realm of words, and Salemenes, the play's hard-nosed man of action, into the camp of "things," Byron makes it clear that the methods of power are never that simple. The irony is apparent even in the play's first scene, where Salemenes criticizes Sardanapalus for failing to make a myth powerful enough to sustain his empire. Empires, he says, are built on stories, not strength: "Semiramis—a woman only—led / These our Assyrians to the solar shores / Of Ganges" (1.2.126–28). And the current Assyrian empire is just as fragile: "thirteen hundred years / Of Empire ending like a shepherd's tale" (1.1.7–8). Meanwhile Sardanapalus, the play's theatrical dandy, extols the power of the concrete. "For my trophies I have founded cities," he counters. "There's Tarsus and Anchialus, both built / In one day—what could that blood-loving beldame, / My martial grandam, chaste Semiramis, / Do more, except destroy them" (1.2.237–40)? There's more than a little mythmaking in Sardanapalus's concrete example: Tarsus and Anchialus were built not only to "make my subjects feel / The weight of human misery less" (1.2.263–64) but to carry Sardanapalus's own self-made myth in their inscription: "Eat, drink, and love; the rest's not with a fillip" (1.2.252). And there's more than a little of the concrete in Salemenes's heroic myth: as Sardanapalus points out, Semiramis caused real deaths on her march to the Ganges, and his own heroic mythmaking will have similar consequences. A few scenes later, Sardanapalus magnanimously spares the lives of the conspirators who are plotting against him and gives them back their swords—clearly the action of a mythical hero, but also an action made real by its dramatic physicality, and with predictable real-world consequences.

The concrete makes the mythmaking real; the myth gives the concrete meaning.

The enemy, then, is not materiality per se. Indeed, *Sardanapalus* shows that materiality can be as pliable and flexible as any dream. Inside the monarch's palace, objects take their direction from Sardanapalus's creativity; even gender is subject to his "construction."[25] Nor is the physical imprisoning in *Sardanapalus* as it is in *Marino*. Like the patrician Lioni, although Sardanapalus is empowered by the physical trappings of power he refuses to be confined by them. In a replay of *Marino*, when Salemenes asks Sardanapalus to stay away from the night's banquet in order to save himself from conspiracy, Sardanapalus refuses. Whether he holds a sword or a distaff, Sardanapalus is fully in control of the trappings of power.

The problem with materiality only comes when the audience expands. Where physicality inside the palace had bent to Sardanapalus's will, outside the palace Sardanapalus, like *Marino*, runs the risk of being a "thing." To present himself as a sovereign is, in essence, not to be himself. Arbaces says of Sardanapalus,

> Methought he look'd like Nimrod as he spoke,
> Even as the proud imperial statue stands
> Looking the monarch of the kings around it,
> And sways, while they but ornament, the temple. (2.1.352–56)

Myrrha begs him not to leave "thy subjects' eyes ungratified" least "the gods [go] unworshipp'd" (1.2.581–82). He fears becoming frozen into his own image, like "my ancestor Semiramis, / A sort of semi-glorious human monster" (1.2.180–81) rather than like Bacchus, "a true man, who did his utmost / In good or evil to surprise mankind" (193–94). To bear the image of the king is to bear the image of Nimrod or Semiramis, or any one of the hosts of other monarchs subject to their subject's command. "Is *this* glory?" Sardanapalus asks, "[t]hen let me live in ignominy ever" (1.2.140).

Indeed, such is the power of this image that Sardanapalus is constantly worried about his humanity. "We are all men" (1.2.266) he says of his subjects; "Those gods were merely men" (1.2.272) of the Greek gods. "I am no soldier, but a man" (5.1.565) he tells Salemenes after battle.

> I feel a thousand mortal things about me,
> But nothing godlike, unless it may be
> The thing which you condemn, a disposition

> To love and to be merciful, to pardon
> The follies of my species, and (that's human)
> To be indulgent to my own. (1.2.272–78)

Why does Sardanapalus need to protest so much? He feels, even within the palace, that he is in danger of becoming a monument, a "god" in a world of "slaves."

Sardanapalus's initial answer, of course, is to create a theatricality of his own making, enslaving himself to avoid becoming a master, feminizing himself in order to avoid becoming a man. But as much as he tries to create the "human," the "man," he finds himself treated as an "object," a "god." His minions bow, Myrrha serves. Even as he proclaims "I seek but to be loved, not worshipp'd" (3.1.36)—and the sincerity of these pronouncements is rightly in doubt—even within his own palace he keeps his status as a "thing," a "pageant."

Worse yet, his attempts to keep himself a "man" rather than a "god" cut him off from the humanity of those around him. In political terms, it cuts him off from his subjects. He is a monarch who "ne'er looks / Beyond his palace walls" (1.2.110), and so does not know that his subjects have less peace and plenty than he believes. And even with those who should be closest, his need to control the circumstances in which he is seen cuts him off from human connection. "There comes / For ever something between us and what / We deem our happiness" (1.2.432–34), he tells Myrrha, and she answers him "[m]y lord!" (436). "Our hearts are not in our own power" (4.1.250), he tells Zarina. "I will not weep for thee; / Thou shalt be mourn'd for as thou wouldst be mourn'd" (5.1.151–52), he says over the body of Salemenes. Alienated from Myrrha, from Salemenes, from the queen, from his sons, and perhaps even from himself, he is trapped in a "theatrical" world of his own making. His very showiness, his self-justification, his constant need for reassurance place him like an actor onstage, separated from the audience from whom he seeks approval.

In this context, it is important to see what Sardanapalus's leaving the palace can and cannot do. It does win him the love of Myrrha, although, as Christensen points out, she is as much in love with an image as with a man. It restores Salemenes's confidence that "[t]here is a careless courage which corruption / Has not all quench'd" (1.1.10–11); it proves to both the troops and the king himself that it is possible for him to "fight as he revels" (3.1.213). It rallies his supporters and provides a target for his enemies. But it does not win the battle or preserve the empire. The first is left to fate—the rise of the Euphrates and the betrayal of Ofratanes—the second to careful planning. For all the rhetoric of amazement and magnificence, Sardanapalus's heroic battlefield appearance seems to be little more than the "pageant" of leadership that his rule has been.

The play's final conflagration, then, is both an act of nostalgia for a theatre where actor and audience could relate on a more human level and a reach toward a newer, more immaterial theatre, one that could reach its audience without making its participants into "things." Pania and crowds of soldiers beg to sacrifice themselves along with Sardanapalus and Myrrha. And Myrrha herself not only takes part in the spectacle but joins in creating it when she brings the torch from Baal's shrine. Far from being a final act of selfishness, it is a gesture that, given its fullest potential, embraces the entire court and the entire nation—indeed, it is memorialized that way in Delacroix's painting, which includes man, horse, and treasure as well as king and woman. As Pania says, it is a pile big enough not only for a king's obsequies but for a kingdom's (5.1.367–68).

But it is also an act designed to make the material immaterial. After giving as much treasure as he can to his followers—"Remember, what you leave you leave the slaves / Who slew me" (5.1.384–85)—the pyre is an attempt to convert the rest into nothingness, "purified by death from some / Of the gross stains of too material being" (5.1.424–25). All the material traces of the empire, "[y]our treasure, your abode, your sacred relics / Of arms, and records, monuments, and spoils" go into the "absorbing" element (5.1.430–34). They are converted first into light and then to ashes, but it is the light and not the ashes that will "lesson ages, rebel nations, and / Voluptuous princes" (5.1.441–42).

The image that Byron uses for the funeral pyre, the "pillar form'd of cloud and flame" (5.1.438) that led the Israelites in Exodus 13:21–22, is the same one he used to describe the fire that burned the theatre in his address for the opening of the new Drury Lane:

> Ye who beheld, (oh! sight admired and moun'd
> Whose radiance mock'd the ruin it adorn'd!)
> Through clouds of fire the massy fragments riven,
> Like Israel's pillar, chase the night from heaven;
> Saw long column of revolving flames
> Shake its red shadow o'er the startled Thames. (5–10)

Like the old Drury Lane, Sardanapalus's theatre has consumed the old theatre of "things" and instituted in its place a theatre that reproduces the spectacle in immaterial form. Interestingly enough, Byron's own experience of the fire that burned the old Drury was spectatorial. He wrote to Lord Holland, "By the bye, the best view of the said fire (which I myself saw from a house-top in Covent Garden) was at Westminster Bridge, from the reflection of the Thames" (*Miscellanies*, 3: 86). Byron's location on a rooftop in Covent Garden, the site of the rival theatre, makes his experience with the pillar of flame almost like the experience of an audience member in the theatre; his opinion that the best view was from the reflection in the Thames makes the burning of the theatre seem (as it was) like a public spectacle. Byron's theatre—spectacular, immaterial, public—consumes the theatre of "things" even as it creates theatre as a public happening, an event that leaves its traces, not on the material but in the collective mind of its viewers.

Byron surely would have known that the final conflagration would have been the most theatrically attractive part of the play: Alexander Calvert, one of the play's nineteenth-century producers, wrote that "the play is a poem over the heads of the people, but the 'conflagration' will make it a financial success" (Wolfson 894). But again, as in *Marino*, he refuses to turn his play into a theatrical event. Instead, he begins his preface by reiterating, "In publishing the following Tragedies I have only to repeat that they were not composed with the most remote view to the stage" (263). And there are signs of the closet in Sardanapalus's conflagration as well. Instead of inviting Pania and the troops to join, Sardanapalus takes only his ideal reader—his "mirror" and Myrrha—for a private experience in his closet.

Thus, for Byron, closet reading and theatrical event converge. Byron's turn to the closet tries to capture the experience of theatrical performance without its material traces—the grossness of audiences and performance spaces that might imprison the poet in time and space. But in giving up the grossness of audiences and monuments—Sardanapalus has tellingly disgraced his own monument by his engraving—Byron might also have abandoned the "fierce political inscriptions" that he admired as he was writing *Marino*. The light might "lesson ages," but it does not involve an audience in creating a revolution, braving the risk of being laughed at for social change. It is telling that most nineteenth-century performances downplayed Sardanapalus's effeminacy—according to George Henry Lewes because "[Kean] instinctively felt that detail would raise a titter!" (Wolfson 894). Byron would rather risk imprisonment in his own "small drop of ink" that might reach the ages than chance the "tramplings" of an audience that might trample his own sovereignty as well as that of the state.

Taken together, Byron and Inchbald suggest that we sell the "closet" dramas of the Romantic period short when we assume a single political valence to stage or closet. Rather than speculate on the effects of closet and stage, then, we might be better off looking at *fantasies* of reading and viewing, and recognizing that those fantasies are often contradictory and conflicted. The closet might represent a turn away from contemporary staging or an attempt to "reform" the stage, but only after a longing glance over its shoulder at a fantasy of what performance might be or mean. These mixed attempts—these crossovers between closet and stage—stage their alternatives more often than not and come to surprising conclusions about the powers and pitfalls of both narrative and stage.

3

Man Seeing

Wordsworth and the Theatrical Voice

The title of Kenneth Johnston's biography, *The Hidden Wordsworth*, might seem an odd choice for the poet whom Keats immortalized as the creator of the "egotistical sublime." But the title does point out something interesting about the poet. For although William Wordsworth's poetry does usually concern the self, the self that we see in Wordsworth's poetry is always partially hidden. We usually find Wordsworth's narrator outside the main current of the action, hanging back, observing. There has rarely been a poet whose greatest moments have so exclusively concerned the act of looking—"Once again / Do I behold" ("Tintern Abbey" 4–5); "Half an hour I watched" (1799 *Prelude* 1.270);[1] "all at once I saw" ("I Wandered Lonely" 3); "I have at all times endeavoured to look steadily at my subject" (1802 preface to *Lyrical Ballads*); "The eye it cannot chuse but see" ("Expostulation and Reply" 17); "Thus have I looked, nor ceased to look, oppressed" (1805 *Prelude* 7.599); "The things which I have seen I now can see no more" ("Ode" 9). And rarely has there been a poet who so compulsively emphasizes his distance from his objects: "I wandered lonely as a Cloud / That floats on high o'er Vales and Hills" ("I Wandered Lonely as a Cloud" 1–2); "I again repose / Here, under this dark sycamore, and view" ("Tintern Abbey" 9–10); "Will no one tell me what she sings?" ("Solitary Reaper" 17); "reascending the bare common, [I] saw / A naked pool that lay beneath the hills,/The beacon on the summit, and more near, / A girl who bore a pitcher on her head" (1805 *Prelude* 11.302–5). Of course, Wordsworth is generally thought to be projecting his personality onto the objects he observes, creatively envisioning rather than passively receiving. But if we think of Wordsworth as a character in his own poems—as, in essence, a poetic persona—by and large he presents himself as a spectator: as Man Looking.

Of course Wordsworth was not the first author to take on a spectatorial perspective—one need only think of *The Spectator* and *The Female Spectator*, or Dr. Johnson's "observation with expansive view." But Wordsworth's spectatorship seems somehow different, simultaneously more distant and more involved. Often he is close enough to speak to his subjects, as in the "Discharged Soldier," "The Thorn," and "Tintern Abbey." But at the same time, he often seems to be a disembodied consciousness, lacking the location in time, place, and social class that Addison and Steele's spectator embodied.

In this chapter, I contend that Wordsworth picked up both perspectives from the theatre. From the street theatres and festivals of the French Revolution, he picked up the idea that the spectator should be part of the action. From the more distant spectacles in the theatres of London, he saw what happened when the spectator was set apart. As early as *The Borderers*, Wordsworth began to develop a theory about the moral force of seeing concrete objects, not to imaginatively reconstruct them but to realize their essence as beings outside oneself. He also begins a sustained critique of the type of theatre where the spectators sit apart from the action in favor of a much older type of theatre where the spectators and actors interact, where they inhabit the same sort of moral world. Wordsworth continues this critique through the *Lyrical Ballads*, where his mini-dramas and scenes of spectatorship are designed to get readers to abandon the distant way of seeing imposed by the theatres and to return to an older world of personal contact, where the act of observing could regain its moral force. And finally, Wordsworth uses his view of an older sort of theatre to create a poetic persona as a hybrid actor-spectator, a figure who combines the public presence and expansive vision of the actor with the human contact of an actor who stands among his audience and the bewilderment of the audience member excluded from the spectacle. This pose allows Wordsworth to retain the power of the actor even as he establishes contact with his audience. He is a spectator among a nation of spectators.

The Theatre: Presence as Knowledge in *The Borderers*

In order to understand why the spectatorship was so important to Wordsworth, we must first look at his earliest experiment with drama, *The Borderers*. *The Borderers* has often been dismissed as an immature work. But I would like to turn the question of its immaturity around to ask why it was that Wordsworth chose the drama as one of his earliest experiments with genre. The Wordsworth who wrote *The Borderers* was only 27. He had written the highly conventional "An Evening Walk" and *Descriptive Sketches*, which had been published in 1793, and he had composed "Salisbury Plain," a poem that Wordsworth himself saw as unstable in its genre.[2] He had experimented with shorter lyrics in his schooldays and with narrative in "Salisbury Plain," but he was far from settled in his choice of genre. We can think of the Wordsworth who wrote *The Borderers*, then, as a poet who had not quite chosen the genre that would define his poetic vocation. At that point in his career, Wordsworth chose to write a play, and the play he chose to write was *The Borderers*.

It is clear from the evidence surrounding the composition of *The Borderers* that it was written for the stage. Wordsworth did several staged readings of the play at Stowey in the summer and autumn of 1797, and after those readings, he showed the play to Thomas Knight, one of the principal actors of Covent Garden, for advice on theatrical production. He traveled to London in the winter of 1797 to alter the play according to Knight's suggestions, and he submitted the play to Covent Garden that same winter, where it was promptly rejected because of the "metaphysical obscurity of one character" (*Borderers* 3–5). Wordsworth later attributed its rejection to the "deprav'd State of the Stage at present," and he never wrote another drama. Nonetheless, it is clear that at the time of composition, Wordsworth thought that the play was stageworthy, and he fully intended it to be produced onstage.

In order to understand why Wordsworth turned to the performed drama at this crucial stage in his career, there are a few things that we need to understand about the difference between lyric, narrative, and drama, and the way that these differences affect the reader—or rather, the audience—of each particular genre. As Susan Edwards Meisenhelder has argued, the way that Wordsworth's work affected his readers was a critical concern for Wordsworth; Wordsworth sought to educate and morally improve his readers by giving them a certain kind of poetic experience that would transform their sensibilities and influence their feelings and responses (Meisenhelder 8). Wordsworth would later set out to transform the lyric so that "feelings connected with important subjects will be nourished . . . [and] such habits of mind will be produced that . . . the understanding of the being to whom we address ourselves . . . must necessarily be in some degree enlightened, his taste exalted, and his affections ameliorated" (*Lyrical Ballads* 8). But at the time he wrote *The Borderers*, Wordsworth was faced with a choice between poetry that was essentially narrative and poetry that was essentially dramatic—that is, poetry that operates through a narrative voice, and poetry that does not. Eve Kosofsky Sedgwick writes in *The Epistemology of the Closet* that one of the conditions of narrative is that "novel-readers voluntarily plunge into worlds that strip them, however temporarily, of the painfully acquired cognitive maps of their ordinary lives (awfulness of going to a party without knowing anyone) on condition of an invisibility that promises cognitive exemption and eventual privilege" (97). This plunge, however willingly taken, creates, "especially at the beginning of novels," a "space of high anxiety and dependence" that leads to an "early overidentification with the novel's organizing eye" (97). The narrator, in effect, is the reader's guide to the party; the reader is the naïf that must be led about by the novel's version of the experienced before she can gain the cognitive perspective that is the narrator's natural right. The drama, however, is a different matter. There, the reader is precisely in the position of the guest who goes to a party without knowing anyone. To be sure, there is an organizing principle in the drama—a "narrative voice" that stands behind the organization of its characters, scenes, and actions. But the reader is left without the explicit comfort of a narrative voice—that scion of cognitive privilege that would reassure her that she is reading the characters properly, and that she is putting the proper valence on each of the things she observes. Left to her own devices, she must figure out the relationships between the characters and their places in the drama all by herself.

But the performed drama offers its own sort of knowledge to compensate for the lack of a narrative voice. The reader of a novel must rely on the narrator to give her the relevant details about character, plot, and setting—peculiarities of dress, or tone of voice, facial expression, or a way of walking, sitting, or holding one's head. In the drama, these facts are all laid out for the viewer to see. If a character comes in *en dishabille*, or talks in a hurried tone of voice, or grimaces at another character's line, or shifts uncomfortably as another character talks, the reader does not need the narrator to point it out. She can see it herself, just as she might see characters performing a certain way in real life, and through that vision, she gains a sort of cognitive privilege that is simply not available to the reader of novels. Reading the physical, then, is the drama's substitute for the narrative voice. The reader/viewer orients herself to the dramatic world by seeing and experiencing the drama's physicality, and through that physicality—viewing the actions onstage, herself, perhaps, unseen—she gains a position of cognitive privilege.

But the type of knowledge that a viewer of the drama gains from context and the type of knowledge that a reader gains from a narrator are of fundamentally different kinds and have profoundly different consequences. For the reader of a novel, knowledge unfolds over time. It is possible to say that the reader learns one thing first, and another second, and another third, and so on. In the drama, by contrast, the viewer learns contextual information all at once. When a spectator sees a character enter a well-furnished salon in modern dress, slightly disheveled, carrying a book, looking worried, she processes a multitude of visual signs all at once. The knowledge she receives has a character of immediacy—of something always and already known—so that she cannot say that "first" she learned that the character was female, then upper class, then a reader, then concerned about something, and so on. And indeed, the language of visual signs is so subtle and complex that a viewer often cannot process exactly what gave her that feeling. It may take a trained actor or set designer to know that a certain turn of the eyebrow, or a certain type of dress, or a certain type of furniture, gave the viewer that impression. Visual knowledge, then, impresses the viewer as both immediate and obvious; it does not have the type of "cause" that the reader can assign to information given by a narrator, who the reader may later learn is unreliable. This immediacy and obviousness can have a dark side as well. We all know from visual puzzles the feeling that one "should have seen" or "should have known" something, that it was "obvious all along" if one had only been sufficiently observant. This feeling is present in narrative as well, but there one can see that the information is clearly more hidden, buried in a casual aside or a subordinate clause. For visual information, the clues are always present on the surface; seeing them or not seeing them is a matter of the viewer's skill. The drama makes that blindness and that anguish concrete by placing the viewer in a situation where—in some cases—he *does* know it. A good deal of Shakespeare's horror—in *Macbeth*'s dagger scene, or when Othello is about to murder Desdemona—comes from the fact that the viewer already knows what is about to happen. All the signs are present on the surface.

This immediacy, this presence, and this horror are all significant to Wordsworth because, in many ways, they characterize an observer's knowledge of outside experience. In real life, we have no narrator to tell us how to process information; we are left with our own judgment of how to read surfaces. And this is the situation in which we so often find Wordsworth's visionary poet: confronting a situation—a landscape, a solitary reaper, the panorama of a city—and trying to make sense of its appearance, to read its heart through its surfaces.

With this in mind, we can better understand why Wordsworth chose the drama as his earliest experiment in genre. Staged drama is the only form that puts the viewer in the position of the visionary poet. It strips him of the comfort of the narrative voice and confronts him with the object in and of itself in a situation where the viewer is charged with reading those objects in order to figure out what the play is about. It opens up the terrifying space of unknowingness, but it does so in order to offer the viewer the possibility of vision. It is no accident, then, that Wordsworth's first drama is all about having vision and about losing vision. It confronts the viewer with the difficult task of figuring out the characters and their world, but it does so in order to illustrate the urgent necessity of doing so, and the consequences that await the viewer who remains in the realm of the ordinary and refuses to see things in their visionary light.

This dependence on seeing the physical surface can often make a drama meant for performance seem strange to readers who come to a drama through the text alone. The characters have a certain sort of knowledge gained from context, gesture, or expression that the reader (at least a reader without good stage directions) does not have. As such, a drama meant for performance can often seem mystifying to readers. This, I believe, is the case with *The Borderers*. As Reeve Parker notes in his seminal essay "Reading Wordsworth's Power: Narrative and Usurpation in *The Borderers*," most readers of the play tend to find it "unreadable and unactable" (299). Michael G. Cooke and Alan Bewell echo the general confusion in their introduction to a special issue of *Studies in Romanticism* dedicated to the play's performance. The characters, they say, "know little of themselves and others," their "identities and motivations are obscure and mysterious," there are "vast discrepancies between rhetoric and action" (353). This inability to understand the play from its language might indicate that there is something going on with its surfaces—that there is something in texture, tone, inflection, and physicality that we miss on paper.

Of course, *The Borderers* is not usually thought of as a play about poetic vision, but it makes sense to think of it that way in light of the place it occupies in Wordsworth's poetic development. As Reeve Parker has pointed out, it is virtually contemporary with "The Ruined Cottage," which many consider to be the first of Wordsworth's major narrative poems, and it was finished less than a year before Wordsworth started composing the *Lyrical Ballads*, which contain some of Wordsworth's most far-reaching statements about vision and the human condition. It makes sense to think that the poet who composed "Tintern Abbey" must have had some practice in the art of vision, and must have thought long and deeply about what it might mean to look at the world and "see into the life of things." *The Borderers* is that practice.

On a more prosaic level, it also makes sense to think of *The Borderers* as a play about knowledge. In the traditional reading, it is about Rivers's attempt to save Mortimer "from the curse / Of living without knowledge that you live" (4.3.204–5). But this reading does not seem quite adequate to a play that is so deeply concerned with knowledge and perception and, on the opposite side, with deception and betrayal. Not only does the plot structure depend on knowledge—what if Mortimer had known that Herbert was really a baron, or that he was really Matilda's father?—but it is also one of the crushing ironies of the play that everyone except Mortimer seems to know the truth. As Kenneth Johnston puts it in Wordsworth's biography, "The trouble with *The Borderers* is that everybody but Mortimer can see right away that Rivers is evil" (496). The question, then, becomes not only what Mortimer knows after he has been betrayed into leaving Baron Herbert on the deserted waste but also why he trusted Rivers, why he fails to believe Matilda and the band of Borderers that are his closest friends, and how he doesn't know that Herbert was Matilda's father in the first place. What does Mortimer know, and when does he know it?

Wordsworth intentionally places the viewer in this condition of uncertainty—intentionally makes the viewer identify with Mortimer—in order to foreground the question of how we know what we know and to advocate one sort of vision, a vision in which one knows people almost intuitively by looking at their faces, over Rivers's sort of vision, a vision that requires them to look "beyond the present object of the sense" (2.1.98–102) by looking at objects from a safe distance, without participation or involvement. And this conflict between the two kinds of vision, the one held by Rivers (and to some extent Mortimer) and the one held by Herbert, Matilda, and the rest of the characters in the play, is a direct result of changes that were in the process of taking place in the theatre during the 1790s and before in England, and that were daily taking place in the theatres of France and especially the theatres of the French Revolution. As I have argued earlier, throughout the eighteenth century changes were taking place at the patent theatres that forced viewers to observe the play from a distance—theatres were growing larger, the action was moving behind the proscenium arch, and the audience was removed from the stage and backstage area. As a result, it was particularly difficult to see detail—particularly to see the actors' faces. F. G. Tomlins recalled in his *A Brief View of the English Drama, from the Earliest Period to the Present Time: With Suggestions for Elevating the Present Condition of the Art, and of Its Professors* (1840) that a spectator in the farthest parts of the house "cannot see the countenances of the performers without the aid of a pocket telescope."[3] And there was also a sense that the actors were separated from the audience, particularly in light of the theatres of the French Revolution, where the actors mixed with the audience and made them a part of the spectacle.[4] Wordsworth would have remembered these festivals and theatres from his residence in France, and in *The Borderers*, he incorporates their vision into a moral system that demands that the spectators be present as part of the spectacle in order to fully see what the characters are like. A spectator removed from the spectacle, Wordsworth implies, can never fully understand. And this is precisely Mortimer's problem.

One thing that makes *The Borderers* difficult to understand—for a reader as well as a spectator—is the atmosphere of almost psychic knowledge that pervades the beginning of the play. The characters seem to know each other intuitively, without the need for exposition or conversation, and the spectators are left trying to figure out how they know what they know from the clues given by their appearance. It is a testament to this difficulty that both readers and viewers have always had a problem understanding the characters' motivation. From Covent Garden's rejection of the play because of the "metaphysical obscurity of one character" (*Borderers* 5) to John Jones's later assessment of its "reckless inattention to coherence of plot and consistency of character" (Whitaker 358) to Cooke and Bewell's assertion that the characters "identities and motivations are obscure and mysterious" (353), critics have always had difficulty untangling the characters from each other. It is difficult to tell where one character's knowledge begins and another's ends, and this makes the dialogue sometimes overly obvious and sometimes completely mysterious. Perhaps the best example of this confusion is the tangled relationship between Mortimer and Rivers. From the very beginning, this relationship has troubled readers of the play. Autobiographical readings, as William Jewett has noted, tend to assume that Wordsworth has depicted some aspect of his past self in "Mortimer, or Rivers, or both,"[5] and more traditional readings tend to focus on River's project to make Mortimer like himself—"A shadow of myself, made by myself" (5.2.33)[6]. But the near identity of hero and villain has its basis in much more than Rivers's philosophical project. Even before Mortimer appears seduced—assuming that we can ever identify such a time—Mortimer and Rivers seem to know each other's thoughts. When Rivers tempts Mortimer, the temptation seems to come from inside rather than outside, a common thread of thought that runs promiscuously from one to another. At the height of the temptation, Mortimer tells Rivers, "Hark'ee, Rivers / You are a man—and if compassion's milk / Be known unto you, you will love this woman / Even as I do" (2.1.82–85), as if Rivers could intuitively share Mortimer's feelings. Rivers functions as a confirming mechanism in a deception (if it is one) that is already well under way by the time the play begins. It is almost as if Mortimer and Rivers have a psychic connection that enables them to read each other's thoughts—or at least enables Rivers to read Mortimer's.

We can see this relationship at work if we compare Rivers's methods to the methods of that other famous tempter, Iago.[7] In *Othello*, we can see Iago leading Othello to his doom, implanting suggestions that Othello has never thought of before, and might never have thought of without Iago's agency ("Did Michael Cassio, when you woo'd my lady, / Know of your love?" [3.3. 95–96]). In *The Borderers*, by contrast, Mortimer often seems to be leading Rivers. Their first exchange—"You saw her write it?" "And saw the tears with which she blotted it." "And nothing less would satisfy him?" "No less." (1.1.25–28)—is a series of rhetorical questions, asked as if Mortimer already knows the answer. And indeed he does. But the oddness of the relationship does not end there. In *Othello*, Iago's doubts seem to be the doubts of an outside observer—the voice of society intruding into Othello's perfect union with his love ("She did deceive her father, marrying you" [3.3.210]; "O, beware jealousy / It is the green-eye'd monster, which doth mock / That meat it feeds on" [3.3.169–71]). But River's doubts seem to be the voice of Mortimer's own consciousness:

> *Mortimer:* This instant will we stop him—a father, too!
> *Rivers:* Nay, Mortimer, I prithee be not hasty,
>   For sometimes, in despite of my conviction,
>   He tempted me to think the story true. [...]
> *Mortimer:* I have been much deceived.
> *Rivers:* But sure, he loves the girl; and never love
>   Could find delight to nurse itself so strangely. [...]
>   There must be truth in this—
> *Mortimer:* False! False as hell—
>   Truth in the story! (1.1.197–210)

By the time Mortimer is at Rivers's mercy in act 3, the understanding between Mortimer and Rivers is so strong that Rivers hardly needs to use words:

> *Rivers:* 'Tis for my peace of mind—
> *Mortimer:* Why, I *believe* you, man.
> *Rivers:* But hear the proofs. (3.2.33–34)

Iago always stands outside, tormenting; Rivers always seems to be inside the relationship, thinking Mortimer's thoughts along with him. The relationship between Iago and Othello binds them together in a common net of intrigue and suffering; the relationship between Mortimer and Rivers seems to create the illusion that they are the same person.

If this were the only relationship of psychic knowledge, of course, we might presume that there is some sort of special bond between Mortimer and Rivers, something like the bond between tormentor and tormented in *Othello* ("I am bound to thee for ever" [3.3.217]) or the reflection of two sides of a single consciousness debating the French Revolution, as the autobiographical reading suggests. But psychic knowledge seems to be the rule rather than the exception in the strange netherworld of *The Borderers*. As Reeve Parker has suggested, the relationship between Matilda and Herbert in many ways parallels the relationship between Mortimer and Rivers, and it parallels it in the special bond of knowledge as well.[8] From the very beginning, Matilda seems able to read Herbert's thoughts—"How chearfully / You paced along while the dim moonlight cloud / Mocked me" (1.1. 80–83)—and Herbert seems to know hers—"That is a silence which I know, Matilda!" (1.1.104). Their dialogue seems but a confirmation of what both already know:

> *Herbert:* Matilda, we must part!
> *Matilda:* Part!
> *Herbert:* Be not alarmed—
> 'Tis but for a few days—a thought has struck me.
> *Matilda:* That I should leave you at the inn, and thence
> Proceed alone? It shall be so; I feel
> You are quite exhausted. (1.1.192–96)

The band of Borderers seems to have a similar sort of psychic knowledge. Kenneth Johnston has observed that they seem to instinctively know that Rivers is evil, but their knowledge of each other and of Mortimer seems to extend well beyond the simple knowledge of Rivers's character. When they do not know instinctively what Mortimer means, they see it as a sort of betrayal:

> *Mortimer:* The world is poisoned at the heart.
> *Lacy:* What mean you?
> *Wallace:* (*Whose eye has been fixed suspiciously upon* RIVERS)
> Aye, what is it you mean? (2.3.344–45)

The band is so accustomed to knowing exactly what Mortimer means—to reading his thoughts in the same way that they read each other's—that the simple act of not knowing opens up a breach in nature that leaves open the possibility of separation, suspicion, and betrayal.

The same principle applies to Robert and Margaret. Robert is a man with a murderous past—"I have done him no harm, but (*hesitating*) Heaven will forgive me, it would not have been so once" (4.3.34)—but Wordsworth suggests that the real consequence of the murder is that it opens up a breach between Robert and his wife—"He has a kind heart, but his confinement / Has made him fearful, and he'll never be / The man he was" (4.3.20–22). Robert and Margaret seem to feel that Margaret should know Robert's thoughts intuitively—that Margaret should know that Robert is innocent, that he feels for the old man, that he has left the old man on the heath out of kindness and not out of greed and a murderous impulse. But the murder has opened up that space of doubt in the world of perfect knowledge. When Robert enters, Margaret immediately assumes the worst—Robert: "It is the blood of an unhappy man." Margaret: "Oh! we are undone forever" (4.3.27–28)—and she refuses to believe him even after he protests—Robert: "I have done no harm." Margaret: "You have not *buried* any thing? you are no richer than when you left me?" (4.3.34–35). Robert rebukes her for her distrust—"Be at peace, I am innocent" (4.3.36). But more than that, her lack of knowledge and her lack of faith make her a conspirator against him: "It is not enough that I have been so unfortunate as to have been abroad to night till this hour; I came home, and this is my comfort . . . You will never rest till I meet with a felon's end" (4.3.58–59, 80).

This is certainly a strange turn of events for a play that is based on deception and betrayal. But *The Borderers*, like *Othello*, is tragic precisely because a perfect bond of knowledge has been broken, or because a character has somehow been persuaded not to know something that he knew all along. In *Othello*, what is at issue is a world of perfect knowledge between Othello and Desdemona— "My life upon her faith" (1.3.294), "I saw Othello's visage in his mind" (1.3.252). *The Borderers* takes that ideal of perfect knowledge between man and woman—that love so perfect that the two of them almost know each other's thoughts—and blows that knowledge up to encompass the whole world. Just as Desdemona sees Othello's visage in *his* mind, Matilda sees Mortimer's visage, Herbert sees Matilda's visage, Wilfred sees Mortimer's visage, Wallace sees Rivers's visage. The world of *The Borderers* revolves around the fact of perfect, transparent knowledge, and when that knowledge fails, chaos is come again.

But studying *Othello* also brings out one important difference between *Othello* and *The Borderers*, one that is crucial to understanding Wordsworth's dramatic project in *The Borderers*. In *Othello*, Iago disrupts the union of perfect knowledge between man and woman by opening up the space of what Othello does not know, and what, indeed, he cannot possibly know: "By heaven I'll know thy thought." "You cannot, if my heart were in your hand" (3.3.166–67). In *The Borderers*, by contrast, Mortimer knows everything he needs to know all along. He knows that Matilda loves him, that she is faithful to her father, that Herbert is innocent, and even that Rivers is evil. But time and time again, we see him denying that knowledge—refusing to know the things that he already knows. We see him rejecting knowledge even in the first scene, where

Wilfred reminds him "You know that you have saved his life"—Mortimer confirms, "I know it"—and Wilfred continues, "And that he hates you!" (1.1.6–8). Mortimer looks displeased, but he never denies that he knows that Rivers is unfaithful. Instead, he brushes Wilfred off—"Fie! no more of this" (1.1.8)—and offers a justification why he associates with Rivers even though he does not "love him"—"I do more, / I honor him" (1.1.11). Mortimer's temptation is an odyssey of denying knowledge. Time and time again, Mortimer knows that Herbert is innocent—"I would fain hope that we deceive ourselves / When I beheld him sitting there, alone, / It struck upon my heart—I know not how" (1.3.1–3), "There is a palsy in his limbs—he shakes" (2.2.131), "[D]id you hear him bless me / When he had gained the other side?" (2.3.24–25), "I look at him and tremble like a child" (2.3.65), "There was something in his face the very counterpart of Matilda" (2.3.272)—and time and time again, Rivers brings him to a point where he can no longer see that. Indeed, Mortimer is finally able to kill Herbert only when he is unable to see the man at all—"Oh! truly / That mole, that weazle, that old water-rat— / Plague on my memory! I had forgot him" (3.3.106–8).

This knowledge, as I have mentioned, seems mysterious to a reader of the play. But Wordsworth makes it clear that the characters get the knowledge they have about each other simply by looking at the body—by being in each other's personal presence. In a play where rhetoric can be deceiving,[9] eyewitness testimony provides a guarantee of truth. Mortimer relies on eyewitness testimony in the play's very first scene—"You saw her write it?" "And saw the tears with which she blotted it" (1.1.25–26). It is the band's first clue that something is wrong with Rivers: "I have noticed / That when the name of God is spoken of / A most strange blankness overspreads his face" (3.4.20–22), and it is Mortimer's first clue about Herbert: "When I beheld him sitting there, alone, / It struck upon my heart—I know not how" (1.3.2–3). Rivers puts this fact to work in his deception. Just as the deception in *Othello* revolves around the presentation of "ocular proof," Rivers's deception revolves around repeated presentations of what should be "ocular proof"—Herbert, Matilda, the Beggar, the wretch who was deceived by Clifford—and around eyewitness testimony of events—Baron Herbert's perishing on the waves, Lord Clifford lurking outside Herbert's cottage, Clifford's servants joking about Matilda. It is as if seeing the thing provides an antidote to tales, a guarantee of truth, and a motivating force that goes beyond thought and into action.

But eyewitness testimony is more than just a way of verifying stories. *The Borderers* also suggests that there is a moral power to personal presence. Seeing the face prevents Mortimer from killing Herbert. When Herbert is physically present, Rivers is powerless; it is only when Herbert is absent that Rivers's tales can work their magic on Mortimer. It is what binds Herbert to Matilda: "When I behold the ruins of that face . . . And think that they were blasted for my sake . . . Father, I would not change this proud delight / For the best hopes of love" (1.1.106–11). It forms the crucial moment of separation in Herbert's narrative of the events at Antioch: "She saw my blasted face—a tide of soldiers / That instant rushed between us" (1.1.153–54). And without it, there can be no certainty about a person's character—Mortimer qualifies his image of Herbert "[t]hough I have never seen his face" (1.1.60). Even the focus on voice that Parker points out becomes subservient to the face.[10] When Matilda tells Herbert, "O could you hear his voice / Alas! you do not know him" (1.1.133–34), she quickly follows it up with a description of his face: "His face bespeaks / A deep and simple meekness" (1.1.136–37). The face awakens compassion—"Could I behold his face, could I behold / The terrible pleading of that face of his / And could I feel his arms and hear him pray / That I would not forsake him nor permit / My heart to abandon him in his old age" (3.5.131–35). It is the mark of charity—"This they can do and look upon my face" (1.3.68)—and the sign of contact with God—"As if he were the only saint on earth / He turns his face to heaven" (1.3.89–90). And when Matilda looks into Mortimer's face, she knows the truth: "I see you love me still" (3.5.162).

Seeing the face brings into focus the nature of vision that *The Borderers* presents. As the traditional reading suggests, the play is about knowledge, but the knowledge that Wordsworth seeks is not the knowledge that can be gained from leaving an old man to die on the barren heath. It is the knowledge that can be gained from seeing the face and realizing, as Mortimer realizes too late, that "[w]e are all of one blood, our veins are filled / At the same poisonous fountain" (4.2.56–57). Although the play was always thought to be Wordsworth's statement against Godwinian rationalism, it is here that Wordsworth's crucial distance from Godwin comes into play. Wordsworth has Rivers spout lines on the equality of man that might have come straight from *Political Justice*: "he is human like ourselves" (2.3.157) or that "[t]here is no justice when we do not feel / For man as man" (2.3.172–73). But Rivers's idea of "man" is hopelessly abstract. Rivers's levelings would take away everything that makes man human:

> Wisdom...
> Spares not the worm.—The Giant and the worm,
> She weighs them in one scale. The wiles of Women
> And craft of age, seducing reason first
> Made weakness a protection, and obscured
> The moral shapes of things. His tender cries
> And helpless innocence, do they protect
> The infant lamb? (2.3.386–93)

Rivers envisions man as an abstract, man without weakness, man without infirmities, man without individuality. As Mortimer ironically comments to Rivers on seeing Herbert's body, "The dead have but one face" (5.3.45). Wordsworth's vision, by contrast, is one that recognizes both individuality and commonality—"There was something in his face the very counterpart of Matilda" (2.3.272)—and imposes, in that commonality, an obligation to recognize weakness. It is this weakness, and this humanness, that Mortimer recognizes when he first spares Herbert at the ruined castle:

> *Rivers:* Plague! is he alive?
> *Mortimer:* Alive! who alive?
> *Rivers:* Herbert! the *Baron* Herbert! since you will have it, he who will be the Baron Herbert when Matilda is Clifford's Harlot.—Is *he* living?
> *Mortimer:* The blind man lying in that dungeon is alive. (2.3.279–83)

Herbert is not leveled by Mortimer's vision; he is not merely "a man," like other men, entitled to the same rights and privileges and subject to the same justice. He is an individual, but yet, within that individuality, Mortimer can see that Herbert is human. It is enough for Mortimer that Herbert is merely "the blind man lying in that dungeon." He does not need for him to be Herbert, the Baron Herbert, Matilda's father, or even the counterpart of Matilda. Simply by being who he is, at the most basic bodily level, Herbert is human, and he is entitled to compassion.

Thus *The Borderers* is a play about the root sources of human cruelty. Wordsworth authorizes this reading in his 1843 note, when he wrote that "while the Revolution was rapidly advancing to its extreme of wickedness, I had frequent opportunities of being an eye-witness of this process, and it was while that knowledge was fresh upon my memory, that the Tragedy of 'The Borderers' was composed." But the root source of cruelty in *The Borderers* is not (or is not necessarily) revolutionary violence, but the failure to see. This fact becomes abundantly clear in the scene where Mortimer and Rivers confront the female Beggar in act 1, scene 3. Few critics have interpreted this scene—Alan Liu is the only one who comes to mind—and this is likely because Wordsworth presents his hero Mortimer in such an unattractive light. The Beggar's physical presence is so literal that Mortimer and Rivers almost trip over her. But despite her concrete insertion into the scene, Mortimer refuses to see her— "We have no time for this"—and gives the Beggar money—"My babbling gossip / Here's what will comfort you" (1.3.34–35)—rather than listen to her story. Even well into the Beggar's speech, Mortimer continues his blindness: "This woman is a prater—Pray, good Lady, / Do you tell fortunes?" (1.3.61–62). Wordsworth suggests this blindness is precisely the problem. Later in the scene, Wordsworth has the Beggar rebuke Mortimer:

> Oh! Sir! you are like the rest . . .
> Well! they might turn a beggar from their door,
> But there are mothers who can see the babe
> Here at my breast and ask me where I bought it:
> This they can do and look upon my face.
> —But you, Sir, should be kinder. (1.3.62–68)

But even after this rather concrete rebuke, Mortimer responds only with sarcasm—"Come here ye fathers, / And learn of this poor wretch" (1.3.68–69). Mortimer never sees the Beggar as human until she is useful to him, and Wordsworth leaves no doubt that Mortimer's failure to see the Beggar is an act of cruelty, perhaps even on the scale of his later murder of Herbert. Indeed, despite the noble ends that he claims for his violence, Mortimer puts the woman in fear of her life:

> *Mortimer:* I must have more of this—you shall not stir
>   An inch till I am answered. Know you
>   aught
>   That doth concern this Herbert?
> *Beggar:* You are angry,
>   And will misuse me, Sir!
> *Mortimer:* No trifling, woman!
> *Rivers:* You are safe as in a sanctuary:
>   Speak.
> *Mortimer:* Speak.

Beggar: He is a most hard-hearted man.
Mortimer: Your life is at my mercy.
Beggar: Do not harm me,
   And I will tell you all. (1.3.125–32)

It is difficult to imagine Wordsworth identifying with a man who threatens a beggar, and it is perhaps all too easy to excuse Mortimer's rage as a fit of passion. But if it is passion, then the particular characteristic of this passion is blindness, and blindness, the scene suggests, almost always leads to cruelty. "This they can do and look upon my face," "There was something in his face the very counterpart of Matilda . . . [i]t sent me to my prayers" (2.3.272, 278). The basis of cruelty is failure to recognize the human, and failure to recognize the human is in essence a failure to see.

This is the politics implicit in Wordsworth's idea of vision, and nowhere is this politics more palpable than in *The Borderers*. *The Borderers* is a statement of neither Godwinian radicalism nor Burkean conservatism, though it has elements of both. Rather, it advocates a new sort of politics based on the idea of seeing properly—a bland and pietistic sort of politics, to be sure, but one that must have seemed an attractive middle ground between a radicalism that promised to liberate man at the expense of turning him into an abstraction and a conservatism that promised to recognize man's place in society at the expense of enslaving him. If Mortimer could only learn to recognize man as human then justice would be not only easy but instantaneous. Kenneth Johnston has argued that "having taken great pains to suggest that established authority is as bad as can be imagined, the play reveals that *it is not so*: violent revolution is not justified, especially by an individual trying to convince himself that his personal motives serve a higher good" (Johnston 503). But rather than showing that violent revolution is not justified, *The Borderers* shows that violent revolution is, in fact, easy: Herbert suns himself before his native doors, the poor and innocent are protected, Matilda is released from her enslavement and free to marry Mortimer, all without the need for murders and violent skullduggery. The play does not necessarily suggest that all is right with the world—as Johnston points out, the play suggests not only that authority is "as bad as can be imagined" but also that injustices take place within the Burkean idealized feudal society. Good men are blinded and dispossessed, daughters are enslaved, the corrupt wield power, the poor are wrongfully imprisoned, and poverty and begging are rife on the barren heath. But what the play does suggest is that the solution to these problems is as easy as a change in perspective—that, as Shelley will later suggest in *Prometheus Unbound*, the shift from tyranny to freedom is as easy as changing your mind.

In Wordsworth's mind, this shift in perspective is intimately related to the type of vision taught in the theatre. Mortimer's shift from revered hero to anguished murderer is the result of a change in perspective, and it is a change in perspective that is taught to him by Rivers. Rivers also looks at the body, but he looks at it from a distance, and from that lofty distance, shapes obscure, so that Rivers believes that he can see general patterns. Rivers tells Mortimer that in his wanderings in Palestine:

> Oft I left the camp
> When all that multitude of hearts was still
> And followed on through woods of gloomy cedar
> Into deep chasms troubled by roaring streams,
> Or from the top of Lebanon surveyed
> The moonlight desart and the moonlight sea;
> In these my lonely wanderings I perceived
> What mighty objects do impress their forms
> To build up this our intellectual being. (4.2.127–35)

The passage concludes "[s]o much for my remorse" (4.2.139) to underscore the consequences of Rivers's vision. From his lofty vantage point, Rivers can see only "mighty objects" that can "impress" him with their "forms," but the result is not an appreciation for the majesty of these forms or his own small size compared to them. Instead, it is to build himself up—"[t]o build up this our intellectual being." The consequence of seeing from a distance is a failure to see. Rivers is always looking for the "mighty objects" and general forms that will give him the universal key. As a result, he is the one who always advocates looking beyond "mere appearance" to find what is underneath. From the very beginning, Rivers attacks the notion of judging things on their appearances: "The tale of this his quondam Barony / Is cunningly devised, and on the back / Of his forlorn appearance could not fail / To make the proud and vain his tributaries / And stir the pulse of lazy charity" (1.1.52–56), and in act 2, he mounts a stunning philosophical defense of ignoring appearances:

> Shall the infirmities
> Which have enabled this enormous culprit
> To perpetrate his crimes serve as a sanctuary

> To cover him from punishment? ...
> Yes, my friends,
> His countenance *is* meek and venerable,
> And by the mass, to see him at his prayers—
> I am of flesh and blood, and may I perish
> When my heart does not ache to think of it! (2.3.386–406)

Rivers's method involves "showing that you calculate, and look / Beyond the present object of the sense" (2.1.109–10), seeing things that are beyond the pale of sight: "The eye / Of vulgar men knows not the majesty / With which the mind can clothe the shapes of things" (2.1.98–100). He wants to "see unveiled the general shapes of things" (4.2.161)—to see the general principles as opposed to the concrete satisfactions that support and nourish man. Mortimer is under his thrall when he says,

> we look
> But at the surfaces of things, we hear
> Of towns in flames, fields ravaged, young and old
> Driven out in flocks to want and nakedness,
> Then grasp our swords and rush upon a cure
> That flatters us because it asks not thought.
> The deeper malady is better hid—
> The world is poisoned at the heart. (2.3.337–44)

All of this only makes Mortimer's failure to see the face more puzzling, and this again raises the question of why Mortimer denies this sort of vision and why Rivers is able to seduce him so easily. It is not simply the strength of Rivers's arguments; Mortimer is already self-seduced before Rivers even gets to him (notice how he cries "I have been much deceived" [1.1.206] before anyone deceives him). Rivers deceives Mortimer and no one else because of Mortimer's mortal flaw, and that flaw is not only his failure to see others but his failure to see himself. We know so little about Mortimer because Mortimer, by his very nature, wants to remain hidden. Mortimer is, in many ways, a stunning nonentity as a character. Although he is supposed to be a Robin-Hood-type hero on the order of Karl Moor in Schiller's *Die Rauber*, we see very little of his heroism, and although his love for Matilda is supposed to motivate most of the action of the play, we see very little of his love. And this is not simply because the exigencies of Wordsworth's psychodrama deny him space to work these things out. Rather, this denial of vision reflects a larger truth about Mortimer. His very first line in the play (and here we might remember that it was Wordsworth's friend Coleridge who inaugurated the practice of reading prophetic significance into Shakespeare's opening lines and scenes), is "I perceive / That fear is like a cloak which old men huddle / Around their love, as 'twere to keep it warm" (1.1.2–4). But in the play itself, it is Mortimer who huddles a cloak around himself. While Rivers speaks his motivation to the audience in no fewer than three soliloquies—four in the late version—Mortimer never reveals his character. His first action in the play is to hide—to observe Matilda and Herbert unseen—"This thicket will conceal us" (1.1.74). And as Peter Manning has observed, the play systematically domesticates Othello's recounting of his own adventures—"moving accidents by flood and field"—by making Matilda the heroic storyteller and Mortimer the passive listener, achieving "harmony" "only at the cost of making the hero feminine and passive" (92). Even in his dialogue we see very little of himself. He tends to phrase things in terms of universal truth instead of his own feelings and agency—"Well! to day the truth / Shall end her wrongs" (1.1.43–44)—and even his most powerful feelings he tends to put into the mouths of others: "Hark'ee Rivers, / You are a man—and if compassion's milk / Be known to you, you will love this woman / Even as I do" (2.1.82–85). The scene where Mortimer gains the band's approval of justice for Herbert is exactly such a scene. Mortimer plays the disinterested storyteller and lets his friends react:

> *Mortimer*: Hark'ee, my friends—
> (*With an appearance of relaxed gaity*)
> Were there a man who, being weak and helpless . . . could . . . look
> To the unnatural harvest of that time
> When he should give her up, a woman grown,
> To him who bid the highest in the market
> Of foul pollution—
> *Lacy*: Hell itself
> Contains not such a monster. (2.3.345–65)

Rivers's type of vision allows Mortimer to stand back and look at generalities without revealing himself. He can see the "deeper malady" that is "better hid," but not the reality open to plain view—the towns in flames, fields ravaged, young and old driven out in flocks to want and nakedness. Wordsworth's vision does not ask for creative reenvisioning, but rather accurate perception filtered through the realm of feeling, and that filtration through the realm of feeling requires a type of self-revelation of which Mortimer seems incapable. Rivers says to Mortimer late in the play, "you talk of solitude— / Ask yourself if you fear a human face" (3.5.13–14). Mortimer does indeed fear the human face; he fears that it will see him.

Mortimer, then, represents what happens when the spectator is hidden from view. Gradually, he becomes addicted to Rivers's way of vision; he becomes accustomed to seeing the general forms of things, not out of any philosophical allegiance, but because it is psychologically more convenient for him. Evil becomes tied to a lack of self-assertion. A spectator who allows himself to become absent from the scene becomes a spectator who is uninvolved, and a spectator who is uninvolved is a spectator capable of cruelty.

It would be convenient for Wordsworth's poetic development if Mortimer eventually came to vision. But Wordsworth has a different fate in mind for his hero. Instead, Wordsworth uses Mortimer to illustrate what happens when a character fails to come to vision— when a man, perhaps like Wordsworth, and certainly like the contemporaries whom he saw "advancing to the extreme of wickedness" in the French Revolution, fails to recognize what is right in front of him. The answer to this question has a good deal to do with another classic Wordsworthian preoccupation—how man comes to lose vision. "I see by glimpses now," he writes in *The Prelude*, "when age comes on / May scarcely see at all" (11.281–82); "The things which I have seen I now can see no more" ("Ode" 9), he writes in the "Intimations Ode." But where those poems make the loss of vision seem like an inevitable result of time and age, *The Borderers* makes Mortimer's loss of vision a sort of poetic justice. Because he has refused to see, he can no longer see. "'Twas in his face—I saw it in his face— / We've crushed the foulest crime" (4.2.194–95), Mortimer protests after Rivers reveals the scope of the plot. But Mortimer already knows that he did not see that at all. The face no longer holds absolute knowledge for him. He sees only by fits and starts; he knows, but only enough to recognize that he does not know. This is what makes Mortimer's recognition scene with Robert so poignant in its Shakespearean hesitation, almost like Lear coming out of his madness: "I believe that there are beings / For unknown ends permitted to put on / The shape of man, and thou art one of them" (5.2.51–53). Like Lear recognizing Cordelia, Mortimer can almost, but not quite, recognize Robert as human (Lear: "Thou art a soul in bliss" [4.7.46]). But unlike Lear, Mortimer does not have a Cordelia to confirm her identity for him—"And so I am, I am" (4.7.70). He intuits the basic fact of unity but misses the point—"Oh monster! monster! there are three of us / And we shall howl together" (5.2.56–57). Their unity does not inaugurate Mortimer into the basic condition of man; instead, it makes man a monster, and the human condition one of blindness and guilt. Mortimer can intuit the primary unity of the world that had previously been his right, but he can no longer experience it. The things that he could have seen, he now can see no more.

But there is another type of punishment that awaits the man who fails to use his vision, one that might be even more important to the poet that we have come to know as the poet of the "egotistical sublime." Just as Mortimer cannot recognize the human in others, others suddenly become unable to recognize him. We can see this lack of recognition beginning in act 2, when the band becomes uneasy when they do not intuitively understand Mortimer ("What mean you?" [2.3.344]). But Mortimer's failure to be recognized reaches its height in act 5, after Mortimer has left Herbert to die on the barren heath. The scenes between Mortimer and Matilda after Herbert's death almost have the quality of farce—Mortimer is racked by guilt; Matilda remains blissfully ignorant that Mortimer played any part in her father's death. But what saves these scenes from metaphysical comedy is the fact that Mortimer so clearly, so touchingly, wants Matilda to know. Indeed, in wanting her to know, he does not want her to simply know the brute fact, "I am the murderer of thy father" (5.3.99). As Reeve Parker points out, the line smacks more of a *coup de grace* by which Mortimer hopes to end Matilda's suffering than an actual confession.[11] He wants her to know the whole thing—his guilt, his innocence, his mistake, his passion. He wants her judgment, he wants her compassion; he wants to deliver the blow in a way that will lessen her suffering, but he also wants her to suffer with him. Finally, he cries out in anguish, "Look on my face" (5.3.97). But her response is not an answer, but a question, "Oh! when has this affliction visited thee?" (5.3.98). Where Mortimer and Matilda once had a psychic unity based on her ability to read his face—"His face bespeaks / A deep and simple meekness" (1.1.136–37)—Mortimer's face is now a mystery to her. It is her failure to recognize him that motivates the cruelty that Parker senses in Mortimer's final confession. He is forced to use words as a blunt instrument since her knowledge of him has failed. Unlike Karl Moor in *Die Rauber*, he is driving a stake into the heart of a relationship that is already dead.

And indeed, being unseen is part of Mortimer's final doom. Parker has noticed that Mortimer's final exile on the barren heath is a rejection of the hero's vocal power, but it is also a condemnation to both blindness and invisibility:

> No prayers, no tears, but hear my doom in silence!
> I will go forth a wanderer on the earth,
> A shadowy thing, and as I wander on
> No human ear shall ever hear my voice,
> No human dwelling ever give me food
> Or sleep or rest, and all the uncertain way
> Shall be as darkness to me, as a waste
> Unnamed by man. (5.3.264–71)

Mortimer recognizes that he must remain unrecognized. Not only does he stifle the reaction from his band—"No prayers, no tears, but hear my doom in silence!"—but he also condemns himself to wander the earth unseen, a "shadowy thing," incapable of producing a reaction—"No human ear shall ever hear my voice"—and incapable specifically of producing the human response of charity—"No human dwelling ever give me food / Or sleep or rest." As he has not seen, he cannot see—"all the uncertain way / Shall be as darkness to me"—and as he has not seen, he cannot be seen. This is the doom that awaits the man who refuses to have vision.

All of this might seem to support David Marshall's hypothesis that Wordsworth condemns spectatorship. But Wordsworth seems to have a different idea of theatre in mind. Throughout the play, Wordsworth constantly seems to insist that it does a body good to look and listen. The line runs through the play like a mantra: Matilda tells Herbert, "Nay, father ... let me hear it all: / 'Twill do me good" (1.1.56–57); Mortimer tells the Beggar, "Nay, be not terrified—it does me good / To look upon you" (1.3.164–65); when Herbert is too long at a story, Mortimer urges him to continue, "Oh let me have it by all means, 'tis pleasant to me to hear you" (2.3.111). And Wordsworth also seems to feel that there is some good in the audience being moved. Mortimer says of Matilda, "It is her virtues / Of which he makes his instruments" (1.1.220–21), the Pilgrim Matilda meets on the road notes that hearing Herbert's story "filled my eyes with tears" (2.2.12). Seeing brings comfort: "I must see / That face of his again—I must behold it— / 'Twere joy enough to end me" (2.3.308–10). Even though Wordsworth recognizes the dangers of contemporary spectatorship, he wants to preserve a spectatorship that will allow a spectator to watch and be moved without succumbing to the temptation posed by Mortimer and Rivers.

With that in mind, Wordsworth does place a figure of the ideal spectator in his play, and that character is Matilda. Matilda has generally been thought of as something of a shadowy figure in the play, beguiled by tales, victimized by figures of rape, betrayed by both her father and her lover, and made to be a McGuffin in the psychodrama between Mortimer and Rivers. But the composition history of *The Borderers* shows that Wordsworth saw her as a much more major character. She figures prominently in two of the five scenes in the drafts of the *Ur-Borderers*: the churchyard scene intended for act 3 and the Matilda-at-the-cottage-door scene in act 5. Indeed, in the early part of the composition process, she played a much more major role than Rivers. And even though Wordsworth cut one of her major scenes, the churchyard scene where Matilda meets a pilgrim in the churchyard, and the part of the prose synopsis where Matilda finds her mother, the Matilda that remains is far from the helpless victim that critics have made her out to be. She fights for Mortimer when she is with Herbert; she fights for Herbert when she is with Mortimer. When Herbert worries that she cannot cross the barren heath alone, she tells him,

> You know, Sir, I have been too long your guard
> Not to have learned to laugh at foolish fears.
> Why if a wolf should leap from out a thicket
> A look of mine would send him scouring back,
> Unless I differ from the thing I am
> When you are by my side. (1.2.22–27)

Matilda represents a figure of strength and self-assertion in a play about weakness, and a figure of compassion in a play about cruelty.

But more importantly, Wordsworth makes it clear that the thing that enables Matilda's tremendous self-confidence is vision. Matilda is a character who is constantly observing. Her very first line is an observation, "Father, you sigh deeply" (1.1.75), and in that very first speech, she rebukes herself for not observing more closely:

> How chearfully
> You paced along while the dim moonlight cloud
> Mocked me with many a strange fantastic shape. [...]
> and yet,
> That you are thus the fault is mine. (1.1.81–86)

Matilda sees the contradictory truth behind Mortimer when no one else does: "His face bespeaks / A deep and simple meekness; and that soul, / Which with the motion of a glorious act / Flashes a terror-mingled look of sweetness, / Is, after conflict, silent as the ocean / By a miraculous finger stilled at once" (1.1.133–41). And her eyes move her compassion for Herbert: "When I behold the ruins of that face . . . And think that they were blasted for my sake . . . Father, I would not change this proud delight / For the best hopes of love" (1.1.106–11). And she is the one who first notices that Mortimer has Herbert's scrip of food around his shoulders (3.5.164–65). More importantly, Matilda is the character who can read people's emotional lives. Even in the midst of her own tragedy, she can look at Mortimer and observe, "Alas! / You too have need of comfort" (5.3.29–30). And her charity is an active, practical sort of charity. Where Mortimer's charity is expressed negatively, and in general principles— "Never may I own / The heart which cannot feel for one so helpless" (1.1.39–40)—Matilda's is expressed positively—she feels sympathy for "the wretches / Who have no roof to shelter their poor heads / Such nights as these" (4.3.1–3). He (generally) feels compassion for "one so helpless" (or rather, does not want to think of a time when he might *not* feel compassion); she would put a roof over their heads.

What distinguishes Matilda's sort of sight from Rivers's and Mortimer's, and what enables her charitable vision, is that she is able to see herself as well as others. Unlike Mortimer and Rivers, she insists that others see her: her parting words to Herbert are "You know me, Sir! Farewell!" (1.2.2), and she insists to Robert "Thou see'st me, what I am" (5.3.8). And she is able to view her situation objectively, without trying to elevate her status in the eyes of others: "I was a woman / Shut out from every noble enterprize (*breaking off*)— / Oh! let me be forgiven!" (3.5.138–40). Because Matilda can see herself— because she knows who she is, and what her relationships are with others—she can see others without the lens of fear or self-interest. She is the one who can see the aspect in the face because she honestly admits that she is the one doing the seeing.

We also see in Matilda an almost compulsive desire to include herself as part of the story. When the old Pilgrim tells the story of his wanderings with Herbert, Matilda interrupts him to insist on her place in the story—"And I was with you" (2.3.31). And indeed, Matilda plays a paramount role in that story. When the pilgrims took refuge in a cave,

> His countenance, methinks I see it now,
> When after a broad flash that filled the cave—

He said to me that he had seen his child
—A face—and a confused gleam of human flesh,
And it was you, dear Lady. (2.2.45–48)

The same is true with Herbert's narrative of the events at Antioch. In Herbert's tale of the events, she is barely there. But in Matilda's own version of events, she plays a paramount role:

But think not, think not, father, I forget
The history of that lamentable night
When, Antioch blazing to her topmost towers,
You rushed into the murderous flames, returned
Blind as the grave, but, as you oft have told me,
You clasped your infant daughter to your heart. (1.1.144–49)

Indeed, her exhortation to her father, "Nay, father, stop not, let me hear it all: / 'Twill do me good" (1.1.156–57) comes at the exact point in the story where her role begins—when "on our return from Palestine, / I found that my domains had been usurped, / I took thee in my arms, and we began / Our wanderings together" (1.1.160–63). It is also the point in the story at which Herbert cedes control of the story to Matilda: "Dear daughter, dearest love— / For my old age it doth remain with thee / To make it what thou wilt" (1.1.157–59). By placing herself into the story, then, as object, as listener, Matilda is able to see herself through the eyes of others and to recognize herself as a seeing subject—she is the subject and the object of the story all at once. And this recognition not only gives her the ethical power to see others; it also gives her the power as a spectator to "make it what she wilt"—to complete the story with her presence and with her action, and to take the story out into the world and make it into action.

Wordsworth's ideal theatre, then, is one in which the spectator can see himself seeing, one in which the spectator is implicitly made part of the production, and his sight made part of the story, so that the spectator can then take control of the tale and bring it to completion in the world of action. It is no secret that after *The Borderers* Wordsworth turned against the stage; very shortly after *The Borderers* was rejected by Covent Garden, Wordsworth wrote that its rejection was due to the "deprav'd State of the Stage at present," and in his 1843 Fenwick note he claimed that at the time of composition he "had then no thought of the Stage" (the word "never" is crossed out). All this may simply be a case of Wordsworthian sour grapes, but it might also reflect a recognition that the stage audience was becoming less and less a part of the production. However much Wordsworth wanted a part in the theatre, he ultimately wanted no part in the theatre of his day. His next task would be to bring his vision of the theatrical relationship between actor and spectator into his lyric poetry, and to create a forum in which the spectator could see himself seeing.

Theatrical Vision in the *Lyrical Ballads*

When Wordsworth complains of the "encreasing accumulation of men in cities" that "blunt[s] the discriminating powers of the mind" and "reduce[s] it to a state of almost savage torpor," he blames the situation on the "craving for extraordinary incident, which the rapid communication of intelligence hourly gratifies." For this he blames not only the urban environment but also "the literature and theatrical exhibitions of the country," which have so "conformed themselves" to this craving that "the invaluable works of our elder writers, I had almost said the works of Shakespear and Milton, are driven into neglect by frantic novels, sickly and stupid German Tragedies, and deluges of idle and extravagant stories in verse" (160). These statements are usually taken as evidence of Wordsworth's antitheatricality. But what Wordsworth is really criticizing is a particular sort of mind-set that is endemic to both urban life and the literature and theatrical exhibitions it produces. Indeed, Wordsworth's attitude toward urban life is somewhat ironic. We might expect a poet who delighted in the language of "man speaking to men," or, more to the point, a man who had the sort of mystical sense of the power of personal presence expressed in *The Borderers*, to glorify the "encreasing accumulation of men in cities," and, perhaps as a side issue, the drama, as a way of bringing people into contact with one another. Indeed, we can see some of this joy at the sheer mass of personal presence in book 7 of *The Prelude*, where Wordsworth delights in simply being in the company of "The Italian, with his frame of images / Upon his head; with basket at his waist, / The Jew; the stately and slow moving Turk, / With freight of slippers piled beneath his arm ... all specimens of man / Through all the colours which the sun bestows, / And every character of form and face" (7.229–38). But the irony of this "encreasing accumulation of men in cities" is that the sheer fact of personal contact does not bind them together into the sort of coherent social whole that

Wordsworth fantasizes in *The Borderers*. Instead, the sheer mass of people, and the variety of their occupations, causes men to look on each other from a theatrical perspective, a perspective that Wordsworth both enacts and deplores in book 7 of *The Prelude*. Men become spectacles to each other—things to be looked at from a distance and observed as curiosities rather than as people to be actually known. The very uniformity of their occupations—and, we might add, the richness of the variety around them ("the great national events which are daily taking place" [160])—produces a craving for "extraordinary incident"—a desire to look at other human beings as something outside oneself, as something extraordinary. We know that one of the things that fascinated Wordsworth about life in London was "how men lived / Even next-door neighbours, as we say, yet still / Strangers, and knowing not each other's names" (*Prelude* 7.115–18)—and here Wordsworth articulates the cause: they look at people as something separate from themselves, as "extraordinary incidents," and therefore they cannot see themselves as part of the picture, or establish a relationship with the human other with whom they are in daily contact. Instead, they look to "the great national events which are daily taking place," "the rapid communication of intelligence," and of course, "frantic novels, sickly and stupid German Tragedies, and deluges of idle and extravagant stories in verse" (160) to satisfy the natural human craving for knowledge through personal presence.

The theatre, for Wordsworth, is both the cause of these ills and their cure. It is the form that satisfies the craving for "extraordinary incident," but it is also the form that allows for physical contact between actors and spectators. In the theatre, the audience could see the actors before them as if they were neighbors; indeed, in Wordsworth's idealized theatre, they could even catch themselves in the act of seeing and learn what it means to see another human being. In 1798, only a few months after Covent Garden had rejected the script for *The Borderers*, Wordsworth embarked on a series of poems that read like dramatic scenes: "The Discharged Soldier" in January–March of 1798, "We are Seven" and "Simon Lee" in April–May of 1798, "Expostulation and Reply" and "The Tables Turned" in May of 1798, and "Tintern Abbey" in July of 1798, as well as his only dramatic monologue, "The Thorn," composed in March of 1798. Each of these poems dramatizes the spectator's act of seeing; each, like *The Borderers*, pictures a spectator in the act of learning to see his immediate surroundings, with various degrees of success, and each envisions the ultimate act of vision as involving both the spectator's ability to notice the other and the spectator's ability to see himself.

Each of these poems revolves around a character who might be called the "idiot spectator," to distinguish him from Blake's "idiot Questioner," who is "always questioning / But never capable of answering" (*Milton*, plate 41.12–13). Just as Blake's "idiot Questioner" uses questions for the wrong end—to "publish ... doubt and call ... it knowledge"—Wordsworth's idiot spectator uses spectatorship for the wrong end. Invariably, he tries to look at the world like a spectator—or like Mortimer and Rivers in *The Borderers*—hidden, out of the picture, set above and beyond the things he observes. And just as invariably, his salvation comes when the object of his contemplation bursts the frame of theatrical vision by looking back at him. The politics of distance becomes the politics of personal contact. By breaching the wall of theatrical vision, the object brings the spectator into its world; the spectator has not only a fuller view of the object but a fuller view of himself. The theatre, then, changes from a space that creates a "craving for extraordinary incident" in order to take the spectator out of himself into a space that self-reflexively puts the spectator into contact with the other by bringing him back to himself.

"The Discharged Soldier," begun only six weeks after Covent Garden rejected *The Borderers*, is a parable that recounts both the danger of theatrical distance and the saving grace of human contact. It is a poem that Wordsworth liked well enough to insert at the end of book 4 of *The Prelude*, along with a short preamble on the "strange rendezvous" that his mind was at the time, "A party-coloured shew of grave and gay, / Solid and light, short-sighted and profound, / Of inconsiderate habits and sedate" (*Prelude* 4.339–42). Yet critics have never thought to take the "Discharged Soldier" as a cautionary tale, a show of the "short-sighted" as well as the "profound," the "inconsiderate habits" as well as the "sedate." Wordsworth further reinforces his moral lesson in the additional preamble he adds to the 1850 version:

> When from our better selves we have too long
> Been parted by the hurrying world, and droop,
> Sick of its business, of its pleasures tired,
> How gracious, how benign, is Solitude;
> How potent a mere image of her sway;
> Most potent when impressed upon the mind
> With an appropriate human centre—hermit,

Deep in the bosom of the wilderness;
Votary (in vast cathedral, where no foot
Is treading, where no other face is seen)
Kneeling at prayers; or watchman on the top
Of lighthouse, beaten by Atlantic waves;
Or as the soul of that great Power is met
Sometimes embodied on a public road,
When, for the night deserted, it assumes
A character of quiet more profound
Than pathless wastes. (*Prelude* 4.353–69)

Wordsworth's preamble neatly draws the tired man from solitude to the public. It begins with the solitary parted from his better self, it recognizes his need to withdraw, but then in the middle of its catalogue of the pleasures of withdrawal, it recognizes that the power of Solitude is "[m]ost potent" when "impressed upon the mind / With an appropriate human centre," and that that "human centre" might appear not only in the places where the solitary might expect to find it—in hermitages, cathedrals, or lighthouses—but also in the common space of the public road, where it assumes "[a] character of quiet more profound / Than pathless wastes."

The "Discharged Soldier" stands as a warning to the solitary not to withdraw, and indeed, stands as a warning to Wordsworth himself about the dangers of taking the wrong perspective in his observations of nature. Wordsworth's solitary narrator—Wordsworth's earlier self within the narrative of *The Prelude*—begins the poem in what we might think of as a typically Wordsworthian situation, walking at night on the deserted way, "my body from the stillness drinking in / A restoration like the calm of sleep / But sweeter far" (22–24).[12] But despite what might seem to be a typically Wordsworthian enjoyment of the quiet evening, this narrator has not yet risen to the level of vision, "all unworthy of the deeper joy / Which waits on distant prospect, cliff or sea" (18–19). The joy that he receives from his senses amounts to no more than "amusement" (13); his pictures "came along like dreams" (31). As Wordsworth's later analysis in *The Prelude* suggests, he knows the worth of the power he possesses, but because his mind is not quite ready, that power remains "slighted and misused" (*Prelude* 4.344–45).

The misuse of that power makes itself manifest in the solitary's conduct. When he sees the soldier, that "human centre ... embodied on the public road" (*Prelude* 1850, 4.359–66), his first instinct is to hide, "stepping back into the shade / Of a thick hawthorn," so that he might "mark him well, / Myself unseen" (39–41). It is not clear how long the poet stays crouching behind the hawthorn bush, but it must have been quite some time—"Long time I scanned him" (68), the poet tells us, and then later in the description, "Not without reproach / Had I prolonged my watch" (83–84). From this privileged viewpoint, the poet makes a minute inventory of the figure—his height, his form, his hands, his legs, his clothing—as if by looking he could find out all he needed to know about the man. But from this vantage point, the soldier appears strange, misshapen, inhuman—an "uncouth shape" (38), "shapeless" (46), "ghastly" (51), "[f]orlorn and desolate, a man cut off / From all his kind, and more than half detached / From his own nature" (58–60): "If but a glove had dangled in his hand / It would have made him more akin to man" (65–66). Even after the solitary emerges from his hiding place to greet the soldier, he treats him as if he were still observing from a distance. Lewis Carroll has famously parodied Wordsworth's habit of questioning his rural subjects:

> I met an aged, aged man
>   Upon the lonely moor:
> I knew I was a gentleman,
>   And he was but a boor.
> So I stopped and roughly questioned him,
>   'Come tell me how you live!'
> But his words impressed my ear no more
>   Than if it were a sieve.[13]

Although Wordsworth's questioning of the soldier is not quite as "rough" as Carroll's parody, it shares something of the same dynamic. It is the one-way questioning of a superior to an inferior: the solitary is seeking information, the man passively provides it. Like a spectator in the theatres of London, Wordsworth's solitary is still looking for "extraordinary incident" that will take him outside himself, not a returned gaze that will bring him back.[14]

But as Wordsworth's description of his mind as a "party-coloured shew" might suggest, the solitary is not totally beyond redemption, and his redemption comes not through transcending the physical but by embracing it. Somehow his way of looking must change, and it changes when the soldier is able to return his gaze—to recognize, to respond, and to reprove. The moment that the solitary's attitude turns is the moment when the Soldier is able to address the solitary narrator not just in answer to the narrator's query but of his own accord. It is also the first moment when the soldier notices something about the solitary narrator. Previously, the soldier's answers have only been about the soldier; now the soldier purports to tell the narrator something about himself: "My trust is in the God of heaven, / And in the eye of him that passes me" (164–65). This moment of recognition converts the solitary narrator's theatrical vision into a moment of personal contact. Once the man has looked back, the narrator can never again look at the man from a distance. Where the soldier started out as an "uncouth shape" (38), he has now become a "comrade" (167) and a "poor unhappy man" (171). The magic of personal presence—the realization that the soldier is not just a shape but a sentient being—turns what had been a distant encounter into a moment of vision. Wordsworth can see not only the soldier but also himself. Their encounter becomes a moment of involvement rather than simply a moment of charity, and perhaps more importantly, it plays an important part in Wordsworth's journey from "short-sighted" to "profound." The return of the soldier's gaze forms Wordsworth from a man of ignorant habits into a poet conscious of the true worth of the powers he possesses.

"The Thorn," composed just as Wordsworth was putting the finishing touches on "The Discharged Soldier," again engages with the drama, but this time Wordsworth's focus is on the way that the physical object can act as a mediating structure that enables human beings to connect with each other in the same way that the solitary connects with the discharged soldier. Seen from the perspective of the drama, the thorn is nothing but an elaborate stage set or prop, the humble analogue of the "impressive" stage sets that dominated the theatre of Wordsworth's day. But from the very beginning, Wordsworth stresses the ability of the physical object to connect rather than to obscure. The poem, as Wordsworth's note tells us, "arose out of my observing, on the ridge of Quantock Hill, on a stormy day, a thorn which I had often passed in calm and bright weather without noticing it. I said to myself, 'Cannot I by some invention do as much to make this Thorn an impressive object as the storm has made it to my eyes at this moment?'"[15] The point of writing a poem about an "impressive object," then, is to create a connection between poet and reader. If the poem succeeds in making the thorn as impressive an object as it was to Wordsworth's eyes at that moment, then poet and reader will have shared a common experience. Wordsworth experiencing the thorn becomes the reader experiencing the thorn; the mediating object allows the reader to get inside Wordsworth's head and share the same experience that Wordsworth experienced.

The "impressive object" works the same way within the poem itself. The thorn, with its accompanying pond and hill of moss, provides a connection between Wordsworth's loquacious narrator, a man of "slow faculties and deep feelings" who Wordsworth tells us "had retired ... to some village or country town of which he was not a native, or in which he had not been accustomed to live" (593), and the tale of Martha Ray, a maiden native to the village and so connected to the land that it has almost become part of her. The thorn, as an object, is not "impressive" in and of itself, despite its lichens, its "beauteous" hill of moss, and the "mossy network" "[a]s if by hand of lady fair / The work had woven been" (11, 36, 40–42). It is impressive because it provides a connection to the tale of Martha Ray. Indeed, it may form the only sort of "connection" that will enable Wordsworth's narrator to see the tale properly. It is one of the great ironies of the poem that Wordsworth's narrator, who constantly protests "I cannot tell; I wish I could" (89), actually knows a good deal about Martha's story: he can rehearse the tale of Stephen Hill, Martha's wedding day, the madness, the child, and her preternatural attachment to the spot as if it were second nature. Indeed, the tale is one of the few spots of knowledge in the poem that is not hedged about with a network of gossip, that complex of "I've heard," "some will say," or "Last Christmas ... Old Farmer Simpson did maintain" (221, 214, 148–49) that qualifies so many of the narrator's claims of knowledge in this poem. The tale is something that the narrator can assert simply from his own knowledge—"I'll tell you every thing I know" (105)—but the tale is not enough. "I cannot tell" may mean that the narrator doesn't know—after all, he "cannot tell" "[f]or the true reason no one knows" (89–90)—but it might also mean simply that he "cannot tell"—that is to say, the story of Martha Ray is a story that cannot be told. It is a story that can only be "known" by being experienced, and in this poem, it can only be experienced through the physical presence of the object. Time and time again, the narrator invites the reader to the thorn, as if the thorn contained the answer to all the reader's questions—"Now would you see this aged thorn" (56), "But if you'd gladly view the spot" (91), "But to the thorn ... I wish that you would go" (106–8). "Perhaps when you are at the place / You something of her tale will trace" (109–10)—the tale is not a tale that can be conveyed by simple narration. It is a story that can only be known by being experienced, and it can only be experienced by coming into the physical presence of the object.

But once again, the physical presence of the object is not important in and of itself, but rather as a way to embody a connection between two worlds, one characterized by intense personal presence and the other characterized by its absence. For Martha Ray does not go up to the mountain to be alone. Instead, her world is a world characterized by a sort of personal contact that the narrator can only imagine. While the narrator and his community of superstitious villagers watch from the churchyard path, Martha Ray communes with "plainly living voices" and "voices of the dead" (171, 173). What is only a heard presence for them is a physical presence for her, which is perhaps why the narrator ends the stanza with a jealous aside: "I cannot think, what'er they say, / They had to do with Martha Ray" (175–76). And then there is the matter of Martha Ray's "communion" with her "stirring child" (145). "[T]he infant wrought / About its mother's heart"—mother and child enjoy a physical communion that is so close that one body is actually inside the other. The child can literally reach its body up into its mother's heart—can commune with her, quite literally, from the inside—and in the process, remake her even as she makes it. The bodily presence of the child is what heals her, and the bodily presence of the voices is what comforts her. Indeed, we might speculate that she habitually visits the thorn, with its pond and hill of moss, to be close to the body of her dead child, like the little girl of "We Are Seven," who sits on the ground and sings to her brother and sister in their graves. But more than that, physical presence is what gives the members of this community of presence exactly what the narrator does not have: knowledge. Because of Martha Ray's presence at the spot, "she is known to every star, / And every wind that blows" (69–70). The stars and wind know what the narrator does not because they experience what the narrator does not—the physical communion with Martha Ray's body—they know her and her story in a way that he cannot access. Physical communion, then, provides comfort, sanity, and knowledge—the very things that Wordsworth's narrator, separated from his own sense of place and his own community, wants.

But there is also another community that develops around the thorn, this time a community that is marked by discourse and physical absence, a community that we might call "the audience." This community includes the narrator and his questioner (though only at its margins), but in a larger sense it includes the entire village—that network of "I've heard," "some will say," or "Last Christmas ... Old Farmer Simpson did maintain" (221, 214, 148–49) that I mentioned earlier. This community is defined by the way it uses Martha Ray. Her tale is integral to them, but only as a way to take them out of themselves. She stands at a distance, as an object lesson in morality or justice, as a bad woman who was betrayed by a bad man, a woman who has (perhaps) killed her baby and should be brought to "public justice" (233). They gather around the churchyard path to hear the voices, they watch her go up the mountain, they see that a child is in her womb, they talk about her madness, they speculate on the fate of the child. But when they talk about Martha Ray, they talk about her fate without a sense of connection. They are the archetypal spectators who watch from a distance, who speculate on the fate of the plot and characters without any sense that they are involved, and who ultimately sit in judgment of right and wrong without feeling the sense of connection to the story. As a result, Wordsworth makes clear, they do not "know"—indeed, they cannot "know"—Martha Ray in the sense that the narrator and his questioner want to know her. "Now wherefore thus, by day and night, / In rain, in tempest, and in snow, / Thus to the dreary mountain-top / Does this poor woman go? ... And wherefore does she cry?" (78–86). The narrator and the questioning voice (which, as Susan Wolfson suggests, may be the inner voice of the narrator himself) seek a deeper sort of knowledge. It is not enough for them to know what happened, not enough to speculate on what demons might be on the mountain, not enough to pass judgment on what Martha Ray might or might not have done wrong—although they use that information to complete their tale. What they want is a different sort of understanding, one that cannot be conveyed by looking at a distance or repeating the tale. What they want, although they may not know it, is the sort of knowledge that can only come from the experience of physical presence, the type of knowledge that the wind and the stars have. And somehow, they intuitively sense that this knowledge might be available to them, and that it might be available through the physical presence of an object: the thorn.

But of course, the thorn is a very difficult figure to read, and this difficulty leads to some of the more ridiculous machinations in the poem. Geoffrey Hartman has noted the narrator's "absurd precision"—"I've measured it from side to side: / 'Tis three feet long, and two feet wide" (32–33). But this absurdity comes from the fact that this is the only way that the narrator knows how to manipulate objects. One can measure, describe, and calculate, but how does one "read" an object—and, more important than reading, how does one experience the presence of the object, or extract the human knowledge that the object contains? As Hartman points out, the narrator is "the ocular man in Wordsworth" (148)—the typical man with a telescope—searching out nature's secrets while watching from a safe distance, trying to get knowledge by magnifying and minimizing, itemizing and categorizing. At times, it seems like the narrator will try almost anything to pry out Martha Ray's story except coming face to face with the woman he seeks. Although he intuits that knowledge can only be had by physical presence, he never dares to confront Martha Ray—"I've never heard of such as dare / Approach the spot when she is there" (98–99). Instead, he tries to make do by listening to the villagers, visiting the spot, and trying to get something of Martha's personal presence through the presence of the objects she visits. Like the audience in the theatre, he seems to be in the physical presence of the knowledge he seeks, but yet locked outside it, condemned to observe from a distance and read the objects he sees, rather than actually coming into the real physical presence of the knowledge of the other.

But of course, since this is one of Wordsworth's instructive poems, the idiot spectator does learn to see, at least as long as he has the proper motivation. The villagers want to know Martha Ray's story out of curiosity or out of a desire to judge, and at least initially, the narrator might have the same motivation. Wordsworth tells us in his note that "[s]uch men having little to do become credulous and talkative from indolence" (593), and the manner in which the narrator begins the poem—"There is a thorn" (1)—makes it sound like the narrator is describing a natural curiosity rather than searching for the truth in the story. Before he can see, the narrator must abandon this distant perspective. He must admit that the thorn and all it represents is more than just a natural curiosity or a curious tale—one that the reader can, in essence, put in his bag and forget about—and he must realize his personal involvement in the tale, the longing that leads the questioner to ask "[b]ut wherefore to the mountain-top / Can this unhappy woman go" (100–101)? The narrator must realize that he is seeking shelter—in this case, physical shelter from the storm—before he can gain the knowledge that will lead him to say "it was enough for me" (200). The narrator's face-to-face meeting with Martha Ray is certainly an odd moment in the poem: running through the rain, the narrator mistakes Martha Ray for a sheltering cliff: "Instead of jutting crag, I found / A woman seated on the ground" (193–94). But Wordsworth has a larger point to make with the comparison. It is not only that the narrator's insight comes at a moment of visual blindness—"A storm came on, and I could see / No object higher than my knee" (186–87)—but also that the narrator is put into the same physical situation as Martha Ray. Just as she goes to the thorn "when the whirlwind's on the hill" (73) and in "winter, when at night / The wind blew from the mountain-peak" (167–68), the narrator also finds himself on the mountain during the storm. He has, in essence, come onstage. He is a part of her physical world. And just as important as their simple sharing of the storm is the fact that they share the same motivation. Just as Martha Ray goes to the mountain to seek comfort, the narrator finds her when he is also seeking comfort—a crag to shelter him from the storm. And finally, even though he might not know *what* he is looking for, he is looking for something. Just like the solitary in the "Discharged Soldier," who senses that he is missing something in his enjoyment of nature, "receiving . . . / Amusement, as I slowly passed along," and "all unworthy of the deeper joy / Which waits on distant prospect, cliff or sea" (12–13, 18–19), Wordsworth's narrator must sense a lack in his distant perspective, must be forced by circumstances to abandon his telescope and seek a closer relationship. Only then can he gain the knowledge that he has been seeking throughout the poem.

And, just as in "The Discharged Soldier," Wordsworth's spectator can only gain that knowledge by allowing the object of his vision to return his gaze. "I did not speak—I saw her face, / Her face it was enough for me" (199–200). This vision is almost too much for the narrator—he immediately "turned about" and "heard her cry, / 'O misery! O misery!'" (201–2). But her cry has changed for him. Before, when he mentions her cry, it is always "to herself she cries" (64, 75). Now her cry is coupled with an observation of her body ("She shudders" [208]) and with an affirmation that her cry has been heard—not only does the narrator say "I turned about and heard her cry" (201), but he also affirms that "all the country know" (207) and that "*you* hear her cry" (208, emphasis added). Suddenly, by virtue of seeing her face, the narrator understands that Martha Ray is conveying some sort of social knowledge. She not only cries "to herself"; all the country around can hear her. He himself can hear her. The cry changes from an isolated act of loneliness to an expression that involves the entire community, and that particularly implicates the narrator and his questioner. They have seen and been seen, therefore they can hear.

Wordsworth's final image of seeing and being seen takes personal presence into the mystical dimension, and suggests the self-reflexivity of the process of seeing both nature and man. Shortly after seeing Martha Ray, and after expounding the theories behind the mystery ("some will say / She hanged her baby on the tree, / Some say she drowned it in the pond, / Which is a little step beyond, / But each and all agree, / The little babe was buried there, / Beneath that hill of moss so fair" (214–20), the narrator and the villagers share a mystical moment:

> Some say, if to the pond you go,
> And fix on it a steady view,
> The shadow of a babe you trace,
> A baby and a baby's face,
> And that it looks at you;
> Whene'er you look on it, 'tis plain
> The baby looks at you again. (225–31)

The image shimmers between self-reflexive viewing and an actual vision of the mystical and the human. As Stephen Knapp has pointed out, it seems likely that what the superstitious narrator sees in the pond is his own reflection (114). But the repetition of the image "the shadow of a babe ... a baby and a baby's face" and the narrator's own double take ("it looks at you ... The baby looks at you again"), coupled with the narrator's recent vision of the face of Martha Ray, suggests that there is something more at work here than a simple parody of self-reflexive gazing of the type seen in *Peter Bell*. Instead, Wordsworth's narration suggests a gradual focusing on the image. The narrator might have peered into the pond out of curiosity, or out of a narcissistic desire to see his own reflection, but gradually that image dissolves, first into "the shadow of a babe," then into "a baby" and finally into "a baby's face," and then finally into the payoff—"it looks at you." If Wordsworth's narrator wants to solve the mystery—as it seems in the poem that he has been trying to do—the "shadow of a babe" and then "a baby" would do it. The forensic certainty of an infant's body lying in the pond would satisfy even the "absurd precision" of Wordsworth's ridiculously scientific narrator. It would satisfy the previous round of speculation—"Some say she drowned it in the pond"—and it would put a fitting end to the story of Martha Ray. Her deeds would be revealed, she would presumably be brought to "public justice" (233), and the villagers could put this portion of the short, sad history behind them. But Wordsworth does not stop with the physical solution. The image dissolves into "a baby's face," which has the capacity to look back at the narrator. The narrator must realize that he is involved, that the mystery he has been dealing with is one with the capacity to look back at him and involve him. He has finally been brought not only into the physical presence of the woman but into the physical presence of the baby, and the shimmer between his own reflection and the baby's face implicates him still further. He can no longer deny the resemblance between the baby and himself, or between Martha Ray and himself. Their story is his story, and he can no longer look at it as a scientific examiner or a curious outsider. He has been brought into the physical presence of that which he seeks.

And the image of the baby also suggests something more radical—that nature, as well as humans, can return the human gaze. As Geoffrey Hartman has pointed out, the thorn that gives the poem its name has always had something of an anthropomorphic character—it stands "[n]ot higher than a two-years' child" (5), it ages like a human being—"It is a mass of knotted joints," "It looks so old and grey" (8, 4)—and it even seems to participate in a human struggle—"It stands erect" although the moss and lichens that surround it "were bent / With plain and manifest intent, / To drag it to the ground" (10, 18–20). But what the thorn lacks, as the poem shows, is the human ability to look back at the narrator, to implicate him, to tell its story. It is, at best, a mute symbol until it is animated by the vision of the baby in the pond. It is the baby's capacity to look back that finally turns mute nature into a dynamic comforter and leads one to understand how Martha Ray can be "known to every star, / And every wind that blows" (69–70). Nature, like man, has the capacity to look back at man. It can see and it can know. Wordsworth tells us in his note that "[s]uperstitious men . . . have a reasonable share of imagination, by which word I mean the faculty which produces impressive effects out of simple elements; but they are utterly destitute of fancy, the power by which pleasure and surprize are excited by sudden varieties of situation and by accumulated imagery" (139). Only the superstitious man, in other words, can see beyond the "pleasure and surprize" that are associated with "sudden varieties of situation and . . . accumulated imagery" and realize the "impressive effects" of simple elements. But this power of the imagination comes not in spite of their superstition, but because of it. The superstitious man is the only kind of man who can be truly "impressed" by objects because he is the only one who can imagine them looking back at him.

There is a general view that when Wordsworth is writing about people, he is usually writing about something else, usually his own perceptions. Jonathan Wordsworth writes that "Wordsworth is of course perfectly clear that the [Discharged] Soldier does not himself possess such wisdom—or rather that he possesses it solely in the eye of the beholder" (14–15); Stephen Knapp slides persons into "personifications," and sees their function as emblematic of self-consciousness. Even Frederick Garber, whose *Wordsworth and the Poetry of Encounter* argues that Wordsworth consistently seeks contact with the other and the unknown, argues that Wordsworth seeks out the other to expand his own consciousness, not out of any particular desire to know the other in and of itself. Seeing Wordsworth's poems as dramas helps us understand the importance of recognizing Wordsworth's people as people—as others in all their embodied otherness—rather than as figures along the poet's path. And although expanding the poet's consciousness is certainly part of Wordsworth's project, so is seeing the faces and figures that inhabit his world. Indeed, this individualized sight is the only thing that permits the poet to see himself as an embodied other, and the only thing that allows him to see through the individualized other into the heart of nature and humanity. Wordsworth's bodies can aid the visionary process only when they remain bodies; Wordsworth's "presences" can only become present when they become persons.

Both Actor and Spectator:
Wordsworth Creates His Own Theatre

To illustrate both how important and how necessary it is to see Wordsworth's poetic persona in explicitly theatrical terms, I would like to point out the similarity in two scenes from *The Prelude* with very different valences: Wordsworth's encounter with Bartholomew Fair in book 7 and his ascent of Mount Snowdon in book 13.[16] In both, the poet begins as a member of a group gathered to see a spectacle: at Bartholomew Fair, he is part of "the city," which "break[s] out / Full of one passion" (7.646–47); on Snowdon, he and his "youthful friend" (13.2) ascend with a guide "to see the sun / Rise from the top of Snowdon" (13.4–5). In both, the poet is lifted up above his companions: at Bartholomew Fair, by the Muse; on Snowdon, by his own effort. And in both, the poet looks down upon a scene that is more or less explicitly an audience: at Bartholomew Fair, "every nook / Of the wide area, twinkles, is alive / With heads" (7.663–65); on Snowdon, "A hundred hills their dusky backs upheaved / All over this still ocean, and beyond" (13.45–46). In both scenes, Wordsworth specifically sets up an actor/audience dynamic (the poet goes to see a spectacle with a group of friends), and in both, the poet is raised up to assume the position of an actor—explicitly at Bartholomew Fair, implicitly on Snowdon—and in both, what the actor does is to look back down at the audience, as if to see the subject position from whence he came. Indeed, the main difference between the two scenes, other than the obvious valence with which Wordsworth treats the two spectacles, is that on Snowdon the elevated Wordsworth remains more or less explicitly part of the audience, as "we stood, the mist / Touching our very feet" (13.53–55) watching "[t]he universal spectacle . . . / [t]he soul, the imagination of the whole" (13.60–65).

This theatrical dynamic points to a conflict in Wordsworth's poetic voice. On the one hand, there is the democratic Wordsworth, the poet who can speak the language of "[l]ow and rustic life"[17] because he has been part of that life, the poet who is, in essence, one of the people he writes about. On the other hand, there is the Wordsworth who is (in this case quite literally) set above and apart from his audience, a "spirit . . . singled out . . . / For holy services" (*Prelude* 1.62–63), a poet, priest or intercessor, an "actor" not so much in the sense of presenting something that is false and fluid (although Judith Pascoe and others have analyzed Wordsworth's role in that sense), but an "actor" in the sense of someone set above the public to play a public role, like the actors on that "great stage / Where senators . . . perform" (7.522–23) that Wordsworth describes in book 7 of *The Prelude*.

Seeing Wordsworth's poetic persona in theatrical terms helps explain why these two roles are closer than one might think, and why Wordsworth so consistently puts himself not in the role of the actor, but in the role of the spectator. The role of the high Romantic poet lifted up above his audience not only offered Wordsworth a confirmation of his poetic destiny; it also offered Wordsworth a model of a public voice, a voice that, like the panoramic artist Wordsworth mentions in book 7, "take[s] in / A whole horizon on all sides—with power / Like that of angels or commissioned spirits" (7.259–60). But on the other hand, the role of the spectator offered

Wordsworth a role in common with his audience. All are spectators in this new spectatorial world, and positioning himself as a fellow spectator allows Wordsworth to make himself a part of his audience. Wordsworth's project in *The Prelude* and his lyric poems is to balance the two roles—to be both outside the crowd and within it—and to do that, he must assume the position of the actor.

In order to understand how the theatre shaped Wordsworth's sense of his poetic role, we must first understand the formative role that Wordsworth's residence in London and his later recording of it in book 7 of *The Prelude* played in his poetic career. His actual residence in London comes immediately after his graduation from Cambridge and his walking tour of Europe with Robert Jones, the journey where Wordsworth would find so many of the "spots" that would later form such a large part of his own narrative of the growth of the poet's mind. Kenneth Johnston titles the section of Wordsworth's biography that begins with his residence in London "Of the Man" (in contrast with his earlier section "The Child is Father"), and indeed, it is in London that Wordsworth first begins to think of himself as embarking on a vocation. Immediately before settling in London, he was beginning to work his notebook jottings into the verses that would become *Descriptive Sketches*; soon after—after a trip to Wales with Jones, a brief sojourn in Cambridge, and his residence in France—he would become a published poet. Indeed, Johnston observes that "[i]f Wordsworth was dilatory in staying so long in Paris, he made up for it by the dispatch with which he attended to his affairs as soon as he returned to London" (329). *An Evening Walk* and *Descriptive Sketches* were both published less than two months after Wordsworth's return from France. We might think of Wordsworth's residence in London, then, as a time when he was just beginning to think about what it might mean to embark on poetry as a vocation.

Like the residence in London that it describes, book 7 of *The Prelude* was also composed at a crucial juncture in Wordsworth's career. As Jonathan Wordsworth has argued, book 7 was probably not originally part of Wordsworth's plan for *The Prelude*.[18] Book 7 literally rose up—almost like Mary of Buttermere in the book itself—after a five-year hiatus. This "rising up" is reported in the book itself—"Five years are vanished since I first poured out, / Saluted by that animating breeze / Which met me issuing from the city's walls, / A glad preamble to this verse" (7.1–4). Wordsworth originally meant this prelude to be a prelude to book 8, a return to nature's bosom, exactly where we might expect a man like Wordsworth to go in the face of severe writer's block. But as Wordsworth wrote book 8, book 7 literally rose up, unbidden, and Wordsworth had to shift his plans for *The Prelude*. In the wake of a five-year break in composition, which saw the publication of eight political sonnets in the *Morning Post*, the growth of Wordsworth's reputation as a poet, and Coleridge's departure for Malta, Wordsworth's thoughts must have turned once again to what it means to be a poet. The result of that thought was book 7.

Book 7 is remarkable for the diversity of the theatrical experiences it portrays: the "fairy cataracts" (125) of the pleasure gardens at Vauxhall and Ranelagh, "the giddy top / And Whispering Gallery of St. Paul's" (129–30), "a raree-show . . . / With children gathered round" (190–91), "a company of dancing dogs, / Or dromedary with an antic pair / of monkies on his back" (192–94), "a minstrel-band / of Savoyards" (194–95), "single and alone, An English ballad-singer" (195–96), the "spectacles / Within doors: troops of wild beasts, birds and beasts / Of every nature from all climes convened" (245–47), the "mimic sights" (248) of the panorama, the "shifting pantomimic scenes" (283) of "[h]alf-rural Sadler's Wells" (289), "singers, rope-dancers, giants and dwarfs / Clowns, conjurors, posture-masters, harlequins" (294–95), "samples, as of the ancient comedy / And Thespian times" (312–13), "dramas"—or rather melodramas—"of living men / And recent things yet warm with life" (313–14), "a theatre," unidentified in the text, where Wordsworth sees the painted mother and her rosy babe set "upon a board" (374, 383), theatres with "lustres, lights / The carving and the gilding, paint and glare, / And all the mean upholstery of the place" (441–43) (presumably the major houses, since they were known for their extravagant decorations[19]), Bartholomew Fair—even the pulpit and parliament, "that great stage / Where senators . . . perform" (522–23). For Wordsworth, "theatre" clearly includes theatres of every kind. But what has not been noticed is the way that Wordsworth consistently favors the "minor" spectacles over the "major" ones. He mentions the "major" playhouses only once, and not too clearly—the "lustres, lights / The carving and the gilding, paint and glare." And more importantly, the "major" theatres, or the theatres that might be major, get the bulk of Wordsworth's negative commentary. The majors, with their "lustres, lights," "carving and . . . guilding" are the places where "the mind / Turned this way, that way—sportive and alert / And watchful, as a kitten when at play" (470–72) and "the imaginative power

/ Languish[ed] within me" (499–500); "a theatre" is the place where Wordsworth observes the painted mother and her babe. By contrast, Wordsworth seems to speak laudably—or at least with interest—of the street theatre "raree-show," the "troops of wild beasts, birds and beasts / Of every nature from all climes convened," and the panorama, which "ape[s] / The absolute presence of reality, / Expressing as in mirror sea and land, / And what earth is, and what she hath to shew" (248–51). He confesses his preference for the minor theatres with some degree of shame: "Need I fear / To mention by its name, as in degree / Lowest of these, and humblest in attempt— / Yet richly graced with honours of its own— / Half-rural Sadler's Wells?" (285–89), and indeed, his disproportionate affection for the minors might be due to the "obstacles / Which slender funds imposed" (439–40). But nonetheless, when Wordsworth criticizes the theatre, he is generally talking about the major houses, and except for the one incident at Bartholomew Fair, when he remembers the minor theatres he does so fondly.

This affection for the minor theatres would have made a distinct political statement in the 1790s—or even in 1804, when book 7 was finally written. As Jane Moody has shown, the term "legitimate" in the theatre had become conflated with political "legitimacy," so that the major theatres' attempt to stifle competition from the minors came to be an analog for the government's stifling of dissent.[20] But Wordsworth's objections to the major theatres seem to have less to do with the overt political implications of the major/minor theatre split and more to do with the different way that the minor theatres related to their audience. As I have mentioned earlier, the major theatres were moving toward a situation where the actors were completely separated from the audience, closed off from the spectacle by a developing "fourth wall." The actor was removed from the audience; the audience was becoming less and less a part of the spectacle and more a passive recipient of it. The minor theatres, by contrast— especially the ones Wordsworth mentions—made the audience part of the spectacle itself. As William Galperin has shown, even the panorama, the spectacle that seemed to be most distant, worked to make its audience part of the scene. The audience was not "plant[ed] ... upon some lofty pinnacle" (261), as Wordsworth and some of the panorama's advertisements would have it; it was a part of the scenery, pictured in details like the crowd crossing Blackfriars Bridge in the *Panorama of London from the Albion Mills* (1792–93) and made a part of the landscape by advertisements that promised that the "whole" would "appea[r] the same as reality" (Galperin 49)—or, as Wordsworth would put it, "All that the traveller sees when he is there" (286). The viewer, in other words, could see himself pictured in the scenery. A panorama of Constantinople (for example) would pretend to situate the viewer (at least for a time) in Constantinople as both a member of the audience and part of the picture.

Wordsworth seems to have the audience very much in mind when he talks about the theatre in book 7 of *The Prelude*. The "raree-show" is not mentioned by itself, but rather "[w]ith children gathered round" (191); Sadler's Wells would not be complete without an observation of the crowd—"Nor was it mean delight / To watch crude Nature work in untaught minds, / To note the laws and progress of belief" (297–99); and even at the majors, Wordsworth's mind transgressively turns to his fellow audience members—the "many-headed mass / Of the spectators, and each little nook / That had its fray or brawl" (467–69). Furthermore, Wordsworth's most trenchant satire of the theatre has to do with the way that the theatre separates the actor from the audience through the mechanics of illusion. The boards that "[p]rate somewhat loudly of the whereabout" (460–61) of the tragic actor, or Jack the Giant-killer, who "dons his coat of darkness" and "atchieves his wonders, from the eye / Of living mortal safe" simply by donning his black garb and wearing the word "INVISIBLE" on his chest (303–10) are both funny precisely because they provide evidence that the body is not really separated from the audience by the world of illusion. The actors' weight and visibility breaks through the structure of the illusion to show the body underneath; the actor is only a body among bodies, not the "mumbling sire / A scarecrow pattern of old age" (455–56) or Jack the Giant-killer working his wonders under the guise of invisibility. The truly troubling thing about these scenes, at least to Wordsworth, is the audience: "To note the laws and progress of belief . . . How willingly we travel, and how far!" (299–301). The body is present among the bodies of the audience, but yet the audience doesn't recognize it.

Of course, this method of relating to the viewer has a politics as well. When Burke showcases the drama in his *Reflections on the Revolution in France*, the drama he praises is the very sort of distant spectacle that was becoming standard at the major houses. The English view the "monstrous tragi-comic scene" from across the channel; the very presence of a "Supreme Director of this great drama" (175) implies that the spectacle takes place outside their ambit and outside their control. By contrast, Burke is very suspicious of personal presence. It is no accident that Burke's attacks on Richard Price's rhetorical style generally sit next to Burke's disquisitions on the "theatre" of the French Revolution. One of his main objections to Price is his "pulpit style," which has "an air of novelty . . . not wholly without danger" (94–95). Price's abandoning his divine calling to preach dissent makes him a sort of an actor—"Those who quit their proper character, to assume what does not belong to them, are, for the greater part, ignorant both of the character they leave, and of the character which they assume" (94). But it is the actor's charisma, not his falseness, that gives him power over the audience. The philosophers "set him up as a sort of oracle" (93); he leads his audience in triumph in "the most horrid, atrocious, and afflicting spectacle, that perhaps ever was exhibited to the pity and indignation of mankind . . . a spectacle more resembling a procession of American savages, entering into Onondaga, after some of their murders called victories, and leading into hovels hung round with scalps, their captives," so different from "the triumphal pomp of a civilized martial nation (159)." "A civilized nation," Burke writes, is not capable of a "*personal* triumph over the fallen and afflicted" (159, emphasis added), but Price's triumph is precisely a "personal" triumph—the triumph of bodily charisma over reason and reasoned passion. It is because of the powerful figure of the orator that "politics and the pulpit are terms that have little agreement" (94). The personal presence of the actor is only safe in a religious context where God upstages the charismatic actor. But when that figure begins to exercise power over politics, the power of the body borders on idolatry.

The situation is even worse in the theatre, where the bodies of the audience mix with the bodies of the actors. The French assemblies

> act like the comedians of a fair before a riotous audience; they act amidst the tumultuous cries of a mixed mob of ferocious men, and of women lost to shame, who, according to their insolent fancies, direct, control, applaud, explode them; and sometimes mix and take their seats amongst them; domineering over them with a strange mixture of servile petulance and proud presumptuous authority. As they have inverted order in all things, the gallery is in the place of the house . . . They have a power given to them, like that of the evil principle, to subvert and destroy; but none to construct, except such machines as may be fitted for further subversion and further destruction. (161)

A good English audience would keep its seats, but at the French assembly, as at the French theatres, fairs, and revolutionary festivals, the audience is exposed to the personal presence of the actor without the buffering effects of illusion and distance. The actors make contact with the revolutionary bodies of the audience and the revolutionaries in the audience make contact with each other without regard to rank or station. Burke recognizes that there is a power at work here—exactly the same power that he fears in Rev. Price's sermons—but that power is even worse because the charismatic bodies of the audience are now part of the equation. There is no regard for the "traditional" distance between actor and audience (although that distance is actually far from traditional) just as there is no regard for rank or history. All is subsumed by the power of the group acting as a communal body, and in Burke's eyes, that power, "like that of the evil principle," is a power that is only "fitted for further subversion and further destruction" (161).

Of course, by the time he wrote book 7 of *The Prelude*, Wordsworth was at pains to disguise his earlier political allegiances,[21] but Wordsworth, like Burke, had seen the actors mixing with their audiences in the French theatres and at the French revolutionary festivals, and like Burke, he remains fascinated by the power of personal presence and by the idea that the actor can play a powerful role in public affairs. What book 7 represents is a conscious trying on of roles—an experiment with types of acting. Wordsworth experiments with the type of acting he saw at the major houses, oddly enough, at Bartholomew Fair. He is separated from his audience, "wafted on [the Muse's] wings / Above the press and danger of the crowd" (657–58). Wordsworth celebrates this position, not because of that separation, but because, like the panoramic artist, it gives him the capacity to "take in" with his "greedy pencil" "[a] whole horizon on all sides" (258–39).[22] From this perspective, Wordsworth can see the entire fair: "every nook . . . alive / With heads" (663–65), the "midway region . . . thronged with staring pictures and huge scrolls" (665–66), "All out-o'-th'-way, far-fetched, perverted things" (689). But his perspective from the top of the showman's platform distorts. From the poet's stately perspective, the remarkable diversity that Wordsworth has witnessed in his walks around London melts into sameness: "An undistinguishable world to men / The salves unrespited of low pursuits . . . melted and reduced / To one identity by differences / That have no law, no meaning, and no end" (700–705)—truly a "parliament of monsters" (692). This spectacle threatens to "lay . . . / The whole creative powers of man asleep" (653–55), not because of any inherent fear of the mob (which after all, Wordsworth has confronted at length at the beginning of the book), but because the poet cannot function without his audience. If the people he is talking to appear to be "melted and reduced / To one identity" (703–4), the poet can have no basis for addressing them. This lofty perspective not only defaces the audience, but it also defaces the tragic actor. He becomes like the senator Wordsworth has seen earlier, who "like a hero in romance . . . winds away his never-ending horn . . . till the strain / Transcendent, superhuman as it is, / Grows tedious even in a young man's ear" (538–42), or the "comely bachelor" in the pulpit, who "[f]resh from a toilet of two hours . . . lead[s] his voice through many a maze / A minuet course" (547–52). The poet set upon a lofty pinnacle becomes an actor in the false sense—a tedious figure, an impersonator, a trivial distraction for the idle—rather than a living part of the mass that he would address.

But Wordsworth remains fascinated by another type of actor, the actor who mixes with his audience. The actor in the midst of the crowd may lose something of his transcendent perspective, but what he loses in breadth, he makes up for in power. We can see this fascination in what is supposedly one of Wordsworth's most antitheatrical scenes, the mother and her rosy babe at the theatre in lines 365–412 of book 7. The mother and her babe "cross" Wordsworth precisely at a point when he is faced with two alternatives in representation—Mary of Buttermere as she is presented by the "daring brotherhood" of melodramatic writers (317), fictionalized and seen from a distance, and Mary of Buttermere as Wordsworth and Coleridge knew her, live and in person, "welcomed, and attended on by her" (331). The mother and her rosy babe literally "rise up" in the midst of this discussion, almost without Wordsworth's volition—"Those days are now / My theme, and 'mid the numerous scenes which they / Have left behind them, foremost I am crossed / Here by remembrance of two figures" (364–67). The appearance of the mother and her rosy babe here, at the juncture between the theatre and the real world, has generally been thought to be a condemnation of the theatre and all that it represents—urbanity, falseness, prostitution—and an endorsement of the real Mary, the rural, unheard-of maiden with "modest mien . . . Unsoiled by commendation and excess / Of public notice" (333, 339–40).[23] But the mother and her rosy babe also suggest a way that theatre can bridge the gap between the real world and its public presentation. Although the painted mother and her rosy babe look quite "theatrical" to modern eyes, their actual place in the theatre is quite ambiguous. James Heffernan suggests that they are at a theatre refreshment stand (437)—"Upon a board, / Whence an attendant of the theatre / Served out refreshments" (383–85)—which, after 1794, would have been outside the performance area. But the child's situation also suggests that he is onstage. "Board" is uncomfortably close to "boards," the term for the stage (recall the "cane, with which [the actor]/ smites . . . the solid boards" [459–60] late in book 7), and the child sits "environed with a ring / Of chance spectators, chiefly dissolute men / And shameless women" (386–88), suggesting that he is part of the show. Indeed, he recalls the rage for child actors like William Henry West Betty, the "infant Roscius," which hit the stage around 1804. The mother, too, although she might be a prostitute, also appears to be an actress, with the false tints on her face, "a painted bloom" (374–75).[24] Already, then, these two figures cross the border between actor and audience—they are neither one nor the other, but both. But if these figures are actors, they are two very different kinds of actors. The infant boy, "environed with a ring / Of chance spectators" (386–87), "treated and caressed— / Ate, drank, and with the fruit and glasses played, / While oaths, indecent speech, and ribaldry / Were rife about him as the songs of birds" (388–91), is the very type of the actor in the midst of the audience. Indeed, even Wordsworth's description of the audience, "chiefly dissolute men / And shameless women" (386–87), recalls Burke's description of the French Parliament, "a mixed mob of ferocious men, and of women lost to shame" (161). His mother, by contrast, seems to be back in the scenery, her "painted bloom" (374) mixing with the painted flats. Of the mother, Wordsworth tellingly does not remember much—perhaps this is a foreshadowing of his later observation that "tragic sufferings . . . pass . . . not beyond the suburbs of the mind" (501–7). But the boy is distinguished from the place by his "lusty vigour, more than infantine" (379), and he walks "[a]mong the wretched and the falsely gay, / Like one of those who walked with hair unsinged / Amid the fiery furnace" (397–99). He later appears to Wordsworth "as if embalmed / By Nature . . . destined to live, / To be, to have been, come, and go . . . no partner in the years / That bear us forward to distress and guilt" (400–405). The actor who walks among the audience, then, even if that audience is "chiefly dissolute men / And shameless women," retains some of that personal charisma that so frightens Burke in the pulpit, a "lusty vigor" that makes him seem "[a] sort of alien scattered from the clouds" (378) in such a place. Where the actor separated from the audience remains a mere show—like the painted woman, or the eloquent senator, or the comely bachelor in the pulpit, whose displays dissolve into mere ornament—the actor who descends into the audience and mixes among them has the power to pass beyond the suburbs of the mind—to live "embalmed / By Nature . . . / no partner in the years / That bear us forward to distress and guilt" (400–405). It is this child actor who has the power to tell the story of Mary of Buttermere—"but he perhaps / Mary, may now have lived till he could look / With envy on thy nameless babe that sleeps / Beside the mountain chapel undisturbed" (409–12). Like Wordsworth himself, he has the power of personal contact with the story, like the actor set above the audience. Like the actor who mixes with the audience, he can make that story real to his hearers. He can bring the innocent Mary to the crowd of dissolute onlookers and make them aware of the presence of something beyond themselves because he has the authenticity that comes from "being there"—both "being" part of the story and "being" part of the audience.

Perhaps for this reason, Wordsworth's persona in book 7 of *The Prelude*—and indeed, in most of his poetic career—lies somewhere between actor and spectator—or, one might say, partakes of elements of both actor and spectator. Wordsworth wants to place his body in the presence of the audience—to be one of them so that he can tell a story to them in a way that will make it part of their experience—but yet set above them so he can teach and be admired. James A. W. Heffernan has noted how important it is for Wordsworth to be both someone who has lived in London *and* someone who has lived outside of it in order to gain the satirical perspective he looks for in book 7—as a resident, he gains the credibility to speak about London life, but as an outsider, he has the capacity to criticize it. But what Heffernan doesn't point out is how consciously Wordsworth establishes this perspective not only by his life history but also by manipulating his position as actor and spectator. Indeed, we might say that book 7 is an extended meditation on what it might mean to be an actor or a spectator, and how the poet might combine those roles to gain the universal perspective of the one with the camaraderie of the other.

As I have mentioned, the opening section of book 7 fairly accurately represents a break in Wordsworth's composition process. But it also represents a turn to a very different sort of creativity, a creativity that both places Wordsworth squarely within his body as a speaking man and locates the source of that creativity in the physical interaction between actor and spectator. The way that Wordsworth describes his initial burst of creativity is very much in accord with traditional Romantic notions of composition—"like a torrent sent / Out of the bowels of a bursting cloud / Down Scawfell or Blencathara's rugged sides, / A waterspout from heaven" (6–9)—an almost involuntary working of the spirit, flowing through an inanimate body that is nothing more than a conduit for the natural force. But Wordsworth's vision of recovery involves not only becoming a spectator but also making himself part of the spectacle. A "quire of redbreasts" appears "somewhere near / My threshold, minstrels from the distant woods / And dells, sent in by Winter to bespeak / For the old man a welcome" (24–27). This is no distant aesthetic spectacle, as William Galperin claims in his analysis of Wordsworth's resistance to spectacle in *The Prelude*. Rather, like the actor who mixes with the audience and takes his seat among them, these redbreasts are sent specifically to address Wordsworth—"sent in by Winter to bespeak / For the old man a welcome" (26–27)—and he sees their song not as a spectacular performance, although they are compared to "minstrels," but rather as an "unthought-of greeting" (32), a one-to-one communication, an act of presence, a performance that tends more toward scenic interaction than to disinterested spectacle. And it is this presence—this mixing of actor and audience—that makes Wordsworth feel that he can become one of them—"listening, I half whispered, 'We will be, / Ye heartsome choristers, ye and I will be / Brethren, and in the hearing of the bleak winds / Will chaunt together'" (34–37). The mixing of actor and audience, then, not only inspires Wordsworth—for his creativity still comes from a source outside himself—but also places him back into his own body. The force of nature does not simply flow through him; it speaks to him, and by gracing him with its personal presence, he finds that he himself has presence. By being a spectator, Wordsworth learns that he, too, can be an actor. Because he has been spoken to, he finds that he can speak back.

From the very beginning, then, book 7 sees personal presence as "sticky"—Wordsworth's initial light satire is on himself, unable to see the body of London because of his fascination with "airy palaces and gardens built / By genii of romance" (82–83), when he could have read the physiognomy of London on his storyteller, a boy, "a cripple from the birth, whom chance / Summoned from school to London" (95–96). Even then, Wordsworth realizes that ideas should stick to the body—"I was not wholly free / From disappointment to behold the same / Appearance, the same body, not to find / Some change, some beams of glory brought away / From that new region" (100–104)—but he is unable to see the changes, or unable to recognize those changes as being caused by London, "every word he uttered, on my ears / Fell flatter than a caged parrot's note" (105–6). Wordsworth is only able to recognize the power of bodies to tell a story when he gets to London—the "look and aspect of the place / The broad highway appearance, as it strikes / On strangers of all ages" (154–56). Even as Wordsworth insists on the "wondrous power of words" (121), the thing that tells the story of London is the bodies—bodies of men and women, bodies of streets, bodies of signs—the outright significant physicality of the place. A good deal has been made of the unreadability of Wordsworth's signs and symbols—"Shop after shop, with symbols, blazoned names, / And all the tradesman's honours overhead: / Here fronts of houses, like a title-page / With letters huge inscribed from top to toe" (174–77)—but Wordsworth's inability or refusal to read the script might indicate a larger truth about the signs—that what matters is not what they say, but their simple physicality, their hugeness, their color, their multiplicity. Physicality outstrips literal signification; the things of London do not mean, but be.

Even the most famous of Wordsworth's incidents from book 7—the blind beggar—outstrips signification with physical presence:

> Amid the moving pageant, 'twas my chance
> Abruptly to be smitten with the view
> Of a blind beggar, who, with upright face,
> Stood propped against a wall, upon his chest
> Wearing a written paper, to explain
> The story of the man, and who he was. (610–15)

The written paper might be "a type / Or emblem of the utmost that we know / Both of ourselves and of the universe" (618–20), but the paper is never quoted. What "smites" Wordsworth in this scene, and what later makes his "mind . . . turn round / As with the might of waters" (616–17), is the simple "spectacle," or the "view"—the man and who he was, with his upright face and his body propped against the wall, rather than the "label" on his chest. And Wordsworth's retelling of the story only reinforces the man's force as a physical presence rather than verbal narrative. Wordsworth has amply shown us that he could entertain us with "the story of the man, and who he was" if he only would—his poetry is littered with stories of the people he meets, and if the story were significant he could have departed from his narrative to tell it—but instead he allows the beggar to stand as a physical presence, significant as a breathing body with an upturned face, who can wordlessly make the mind turn round and convey "the utmost that we know / Both of ourselves and of the universe."

Because book 7 is a chapter about the development of Wordsworth's poetic mind, the question for the young poet becomes how he can obtain this power—how he can convey the power of physical presence through mute words—and this is where the theatre comes in. Wordsworth's description of London is almost cinematic in its use of zoom shots. He starts with a broad view of London seen from a great height—the "fairy cataracts / And pageant fireworks" of Vauxhall and Ranelagh,

> The river proudly bridged, the giddy top
> And Whispering Gallery of St. Paul's, the tombs
> Of Westminster, the Giants of Guildhall,
> Bedlam and the two figures at its gates,
> Streets without end and churches numberless,
> Statues with flowery gardens in vast squares,
> The Monument, and Armoury of the Tower. (129–35)

It is as if Wordsworth himself were painting a panorama or giving a global view. But quickly this view from a disinterested height gives way to the familiar perusal of the day to day, "For hour to hour the illimitable walk / Still among streets" (159–60), focusing first on distant objects moving away from him—"the glittering chariots with their pampered steeds" (162)—and then on large objects up close—"Face after face—the string of dazzling wares" (173–74)—then on shows and spectacles—"a raree-show is here" (190–91)—and then finally on the human face—"Behold a face turned up towards us, strong / In lineaments . . . / A travelling cripple" (216–19) and all the broad diversity of life—"The Italian, with his frame of images / Upon his head . . . And Negro ladies in white muslin gowns" (229–43). With each of these successive focusings, Wordsworth's self becomes more powerful. In the first broad section, where he is still focused on the "wondrous power of words," Wordsworth himself does not appear. He only enters the narrative as he begins to focus in: "These fond imaginations, of themselves, / Had long before given way in season due . . . / And now I looked upon the real scene, / Familiarly perused it day by day" (136–40). But even then, Wordsworth gives way to the telling of tales: "Shall I give way / Copying the impression of the memory— / Though things remembered idly do half seem / The work of fancy" (146–48). He does not fully realize himself as a character—does not place his body into the scene he describes—until line 184, when he is overwhelmed by the "roar" of objects and "[e]scaped as from an enemy," "turn[s] / Abruptly into some sequestered nook" (185–87). At this point, Wordsworth's walk through London becomes an embodied quest—"Thence back into the throng" (205), "on the broadening causeway we advance" (215), "'Tis [a face] perhaps already met elsewhere" (218), "Now homeward through the thickening hubbub" (227), and finally into the theatre, where Wordsworth's experience becomes completely his own—"At leisure let us view from day to day" (244), "I do not here allude" (252), "Need I fear" (285), "Though at that time / Intolerant, as is the way of youth / Unless itself be pleased, I more than once / Here took my seat" (289–92). It is only by focusing in, by seeing the details, by making himself one of the masses he sees, that Wordsworth can fully realize himself as an embodied character, a speaking voice among other speaking voices, a presence among presences. Wordsworth must descend from his podium as an actor—or from his even more rarified position as a disembodied narrator pouring forth inspiration from the purest of sources—before he can obtain presence. He must become a spectator in order to become an actor.

Wordsworth's subjectivity, then, is a subjectivity that is formed by contact. His creative power is not a power that flows out of nowhere like the "deep / But short-lived uproar" (5–6) of the initial burst he describes, but rather a submission to a fundamentally different sort of power, the power of the object outside himself—"pleased / Through courteous self-submission, as a tax / Paid to the object by prescriptive right" (142–44). What Wordsworth gains through this self-submission is a picture of his own body—a body seeing—that has the sort of power that he imagines belongs to an actor, or the artist, "fashioning a work / To Nature's circumambient scenery, / And with his greedy pencil taking in / A whole horizon on all sides" (256–59). It is important to realize what a struggle it was for Wordsworth to picture that body. Already, the spectacle was threatening to wipe the seeing body offstage—to eliminate the audience in pursuit of an ever more complete spectacle. But Wordsworth takes pains to put the seeing body back in—not only just his own seeing body in its journey around London but also the seeing bodies of the audience. The raree-show is not a raree-show without "children gathered round" (191); the panorama is not a panorama without the "traveller" who "sees when he is there" (280); the pantomime, not a pantomime without a reflection on the audience: "Nor was it mean delight / To watch crude Nature work in untaught minds, / To note the laws and progress of belief— / Though obstinate on this way, yet on that / How willingly we travel, and how far!" (297–301). Even the long-winded senator and the dandy in the pulpit cannot be mentioned without their bored and delusional audiences—"till the strain / Transcendent, superhuman as it is / Grows tedious even in a young man's ear" (541–43); "This pretty shepherd, pride of all the plains, / Leads up and down his captivated flock" (565–66). Indeed, this may be the reason why Wordsworth turned away from the drama and into poetry: only poetry allows him to picture the body seeing, and to give the body of that audience power.

Throughout his poetic career, then, Wordsworth would return to the pose of the actor/spectator, a figure who mixes with his audience and takes his seat among them, and shares with them their common act of seeing. In "I Wandered Lonely as a Cloud," the poet moves from a station high above the flowers—"I wandered lonely as a Cloud / That floats on high o'er Vales and Hills" (1–2)—to take his place among them—"A Poet could not but be gay / In such a laughing company" (9–10). Even when the poet's thoughts move to "that inward eye" (15), the actor/spectator dynamic remains the same. The poet, lying on his couch "[i]n vacant or in pensive mood" (14), sees the daffodils "flash upon that inward eye" (15), like a spectator watching a play. But in that watching, there is interaction—the spectator "dances with the Daffodils" (18). Wordsworth's imagination—his inner eye—provides a way, illusory in his own culture, for the isolated spectator to become an actor, to mix and dance among the figures he watches, in a spectacle of distance dissolved into absolute presence. Even Wordsworth's more distant poems, like "The Solitary Reaper," imagine the solitary interlocutor as part of a community of watchers. "No Nightingale did ever chaunt / So sweetly to reposing bands / Of Travellers in some shady haunt, / Among Arabian Sands" (9–12) places the solitary listener, listening "[i]n spring-time from the Cuckoo-bird" (14) in the same situation as the watching group; "Stop here, or gently pass!" (4) imagines Wordsworth in the presence of a company of listeners. The physical presence of the Highland Lass brings the community of listeners together, and brings the song—however distant—into their presence and into their hearts, so that "[t]he music in my heart I bore / Long after it was heard no more" (31–32).

But perhaps the truest test of Wordsworth's relationship to distance and the situation of the distant spectator lies in his sonnet

"Composed Upon Westminster Bridge." In all readings, both critical and celebratory, the poem has been taken as sort of a celebration of distance. Written on Wordsworth's way out of town, on a bridge that both separates and connects country and city, at a time when "all that mighty heart is lying still" (14), the sonnet seems to be the very antithesis of book 7 of *The Prelude*. Indeed, a rough summary of the traditional take on "Westminster Bridge" as opposed to book 7 might be that London seen from a distance is beautiful and majestic, while London seen up close is a "blank confusion," an "undistinguishable world to men," a "parliament of monsters" (*Prelude* 7.696, 700, 692). But I would argue precisely the opposite—that "Composed on Westminster Bridge" is an attempt to regain the personal presence of London from a distant perspective, and to appropriate some of its personal power for the poet, who acts as both an actor and a spectator in the poem. As Alan Liu has noted, "Westminster Bridge" is a poem that crosses genres: a sonnet that is also a love poem, an epitaph, a pastoral, an apocalyptic cityscape, a tour poem, a portrait, and a silent picturesque landscape (460). But most importantly, it is also a drama, with a silent spectator watching a distant actor, the city personified. And it is also a call to action to a passive audience—"Dull would he be of soul who could pass by" (2)—that recalls the spectacle that "lays ... the whole creative powers of man asleep" (653–55) in *The Prelude*. It is a call to that audience, above all, to do as he does: to look, but to look in a certain way; not to "pass by," but rather to feel the city as a personal presence. To see the city is to see a body, and not a body closed, but a body "open," "all bright and glittering in the smokeless air" (7–8). This is a body that one can get inside, and indeed, Wordsworth does get inside the body of the city in this sonnet. As Liu again has noted, the panorama Wordsworth presents does not represent either a clockwise or a counterclockwise view of the London skyline. Instead of the "dome" of St. Paul's, it gives us "domes," and randomly scattered, it gives us "Ships, towers ... theatres, and temples" (6). This view, then, is a view that one could only get from *inside* the city—from "[f]amiliarly perus[ing] it day by day" (*Prelude* 7.140) as Wordsworth does in *The Prelude*—from wandering among its multiplicity of ships, towers, domes, theatres, and temples rather than observing them from afar. This, Wordsworth implies, is what it takes to know the body—to see it both clothed and bare, static and moving, newly born and freshly dead, glitteringly awake and peacefully asleep. But above all, it is to be able to see the inside through the outside, to glimpse the "mighty heart" (14) through the "garment" (4) and the body, to come into the full personal presence—to know the body and heart completely—simply by the act of looking.

All of this may seem to fall into the realm of New Critical irony and ambiguity, or perhaps deconstructive ambivalence. But it is important to remember that it is not figures we are talking about here, but bodies. Figures might seem to melt into air, but if we look at the city as a body, as Wordsworth invites us to do, we can see Wordsworth's examination of the figurative city as part of the same sort of fantasy about bodily presence that we saw in *The Borderers*. The sight of the city's body gives instant access to the city's heart; we know immediately through sight what we could only find out meanderingly (if at all) through narrative. The sight is "touching," a metaphor that works somewhat oddly in the phrase "touching in its majesty" (3), not only because "touching" is a word often used to describe spectacles but also because it conveys the feeling of literally being touched, as if the city could literally reach out and touch the viewer and convey in this most bodily of ways its power and "majesty."[25] The power that Wordsworth feels from the city—and that we as readers feel in reading the poem—comes from a sense of being in the personal presence of the city—not just seeing ("Earth has not any thing to shew more fair" [1])—but being "touched" by it and, in return, "touching" it to the very heart.

But where is the spectator in all of this? Both precisely located and promiscuously distributed. The sonnet is written from the bridge, but the spectator is invited to roam freely among the "[s]hips, towers, domes, theatres, and temples" (6), the open fields, and the sleeping houses. Although the poem might seem to have no audience at all, or at least an audience so abstract that it is only addressed by its absence ("Dull would he be of soul who could pass by" [2]), it implies a view that comes from everywhere, a view that one might have only if one were an audience of many—perhaps only an audience of the collective inhabitants of London. And Wordsworth himself plays the role of the actor/spectator who mixes and moves among them. He is an actor in terms of presenting the city to its audience—we might almost see him in the showman's role he assumes at Bartholomew Fair, lodged "above the press and danger of the crowd— / Upon some showman's platform" (*Prelude* 7.658–59)—but he is also among them, a spectator just as they are spectators, touched by the mighty hand of the embodied city.

Indeed, in his moments of vision, almost all of Wordsworth's objects are "presences"—presences that can literally reach out and take his hand, and presences too that the audience can feel as presence. At the end of book 7, after seeing the "picture[s]" that "weary out the eye" (708), Wordsworth reaffirms that "[a]ttention comes, / And comprehensiveness and memory, / From early *converse* with the works of God" (717–19, emphasis added). The mountain's "presence" (724) shapes "[t]he measure and the prospect of the soul / To majesty" (725–26), virtues have "the forms / Perennial of the ancient hills" (726–27) and the "changeful language of their countenances," which "[g]ives movement to their thoughts" (728–30). When Wordsworth speaks of nature, he is speaking of a distinctly *personal* presence, a presence that has the power to reach out and look and touch, and the power to give the spectator his body back even as she reveals her own to him.

All of this, of course, may seem to be a body so figural and attenuated that it is almost no longer a body at all—and a theatre so figural and attenuated that it is no longer a theatre. But Wordsworth faced a world in which there was no choice. Not only had he been rejected in his early attempts at theatre, but the theatre seemed to be developing toward exactly the sort of spectatorial situation he deplored. His only choice was to figure the theatre in the world of poetry—to build a world of personal presence in a world in which spectatorship seemed to have become the norm, and to rebuild the body of the spectator in a medium in which that body could be seen. Wordsworth's early fascination with the theatre, his turn to it in his most famous and socially conscious work, the *Lyrical Ballads*, and his return to the theatre to restart his magnum opus show how crucial the theatre was in shaping his vision of the way that bodies relate to each other and his attempts to bring those bodies into the disembodied world of print. And those bodies, in turn, show how conscious Wordsworth was, not only of genre, but also of medium—the form in which his thoughts would reach his audience—and of power—how his works would ultimately touch them. Seeing Wordsworth's work in this way also leads to a more personal and embodied view of Romanticism. His bodies are not just figures or reflections of consciousness. They are, first and foremost, bodies, with an almost mystical bodily presence. They are not self but are fundamentally other, and Wordsworth's struggle is not to convert them into self, but rather to rebuild himself in the face of their presence. It is axiomatic that Romantic poetry is a poetry that is fundamentally about the self, but Wordsworth's dramatic perspective ultimately leads to a new kind of self, and with it a new type of poet. By uncovering the dramatic roots of that vision, we can see that Wordsworth's perspective is not individual but fundamentally social—he is an audience member among audience members, not an actor who stands above them. And we can also see what a struggle it was for him to develop that type of self.

4

"The Great Master of Ideal Mimicry"

Shelley's Struggle with the Actor

In "The Sensitive Plant," Percy Bysshe Shelley's allegory of death, renewal, and perception, Shelley posits a world of perfect expression, where things can express their essence through their very bodies. The breath of the snowdrop and the violet is their "voice and ... instrument" (1.16); the "sweet peal" of the hyacinth "was felt like an odour within the sense" (1.26, 28); the rose "unveiled the depth of her glowing breast" until "[t]he soul of her beauty and love lay bare" (1.30, 32); the stream "did glide and dance / With a motion of sweet sound and radiance" (1.47–48); and even the lady's "form was upborne by a lovely mind / Which, dilating, had moulded her mien and motion, / Like a sea-flower unfolded beneath the Ocean" (2.6–8). Each "[s]hared joy" (1.65) because "each one was interpenetrated / With the light and the odour its neighbor shed" (1.66–67). All, that is, except for the sensitive plant. Even though it "[r]eceived more than all" and "loved more than ever" (1.73), it "has no bright flower; / Radiance and odour are not its dower" (1.74–75). Everything in the garden—nature, plant, and human—expresses the love within it by the very frame of its body. Only the sensitive plant, which "loves— even like Love" (1.76), has no capacity to express.

I want to hazard a claim that may seem controversial: there is something curiously hollow about Shelley's rhetorical heroes. Although Shelley's poetry and drama are full of passionate stands and stunning speeches, his speakers seem strange and insubstantial, outcasts and phantoms pronouncing justice on an alien world. Often they are phantoms of mythological figures—Prometheus,

Ahasuerus, Demogorgon, Rousseau—and even when they are real historical figures, like Beatrice Cenci, they can seem inhuman and impervious. It is as if the very act of speaking alienates characters from themselves, removes them from the human, and turns them into something preternatural. Ordinary humans, it seems, are in the position of the sensitive plant: loving like love itself, but without the means to tell it.

In fact, the strangeness of Shelley's heroes stems from Shelley's ongoing and contradictory relationship with the theatre. For Shelley, the ideal theatre was the work of many hands. It mixed the talents of artists, writers, set designers, dancers, musicians, actors, singers, and creators of spectacle. The perfect theatre piece, like the perfect society, involves the combination of different voices into the whole. But in print, the talents of visual and kinetic artists are shorn from the production. The voice that is left is the voice of the sole writer/actor left alone onstage, "some great master," as Shelley says in *A Defence of Poetry*, "of ideal mimicry" (518). But can a lone voice inspire sympathy? Can it connect with an audience? Can it inspire a better world? In his poetry and drama, Shelley experimented with ways that the body might be opened or combined so that it represents not just the individual but her social sympathies. His speakers have bodies masochistically torn apart, as if showing their insides would reveal that they, too, were assemblages of many hands. Often Shelley's bodies are ghostly bodies, bodies that perform the drama's function of combining different arts into a single harmonious whole. Ironically, Shelley's vision of the drama as the ideal social art could only be made possible in the nonphysical world of print.

Social and Bodily Language in *Defence* and *Alastor*

Of course, the very notion that the body is Shelley's primary form of expression must overcome some hurdles, and one of them comes from looking at Shelley primarily as a poet rather than a dramatist. As Jerrold Hogle suggests, Shelley has always stood for a certain complexity in poetic language, and perhaps for the uncertainty of language itself. But for Shelley, language in general—and writing in particular—represents only the most restricted sense of poetry. As Shelley himself admits in *Defence of Poetry*, "Language, colour, form, and religious and civil habits of action are all the instruments and materials of poetry" (483). Indeed, language is fading and unnatural. Once "composition"—a distinctly written term—begins, "inspiration is already on the decline" (504), and if language is not constantly renewed, "the words which represent [thoughts] become through time signs for portions or classes of thoughts instead of pictures of integral thoughts; and then if no new poets should arise to create afresh the associations which have been thus disorganized, language will be dead to all the nobler purposes of human intercourse" (482). Even the plastic and pictorial arts arise more naturally: "a great statue or picture grows under the power of the artist as a child in the mother's womb, and the very mind which directs the hands in formation is incapable of accounting to itself for the origin, the gradations, or the media of the process" (504).

By contrast, Shelley's account of poetry's origins makes it clear that the purest form of poetry is not language but bodily expression. In the beginning, he says, "Man is an instrument over which a series of external and internal impressions are driven, like the alternations of an ever-changing wind over an Æolian lyre, which move it by their motion to ever-changing melody" (511). The first form of poetry is the child's own body: "A child at play by itself will express its delight by its voice and motions, and every inflexion of tone and every gesture will bear exact relation to a corresponding antitype in the pleasurable impressions which awakened it" (511). All other forms of expression develop to augment the original force of language and gesture. The child and the savage first develop "plastic and pictorial imitation" to prolong their memory of the original delight. Once man comes into awareness of his society, a new class of arts comes into being to express the new set of passions and pleasures that come with social life. The original gesture contains both the perfect form of individual expression and the perfect form of expression of society, for in every individual there is a principle that "produces not melody, alone, but harmony" (511). Thus for Shelley the drama is not only the most developed of the social arts but the closest to man's original artistic impulse.

This is why Shelley chooses the drama as the art that produces the greatest effect on society. The "dramatic and lyrical Poets of Athens" (518), which is where "the Drama had its birth" (518), not only "flourished contemporaneously with all that is most perfect in the kindred expressions of the poetical faculty; architecture, painting, music, the dance, sculpture, philosophy, and we may add the forms of civil life" (518), but also "coexisted with the moral and intellectual greatness of the age" (519–20). For no other form is Shelley so confident about the direct connection between excellence in poetry and excellence in society: "The connexion of scenic exhibitions with the improvement or corruption of the manners of men, has been universally recognized: in other words, the presence of absence of poetry in its most perfect and universal form has been found to be connected with good and evil in conduct and habit" (519). In Athens, the drama not only "flourished contemporaneously with all that is most perfect in the kindred expressions of the poetical faculty: architecture, painting, music, the dance, sculpture, philosophy and we may add the forms of civil life" (518); it actually made use of those forms. The dramas of ancient Athens "employed language, action, music, painting, the dance, and religious institution to produce a common effect in the representation of the highest idealisms of passion and of power" (518). By combining all the arts together, the ancient Athenians replicated the synthesis achieved by the first primitive artists. By combining language and gesture with plastic or pictorial imitation, they combined the artist's forms with his imagination—"the image of the combined effect of those objects and of [the artist's] apprehension of them" (511). The final product is the synthesis of many arts and many hands: "each division in the art was made perfect in its kind by artists of the most consummate skill, and was disciplined into a beautiful proportion and unity one towards the other" (518). Thus the value of the ancient drama was in its unity: not unity in the Platonic sense, but in the more prosaic sense of everyday cooperation. The Athenian drama produced a "common effect," its artists "disciplined" their art "into a beautiful proportion and unity one towards the other" (518); its unity is "universal, ideal and sublime." Like Shakespeare's *King Lear*, its aim is "equilibrium" (519). By using all the media available to it, the drama not only disciplined the artist's "apprehension" to the media around him—pencil and pen, hammer, stone and chisel. It also forced him to combine his talents with the talents of other artists around him, producing an effect that was truly "common."

It is unclear why Shelley thought this type of theatre had disappeared from the modern world. Contemporaries were more likely to complain that sets and songs distracted from the focus on actors and language. But when Shelley looked at the theatre, he saw the sister arts fading in favor of a single voice: "On the modern stage a few only of the elements of expressing the image of the poet's conception are employed at once. We have tragedy without music and dancing; and music and dancing without the highest impersonations of which they are the fit accompaniment, and both without religion and solemnity" (518). Even the traditional device of the mask has been stripped away, so that the actor truly is a lone individual: "Our system of divesting the actor's face of a mask, on which the many expressions appropriated to his dramatic character might be moulded into one permanent and unchanging expression, is favourable only to a partial and inharmonious effect; it is fit for nothing but a monologue, where all the attention may be directed to some great master of ideal mimicry" (518). Perhaps like the single poetic voice in print, the single actor is "fit for nothing but monologue." If it expresses anything, it expresses only the lonely self. Rather than combining the expressions that would be needed for members of the audience to "put [themselves] in the place of another and of many others" so that "the pains and pleasures of [their] species ... become [their] own" (488), it focuses their attention on the single "great master." And the problem with that "great master" is not so much his "ideal mimicry," since the natural face replaces an artificial mask. It is that the one face and one voice can only be "partial" and "inharmonious." It cannot mold the "many expressions" appropriate to the dramatic character together into something harmonious and communal. The single natural face bears the burden of communicating all social sympathies. But can the single voice carry the drama? And if it can, can it do it without becoming inhuman?

This is the problem Shelley addresses in *Alastor, or The Spirit of Solitude*. The poem comes as close as any of Shelley's poetry to having a moral: in quest of deeper truths, Shelley's poet has rejected the spirit of sweet human love, who sends him a haunting vision that he pursues until his death. But the tragedy is not simply that the *Alastor* poet rejects human love, but that human love is unable to communicate itself to him. Both Poet and Narrator search for meaning in the bodies of things, only to be disappointed. The Narrator has "watched / [Nature's] shadow, and the darkness of [her] steps," in order to "still these obstinate questionings / Of thee and thine" by "forcing some lone ghost ... to render up the tale / Of what we are" (20–29). He ends by trying to find truth through the largely mute and uncommunicative Poet, watching his quest through nature and history, trying to find his own emotional truth by watching the Poet's quest. The Poet, too, searches for truth through contact with nature and the physical shapes of the past: "Nature's most secret steps / He like her shadow has pursued" (81–82); "Among the ruined temples ... / He lingered ... / Gazed on those speechless shapes ... / till meaning on his vacant mind / Flashed like strong inspiration, and he saw / The thrilling secrets of the birth of time" (116–28).

But even though the Poet is able to read the "thrilling secrets of the birth of time" through the artifacts of human history, he is unable to see and relate to human beings. While bodies can express emotions, in this poem the truth is only seen in rare, unguarded moments. This is what happens to the Arab maiden who courts the Poet as he sleeps, perhaps the only time when his body is fully expressive of himself, "his lips / Parted in slumber, whence the regular breath / Of innocent dreams arose" (135–37). Her daily actions are inexpressive, almost mechanical: she brings food, "[h]er daily portion," spreads her matting for his couch, and "stole / From duties and repose to tend his steps" (129–32). But the authentic expression of her body, returning "wildered, and wan, and panting" (139), she never allows the Poet to see. Even the Poet's own body is curiously inexpressive. Like an actor, he uses his expressive intensity to earn his keep: "he has bought / With his sweet voice and eyes, from savage men, / His rest and food" (79–81). But in the process, the Poet reveals none of his secrets. Like the "great master of ideal mimicry" in the *Defence*, he gives the audience the product it wants, leaving the authentic self, if indeed there is one, to languish outside of the performance. Even his poetry is alienated: "Strangers have wept to hear his passionate notes," and "virgins ... have pined / And wasted for fond love of his wild eyes" (61–63), but the Poet passes by "unknown" (62).

A good deal has been made of why the Poet rejects the Arab maiden's expression of "sweet human love." But it is not simply a longing for the "infinite and unmeasured" (69) that the human form cannot satisfy. It is rather that the human form, in its isolated condition, cannot accomplish the kind of interchange that Shelley imagines between the Poet and nature or history. Not only are the Poet and the Arab maiden afraid to allow the other to see their bodies as truly expressive of themselves, but those bodies, once they do express, are "partial and inharmonious" compared to the multiple and intertwined beauties of nature and the secrets of time. The Arab maiden's expressive powers are limited to domestic tasks—bringing food, spreading mats—even though the fact that she leaves her domestic tasks to attend to the Poet, like a Mary or a Desdemona, suggests that she might have a more spiritual dimension. Her bodily expression bespeaks only her disappointed love for the Poet, not the wider dimensions of her character. And even though his body is somewhat more expressive, the Poet is in the same boat. Although his "sweet voice and eyes" (80) purchase rest and food from savage men, his "passionate notes" and "wild eyes" (60, 63) charm strangers and virgins passing by, and his "graceful" (106) form enchants the antelope, he searches for "intercourse" with an intelligence similar to himself—an interaction that can "run between" the self and the other. Although his expression combines some of the diverse aspects of his personality—at once "sweet" and "wild," natural and cultured, gentle and passionate—he never reveals enough of himself to mingle with his audience. Indeed, we might say that the Poet's combination is merely a projection or a persona, a combined figure marketed to the audience while the Poet himself remains "unknown." Shelley needs a more fluid figure, a figure capable of mingling itself with the other, in order to create the social interchange for which the Poet thirsts.

The figure that can create that "intercourse" is, of course, the dream vision. But that vision cannot be, as critics have supposed, a simple reflection of the Poet's consciousness. Instead, she is an integrative vision, a vision that, as Shelley puts it in *Defence*, can "employ[ ] music, painting, the dance, and religious institutions to produce a common effect in the representation of the highest idealisms of passion and of power," and can combine "the many expressions appropriated to ... dramatic character ... into one permanent and unchanging expression" (489). The vision begins with a change in the way that the Poet sees nature. Where before, nature and history proceed in linear sequential fashion—the Poet wanders from "wide waste and tangled wilderness" (78) to "awful ruins of the days of old" (108), and then "Arabie / And Persia, and the wild Carmanian waste" (140–41)—the physical surroundings that the Poet sees in the vale of Cashmire are intermixed: "odorous plants entwine / Beneath the hollow rocks a natural bower" (146–47). The vision he sees there likewise "entwines" moods, voices, and arts, history and the present, nature and culture, self and other, veiled and naked. She uses voice, movement, song and sight, philosophy, music and poetry, reason and emotion. Even when she only uses a single medium, her voice is like the "woven sounds of streams and breezes, [which] held / His inmost sense suspended in its web / Of many-coloured woof and shifting hues" (155–57). She appeals to the Poet by speaking in a voice "like the voice of his own soul" (153), but at the same time she emphasizes her distance from him by her embodied form (she sits "near" him) and by the series of veils that covers her. Unlike the Arab maiden's bare and inexpressive body, the dream vision unites nature and culture, reason and passion, male and female. The sound of "streams and breezes" (155) mixes with "knowledge and truth and virtue ... / And lofty hopes of divine liberty" (158–59); "low solemn tones" (151) mix with "wild numbers"163); "long" music (155) with a heart that "impatiently endured / Its bursting burthen" (173–74); a "pure" and "eloquent" mind that is nonetheless "stifled" and "subdued" (162, 168, 164–65). But above all, the vision unites self and other, the Poet's ideal expressivity—"[h]erself a poet" (161)— with the human sympathy he desires.

Unlike the Arab maiden, whose body can only express her isolated emotion, and only in private, coming into contact the combined body of the dream vision finally gives the *Alastor* Poet the capacity to express. Where the Poet's youth had been "nurtured" "[b]y solemn vision, and bright silver dream" (67–68) and later by the shapes of nature and the past, the food of the vision—and the somewhat earlier food of the Arab maiden—empties nature and makes the Poet turn inward—"the Poet kept mute conference / With his still soul" (223–24). And although the vision partially destroys the Poet's body, it also makes him aware of himself as an embodied creature. The sections of the poem before the vision appears contain only the sketchiest descriptions of the Poet's body, usually seen through the eyes of others, and often himself consumed, as when "[s]trangers have wept to hear his passionate notes / And virgins, as unknown he past, have pined, / And wasted for fond love of his wild eyes" (61–63). The vision, however, gives the Poet the capacity to fashion his own body. He "longed / To deck with [the flowers'] bright hues his withered hair" (412–13), and "[h]is eyes beheld / Their own wan light through the reflected lines / Of his thin hair" (469–71) in the still water of a pool, a narcissus gazing at his "own treacherous likeness" (475). Even broken as it is, the Poet's body has the capacity to express: "his scattered hair / Sered by the autumn of strange suffering / Sung dirges in the wind" (248–50). Only after he has seen the vision does his body have the capacity to "impress / On the green moss his tremulous step" (515–16).

And through the power of bodily expression, the Poet also gains the capacity to speak. The Poet's only words—the address to the swan at 280–90, the address to the vision at 366–69, and the address to the stream at 502–14—come after he has met with his dream vision. His world is now intertwined—"tangled swamps" (235), "whirlwind" (320), twilight "[e]ntwin[ing] in duskier wreaths her braided locks / O'er the fair front and radiant eyes of day" (338–39), "[t]he winding of the cavern" (370), parasitic vines that "[w]ith gentle meanings, and most innocent wiles, / Fold their beams round the hearts of those that love, / . . . twine their tendrils with the wedded boughs, / Uniting their close union" (442–44)—and he is intermingled with it. The Poet has become the same sort of intermingled form as the maiden, and has achieved through that form both sympathy and the capacity to speak.

This mixing of bodily forms is particularly important to Shelley given his concern with the problems of solipsism. The body, after all, is that which, above all, remains separate, frozen in the self, beyond penetration by the other. This is part of the reason behind the eroticism of Shelley's vision. The body is not only the root of the vision's expressive power:

> In their branching veins
> The eloquent blood told an ineffable tale.
> The beating of her heart was heard to fill
> The pauses of her music, and her breath
> Tumultuously accorded with those fits
> Of intermitted song. (167–72)

But it is also the root of her combining power. Her voice is both essential—in the sense of being rooted in her body and blood—and intermixed. And eroticism is also a way of calling forth a bodily response from the Poet—"He reared his shuddering limbs and quelled / His gasping breath, and spread his arms to meet / Her panting bosom" (184–86)—that combines (or threatens to combine) the two bodies (at least temporarily) into one. By mixing with the multiple and intertwined vision, Shelley's Poet cannot only "put himself in the place of another and of many others" (488), as Shelley says in the *Defence*, he can actually combine himself and the other. The vision's very otherness both takes him out of himself—"The great secret of morals is Love, or a going out of our own nature, and an identification of ourselves with the beautiful which exists in thought, action or person, not our own" (517)—and puts him back into himself, so that he can have his own bodily power and bodily voice. The vision can accomplish this because she combines the Poet's self with her otherness in a way that an ordinary body cannot. The integrated vision, then, not only brings the Poet into sympathy with others, but it also brings him more fully into contact with nature and gives him both the body he needs to express and the voice he needs to speak.

But the composite vision also holds danger for Shelley. For in its very multiplicity—its capacity to express all of its "many expressions" in one complete and harmonious form—it also threatens to penetrate and dissolve the self. When the "pains and pleasures of [man's] species ... become his own" (517), the actor walks a fine line between fully realizing his own humanness and dissolving into the more general and all-encompassing human. Thus when the vision "[f]olded [the Poet's] frame in her dissolving arms," "blackness veiled his dizzy eyes, and night / Involved and swallowed up the vision" (188–89). The Poet is only saved by not succumbing to the vision, by refusing to be "involved" and "swallowed up" even as he is "intertwined," "mingled," and "inwoven."

The Poet, then, must always be close enough, but never too close. As Shelley speculates in the *Defence*, "[f]ew poets of the highest class have chosen to exhibit the beauty of their conceptions in its naked truth and splendour; and it is doubtful whether the alloy of costume, habit, etc., be not necessary to temper this planetary music for mortal ears" (516–17). The Poet must come close enough to others to bring him into his body and create his voice, but not so close that he is consumed. This is why the Poet must always to some degree be withheld from human sympathy, misunderstood by the "cottagers, / Who ministered with human charity / His human wants" even as they "beheld with wondering awe / Their fleeting visitant," the mountaineer, who "deemed that the Spirit of wind / With lightning eyes, and eager breath, and feet / Disturbing not the drifted snow," the infant who "conceal[s] / His troubled visage in his mother's robe / In terror at the glare of those wild eyes," and the "youthful maidens," who "would interpret half the woe / That wasted him, [and] would call him with false names / Brother, and friend" (254–69). If the Poet were able to mold all the "many expressions appropriated to his dramatic character ... into one permanent and unchanging expression" (489), that unity might consume the very individuality that he has fought to maintain.

Alastor, then, shows Shelley quite conflicted about both the natural body and the combined body that is the poetic mask. On one hand, Shelley sees the natural body dissipated by its focus on consumption, a body that drinks in the "thrilling secrets of the birth of time" (128) but that keeps its own secrets in a private space, where they can be limited and contained, and where they can convey neither poetry nor sympathy. A human being can hope for nothing better than the one-way contact of the Arab maiden who watches him while he sleeps or for contact with the inert bodies of the "thrilling secrets of the birth of time" (128). In response to this dissipated body, which is "fit for nothing but a monologue, where all the attention may be directed to some great master of ideal mimicry" (519), Shelley creates a composite body that can mold "the many expressions appropriated to . . . character" into "one permanent and unchanging expression" (519). But while the combined body has the capacity to create sympathy and form the individual voice, it also threatens to dissolve the Poet, to extinguish his individual identity, and to destroy the very voice that it had a hand in creating. The Poet must negotiate a distance between poetry and its veils that allows him to create without dissolving his individual voice into the voice of the whole. While the vision is a physical composite, the Poet's expression is mainly internal: "Life, and the lustre that consumed it, shone / As in a furnace burning secretly / From his dark eyes alone" (252–54).

Prometheus Unbound and the Broken Hero

But the best form for Shelley to explore the possibility of composite bodies is the drama, and especially his master drama, *Prometheus Unbound*. As Jeffrey N. Cox has argued, *Prometheus* engages with many of the issues raised by members of the Hunt circle in their exploration of mythological drama: an ecstatic movement from tragic entrapment, through nonviolent reformaton, into universal revelry. It also engages with dramatic forms as diverse as tragedy, melodrama, opera, and pantomime.[1] But the choice of Prometheus as a hero and Aeschylus's *Prometheus Bound* as a source indicates a special concern with whether a suffering body could elicit sympathy from a modern audience. Like so many Greek dramas, the original *Prometheus Bound* exhibits a perfect interchange of sympathy between the tortured hero and his community. The hero suffers; the chorus responds. The tortured body of Prometheus exhibited on the rock brings forth a perfect response. The Chorus affirms that "a mist of fear and tears / besets my eyes as I see your form / wasting away on these cliffs" (145–47), and when Prometheus speculates that "[n]ow as I hang, the plaything of the winds, / my enemies can laugh at what I suffer," the Chorus responds, "Who of the Gods is so hard of heart / that he finds joy in this? / Who is that that does not feel / sorrow answering your pain— / save only Zeus?" (158–64). Universal sympathy for Prometheus's sufferings is one of the play's major themes. Even as Prometheus fears that the spectators will get it wrong—"Have you, too, come to gape / in wonder at this great display, my torture?" (300–301)—the Chorus sings,

> He would be iron-minded and made of stone, indeed,
> Prometheus, who did not sympathize with your
> sufferings. I would not have chosen to see them, and now
> that I see, my heart is pained. (245–48)

And again:

> I cry aloud, Prometheus, and lament your bitter fate,
> my tender eyes are trickling tears:
> their fountains wet my cheek.
>
> Now all the earth has cried aloud, lamenting:
> now all that was magnificent of old
> laments your fall, laments your bretheren's fall
> as many as in holy Asia hold
> their stablished habitation, all lament
> in sympathy for your most grievous woes. (399–413)

The Chorus's prediction of universal sympathy is correct. Oceanus affirms "my heart is sore / for your misfortunes" (289–90); even Hephaestus, who binds Prometheus, exclaims, "Alas, Prometheus, I groan for your sufferings," and in response to Might's question—"Are you pitying again?"—takes the pain from the sufferer to the spectators—"You see a sight that hurts the eye" (65–69). The introduction of Io also advances the theme of sympathy. At first, the Chorus reacts salaciously:

> *Prometheus*: Since you are so eager, I must speak; and do you give ear.
> *Chorus*: Not yet: give me, too, a share of pleasure. First let us question her concerning her sickness, and let her tell us of her desperate fortunes. And then let you be our informant for the sorrows that still await her. (630–34)

But once it hears the tale, the Chorus cries, "Alas, Alas, for your fate! / I shudder when I look on Io's fortune" (690–95). Prometheus even encourages Io to tell her tale, despite her unsympathetic audience: "[t]o / make wail and lament for one's ill fortune, when one will / win a tear from the audience, is well worthwhile" (637–39). It is almost as if the play were a civic primer, instructing its audience not to laugh or be amused at its characters' misfortunes, but instead to show the pity due to them.

Shortly before writing *Prometheus Unbound*, Shelley experimented with the idea that sympathetic presence is the ultimate physician. In "Julian and Maddalo," the poem that grew out of an attempt at a poetic drama on Tasso, Julian speculates that

> 'twas perhaps an idle thought,
> But I imagined that if day by day
> I watched him, and but seldom went away,
> And studied all the beatings of his heart
> With zeal, as men study some stubborn art
> For their own good, and could by patience find
> An entrance to the caverns of his mind,
> I might reclaim him from his dark estate. (567–74)

It is odd, then, that at the beginning of *Prometheus Unbound*, the presence of the wounded Prometheus provokes no such sympathy. Instead, "shapeless sights come wandering by, / The ghastly people of the realm of dream, / Mocking me" (1.1.36–38). This lack of sympathy is mirrored by Prometheus himself, "eyeless in hate" (1.1.9), as he and Jupiter look out on "this Earth / Made multitudinous with thy slaves" (1.1. 4–5) ("Which Thou and I alone of living things / Behold with sleepless eyes!" [1.1.3–4]). It would be easy to say that *Prometheus Unbound* is a narrative about Prometheus learning to see—once he has seen the vision of Jupiter physically dragged "to kiss the blood / From these pale feet, which then might trample thee" (1.1.50–51) he can behold the form of Love and see the car of the hour arrive—as Michael Simpson has observed that it does—with an almost comic literalness.[2] But the body—and bodily sympathy—is not that easy in *Prometheus Unbound*, which is why the narrative cannot stop at its apparent climax in Prometheus's forgiveness in act 1. Shelley's project in *Prometheus* is to experiment with building an Aeschylean world in a non-Aeschylean context, to create a body able to express and be seen. The focus of that project is Prometheus himself.

Before we get to Shelley's project of building the body, however, it is important to note how important a function the gaze plays in *Prometheus Unbound*. The furies torture Prometheus with visions— not only the painful vision of Jesus Christ but also the forms of the furies themselves: "Whilst I behold such execrable shapes, / Methinks I grow like what I contemplate / And laugh and stare in loathsome sympathy" (1.1.449–51). On earth, "men were slowly killed by frowns and smiles: / And other sights too foul to speak and live" (1.1.590–91), and the condition of the fallen world is that they are unable to see or read each other's bodies: "Many are strong and rich—and would be just— / But live among their suffering fellow men / As if none felt: they know not what they do" (1.1.629–31). But good sights—or even neutral ones—have the power to change the world. Demogorgon's famous pronouncement of formlessness and skepticism, "the deep truth is imageless" (1.4.116), is not the final word on such matters, but rather an encouragement to look where the truth really lies: "For what would it avail to bid thee gaze / On the revolving world?" (1.1.117–18). Prometheus's curse must be given not only a voice but also a form—the form of Jupiter, speaking the words of Prometheus. Salvation lies in being able to see the actual human body—"How fair these air-born shapes! and yet I feel / Most vain all hope but love, and thou art far, / Asia!" (1.1.807–9)—and the human presence has the capacity to transform the world—"Asia waits in that far Indian vale, / . . . rugged once / And desolate and frozen like this ravine, / But now invested with fair flowers and herbs / And haunted by sweet airs and sounds, which flow / Among the woods and waters, from the ether / Of her transforming presence" (1.1.826–32).

The question that I want to ask is why it is Asia, not Prometheus, who transforms the world through her presence, and what it is about gazing upon the revolving world, or being gazed on in turn, that has the capacity to fragment and reunify the self. The answer, I think, is that Prometheus needs to betray himself and the world before he can become the kind of composite body that Shelley imagines. Elaine Scarry has written that intense pain has the capacity to "unmake" the world, and that torture in particular obliterates everything in its victim's world except for the suffering body. That is certainly the case with Prometheus. If the ostensible purpose is to make the victim "betray" the remaining world by answering the torturer's questions, thus putting the torturer in possession of the world and confirming the unimportance of the world to the tortured, Prometheus does give in to the betrayal. Mercury uses the torturer's strategy when he makes his questions commensurate with the world—"There is a secret known / To thee and to none else of living things / Which may transfer the sceptre of wide heaven, / The fear of which perplexes the Supreme" (1.1.371–74)—and Prometheus, though he protests "[o]r could I yield?—which yet I will not yield" (1.1.400), still gives his torturer the best answer that he knows, "I know but this, that it must come" (1.1.413). But the real betrayal of the world comes earlier, in Prometheus's curse, "Let thy malignant spirit move / Its darkness over those I love: / On me and mine I imprecate / The utmost torture of thy hate" (1.1.276–79). In the depths of his pain, Prometheus can sense nothing but himself, and he is willing to cede the entire world to his torturer in order to retain "torture and solitude, / Scorn and despair" as "mine empire" (1.1.14–15).

But there is one thing that makes Prometheus's torture different from the tortures that Scarry describes, and that is the presence of spectators. Kaja Silverman, in her excellent study of male masochism, notes that one pervasive feature of masochistic fantasies is exhibitionism. In order for pain to be pleasurable, as opposed to the simple torture that Scarry deals with, there must be an audience, so that the victim's "suffering, discomfort, humiliation and disgrace are being shown and so to speak put on display" (197). This feature of masochism is in marked contrast to another prominent feature, the solipsism of the masochistic experience. In moral or social masochism, according to Silverman, "the subject functions both as the victim and as the victimizer, dispensing with the need for an external object" (196). Ego and superego, victim and victimizer, crime and punishment are all rolled into a single package. The exhibitionism of the masochist works against this solipsism by letting in the world. It confirms the subject's desire to be rewarded for good behavior or punished for bad. In Christian masochism, it even makes the suffering figure a rebel or a revolutionary of sorts. The suffering body on display, unlike the body suffering silently in the torture cell, has the capacity to "speak" not only its suffering, but the moral system that produced it. It speaks not only for itself but for (and to) an entire system of moral behavior, a system that is confirmed (as Scarry would appreciate) by the very bodily reality of its suffering.

Prometheus is exceptionally heroic when he transcends his pain to let in the world, both in the revocation of his own curse and in his pity for the figures he sees being tortured, and the display of his suffering body acts as a physical confirmation of the unjustness of Jupiter's system and a living monument to Prometheus's own rebellion against it. But the force of Prometheus's masochism comes not solely from the spectators around him, but from the force of the body opened up for display. Prometheus's body must not only be his own, but like the body of the dream maiden in "Alastor," it must become the body of "another and of many others" (488), the body that molds "the many expressions appropriated to his dramatic character... into one permanent and unchanging expression" (489). Because of this, it is important for the body of Prometheus to be torn apart—"pierced," as he puts it—not only by "crawling glaciers" (1.1.31) but by the looks of Mercury and the furies, the sorrows of the Earth and her spirits, and finally, by the forms of Asia and Love. This is why the particular nature of Prometheus's torture appeals to Shelley. The body is opened; its inside becomes its outside. The same is true of the body of Christ on the cross: his blood "mingles" with his tears, and his "pale fingers play... with [his] gore" (1.1.599–602). What is most inside of him not only comes outside to be seen but also mingles with what is naturally outside—blood mingling with tears—so that exhibitionism constitutes both a literal going outside of the self and a figurative mixing of what is most intimate with the self with the world outside. This is also the force of the furies' torture. Prometheus fears "grow[ing] like what [he] contemplates" (1.1.450)—partaking of the evil he sees—but even this contemplation of evil takes him outside his body. The furies' threat that

> we will live through thee, one by one,
> Like animal life; and though we can obscure not
> The soul that burns within, that we will dwell
> Beside it, like a vain loud multitude
> Vexing the self-content of wisest men
> That we will be dread thought beneath thy brain
> And foul desire round thine astonished heart
> And blood within thy labyrinthine veins
> Crawling like agony (1.1.483–91)

is not a threat to be resisted, as Prometheus does when he proclaims, "Yet am I king over myself" (1.1.492), but rather a promise to be embraced, as Prometheus affirms at the end of his torture—"The sights with which thou torturest gird my soul / With new endurance" (1.1.644–45). Prometheus must be a combined force rather than a single individual before he can fulfill his promise as a voice of rebellion.

Shelley's combinatory aesthetic also accounts for the play's peculiar form, the "Lyrical Drama." As several critics have noted, the play is, in many ways, a psychodrama: its various characters, Prometheus, Jupiter, Earth, Asia, Panthea, Ione, Demogorgon, are all aspects of Prometheus's own mind, and the action of the play, like the action of a lyric poem, is the action of Prometheus's own consciousness. But in the dramatic portion of the lyrical drama, the characters are also separate—all the various "expressions" of Prometheus, his tyrannical will (Jupiter), his liberatory force (Demogorgon), his connection with mortality (Earth), and his love (Asia) stand out in relief, like expressions on a Greek mask, because they can be delineated separately. And because they are delineated separately, they can perform the function of others. They can watch, they can provide comfort, they can speak in their own voices. Their bodily form gives content to abstractions—Prometheus can embrace his mother Earth in act 3, scene 3, not only by kissing the ground, as the stage direction prescribes, but by actually embracing a person—at the same time that their lyricality makes them a part of the whole, speaking Prometheus.

The necessity for a suffering body also accounts for the play's peculiar pacing. As Silverman points out, suspense is also an important part of masochistic fantasies—the prolonging of forepleasure, false climaxes, pleasurable and unpleasurable anticipation, and apparent interminability of the pain. This suspense subverts the narrative order of forepleasure and climax, and makes, in essence, the anticipation of the climax the story in itself. If *Prometheus Unbound* is, as I have been suggesting, a story about the building of Prometheus into an ideal speaking body—the creation of a composite Promethean mask—rather than a story about Prometheus's forgiveness of Jupiter and the sudden renewal of the world, the delay in the narrative serves to accentuate Prometheus's suffering, to focus on the building rather than the climax, so that the climax, when it comes, is anticlimactic, a building block in a continuing (and possibly endless) narrative of pain. This is why readings like Abrams's and Bloom's, which make the play, in essence, over before it begins, do the play such a disservice. Not only do they mistake the climax of the narrative, but they also mistake its purpose and make the rest of the play into an addendum to the "main action" that happens in the first speech of act 1. The play continues, as it must continue, because the simple forgiveness of Jupiter is not enough to effect the revolution Shelley hopes for. What is necessary is the continued suffering that builds Prometheus into a composite mask—that pierces him and strips him down in order to build him up—so that he can speak the words of revolution rather than the words of curse.

But while this type of narrative structure can stand as a powerful subversive force in itself, as Silverman has shown—a perversion that stands in contrast to the *père-version* of linear narrative, the pleasure principle, and exemplary male subjectivity (213)—Shelley's attempt to mold Prometheus into a multiple speaking body is not altogether successful. Although the suffering Prometheus is able to stand as a symbol of revolution for the Earth, Ione, and Panthea, Prometheus can only achieve Shelley's ideal combined form in a dream—the dream that Panthea recounts to Asia in the first part of act 2. There, finally, Prometheus's "pale, wound-worn limbs" fall from him, and he is finally able to produce the same sort of radiance that Asia does when her "transforming presence" reinvigorates the world: "the azure night / Grew radiant with the glory of that form / Which lives unchanged within" (2.1.63–65). Prometheus's ideal form combines light, voice, and music with the bodily form purged through pain, and more importantly, it makes the viewer combine with him. Panthea feels love as

> an atmosphere
> Which wrapt me in its all-dissolving power
> As the warm ether of the morning sun
> Wraps ere it drinks some cloud of wandering dew.
> I saw not—heard not—moved not—only felt
> His presence flow and mingle through my blood
> Till it became his life and his grew mine
> And I was thus absorbed. (2.1.75–82)

Panthea and Prometheus become each other, and that makes both capable of becoming more fully themselves. Panthea goes on:

> And like the vapours when the sun sinks down,
> Gathering again in drops upon the pines
> And tremulous as they, in the deep night
> My being was condensed. (2.1. 83–86)

Becoming part of Prometheus brings Panthea back to her fullest self, combines and dissolves her in order to make her condense, and in that condensing, she can fully realize not only Prometheus's voice but also Ione's, asking "Canst thou divine what troubles me tonight?" (2.1.94), and Asia's: "for when just now / We kissed, I felt within thy parted lips / The sweet air that sustained me; and the warmth / Of the life blood for loss of which I faint / Quivered between our intertwining arms" (2.1.102–6). Being combined and dissolved into the multiple form of Prometheus allows Panthea to hear and see and know, unlike the people of the world who "know not what they do" (1.1.631). The dramatic form produced by pain produces seeing spectators, and creates that ideal sympathy by which, as Shelley says in *Defence*, a viewer can "put himself in the place of another and of many others," and the "pains and pleasures of his species . . . become his own" (488).

But it is instructive that Prometheus can only appear in this combined form in a dream and not onstage. Shelley's optimism about writing the drama could lead him as far as experimenting with a play, but it could not ultimately make him envision the way that the combined body would look onstage. Accordingly, as befits a closet drama, the action moves back and forth between showing and narration. Prometheus sees the torturing forms, but the Oceanides must describe them for the reading audience. Even in a play that can envision in the most graphic terms throwing Jupiter into the bottomless void, Shelley cannot imagine putting onstage the combined body that the Greek drama inspired. Moreover, the play depends more on narration as the ideal world approaches. Jupiter's downfall is the last scene of action in the play (at least until act 4); the remainder of the revolution must be told secondhand rather than observed.

Furthermore, the combined form, with all its power, tends to dissolve, just as it does in *Alastor*. We have already seen Panthea dissolve into Prometheus, only to recover a "condensed" form of herself that can live in sympathy, but Prometheus's own fate is not so fortunate. After Panthea's dream vision dissolves her into Prometheus's ideal form, Prometheus all but disappears from the play. He appears again only in act 3, after Jupiter is deposed, and his sole act is not to assert his own voice, but to instruct the Spirit of the Hour to blow the shell announcing the new age. Prometheus himself is caught in a harmonious but self-enclosed world, a cave that mirrors Plato's, and like Plato's cave, Prometheus's only contains the shadows of the world outside, "echoes of the human world" (3.3.44) rather than interaction with the world itself. The combined form that would encompass all the expressions appropriate to Prometheus's dramatic character narrows into "one permanent and unchanging expression" (489), with mere "visits" from "the progeny immortal / Of Painting, Sculpture and rapt Poesy / And arts, though unimagined, yet to be" (3.3.54–56). Prometheus's harmony with Asia, Panthea, and Ione, while it mixes the three, effectively excludes anyone else, and with it excludes all but the shadowy forms of the changing human world. This is the problem of acting. Prometheus must retain some of the "great master of ideal mimicry" in order to project his suffering image; when he combines with the audience in the ideal world, his suffering body disappears.

Shelley's figure of self-assertion is, ironically, Asia, and far from being tortured into a composite mask, Asia returns to her purest form: her own original body. As she rides toward the hour when Jupiter's power must end, she moves backward, not forward, in time:

> Some good change
> Is working in the elements which suffer
> Thy presence thus unveiled.—The Nereids tell
> That on the day when the clear hyaline
> Was cloven at thy uprise, and thou didst stand
> Within a veined shell, which floated on
> Over the calm floor of the chrystal sea,
> Among the Ægean isles, and by the shores,
> Which bear thy name, love, like the atmosphere
> Of the sun's fire filling the living world,
> Burst from thee, and illumined Earth and Heaven
> And the deep ocean and the sunless coves
> And all that dwells within them; till grief cast
> Eclipse upon the soul from which it came. (2.5.18–32)

Shelley's Asia is able to speak like a child because her body is new, perfectly formed without the intervention of time, change, or others. Asia's body, at this point, is nothing but itself, newly arisen and purely formed, not tortured or interpenetrated, but purely itself. Where Prometheus has to become a form of everything to obtain a speaking voice that can promote sympathy in his hearers, Asia does so spontaneously: "nor is it I alone, / Thy sister, thy companion, thine own chosen one, / But the whole world that seeks thy sympathy" (2.5.32–34). Asia's body, unbroken and unscathed, produces life and sympathy in a way that Prometheus's cannot.

But could such an innocent body carry the voice of revolution? Would one body be powerful enough? Shelley broke off composition of *Prometheus Unbound* after act 3 to begin work on *The Cenci*, and after finishing *The Cenci*, he renewed his work on *Prometheus*, adding the play's final hymn to the marriage of the Earth and the Moon. Shelley turned to *The Cenci* to solve the problems with rhetorical heroism that had arisen during the composition of *Prometheus*. *The Cenci* is famously more dramatic than *Prometheus*—not only is it styled a "tragedy" rather than a "lyrical drama," but it also ties itself more closely to the bodily and embodied world of history, with bodies natural and whole rather than combined as masks as they were in Greek drama. *The Cenci* is an attempt to examine the effects of the tortured body in a real political situation, and an attempt to come to grips with the role it plays in action and suffering.

The Cenci and the Politics of Acting

It is intriguing to think of the similarities between *Prometheus Unbound* and *The Cenci* in light of their interwoven composition process. Both address resistance to an omnipotent tyrannical power. Both involve a woman raped and in danger—Thetis in *Prometheus Unbound*, Beatrice and (to a lesser extent) Lucretia in *The Cenci*. Both involve a powerful scene where an innocent female figure confronts a figure of power—Beatrice Cenci confronting her father, Asia confronting Demogorgon. And in both, the confrontation between the woman and the powerful figure sets the process in motion that leads to the tyranny's overthrow and the world's renewal. But within that framework it is difficult to imagine two confrontations more different. In *Prometheus*, the meeting between Asia and Demogorgon feels like a catechism. Asia, newly made innocent by her journey through time, gains the confidence to answer even as her own heart would answer; Demogorgon, for his part, gently leads Asia to ask the questions that lead to their own answers. In *The Cenci*, Beatrice, though innocent, challenges her evil father. She must possess a confidence already formed from her own innocence, a confidence that her father does everything within his power to quash. And where Asia's confrontation effortlessly leads to the hour where Jupiter's power will be overthrown, Beatrice's confrontation sets in motion an arduous process that leads down two different paths: the first in the Legate's office, where her speech has moved the officials' hearts to finally do something about Count Cenci's crimes, and the second within her own heart, where Cenci's tortures finally lead her to take her own action.

Beatrice's tragedy, I would argue, is what comes from having a broken body speak in an imperfect world. Her brokenness allows her to speak powerfully, and perhaps even carry the day without the need for action. But the brokenness that allows that speech also makes her subject to desperate mistakes and even wickedness. If Beatrice had been whole, she might have realized that "the fit return to make to the most enormous injuries is kindness and forbearance, and a resolution to convert the injurer from his dark passions by peace and love." But if she had been whole, she "would never have been a tragic character": "The few whom such an exhibition would have interested could never have been sufficiently interested for a dramatic purpose, from the want of finding sympathy in their interest among the mass who surround them" (240). Only a body that is broken and torn can obtain sympathy from "the mass" that surround them. The tragic author must take risks.

If this seems unlikely, we only need to think of the way that bodies and objects are inexpressive in *The Cenci*—or that their expression goes unheard. The first lines of the first two scenes of act 1 have to do with silence and secrecy: "That matter of the murder is hushed up" (1.1.1); "Pervert not truth, / Orsino" (1.2.1–2). One of Count Cenci's satisfactions in his tortures is to see "[t]he dry fixed eye ball / [and] the pale quivering lip, / Which tell me that the spirit weeps within" (1.1.111–12). Appearances are deceiving: Camillo tells Cenci, "How hideously look deeds of lust and blood / Through those snow white and venerable hairs!" (1.1.38–39). Bodies, it seems, must be tortured before they can give up their truth.

How, then, is Shelley to "clothe [the story of the Cenci] to the apprehensions of [his] countrymen in such language and action as would bring it home to their hearts" (240)? A "dry exhibition" onstage, he says, would be "insupportable"; the characters' suffering is simply too horrible for the audience to be able to see the ideas beneath (240). This imagination must be "clothed" in exactly the right way to bring its point home to an audience. It must appear in "flesh"—"Imagination is as the immortal God which should assume flesh for the redemption of mortal passion" (241)—but flesh of a special kind. In a dramatic composition, Shelley says, "the imagery and passion should interpenetrate one another" so that the body shows "all of the feelings of those who once acted [the drama], their hopes and fears, their confidences and misgivings, their various interests, passions and opinions acting upon and with each other" in order to "make apparent some of the most dark and secret caverns of the human heart" (239).

This "interpenetration" of imagery and passion, I would argue, is the reason why critics have always found the character of Beatrice so puzzling. Jerrold Hogle argues that her own "will to power" mirrors her father's; Julie Carlson sees Beatrice's commanding stage presence as a critique of the power of actresses onstage. Margot Harrison suggests that Beatrice adopts the pose of the "insincere" Diderotian actor as a form of self-protection; Laurence Lockridge argues that Beatrice splits her consciousness between being and doing—although she has done the crime, in her heart she remains "innocent." All assume that if Beatrice had clear motivations she would be wiser and better, if not a better tragic character.

Shelley, however, meant Beatrice to be cloudy, her motives mixed and tangled, the better to represent the complex social sympathies of the drama. Thus, when Beatrice confronts her father, her voice has power not because she is innocent, but because she bears part of his guilty flesh. Where Cenci hides in false innocence, Beatrice does not hesitate to show her guilty body:

> What, if 'tis he who clothed us in these limbs
> Who tortures them, and triumphs? What, if we,
> The desolate and the dead, were his own flesh,
> His children and his wife, whom he is bound
> To love and shelter? Shall we therefore find
> No refuge in this merciless wide world? (1.3.102–7)

Her power does not lie, as Cenci believes, in her "fearless eye," her "brow superior," or "unaltered cheek" (2.1.116–17). Instead, her calling card is her suffering. She is not only trapped by the structures of power; she *is* the structures of power. Her very body, the instrument that she would use to present herself, is constructed of those structures. It is not simply, as Hogle claims, that the rape makes her *like* Cenci. For Shelley, she already *is* Cenci. She is "clothed" in these limbs, and indeed, she "is" his own flesh. Cenci makes the equation as well in his answer to her speech. He asks his auditors first to "think of their own daughters," and then "perhaps / Of their own throats" (1.3.130–31)—their daughters' flesh is equated with their own, and indeed with their own voices ("throats"). To allow one's daughter to speak in her own voice would be like allowing a piece of one's own body to rebel. Cenci might be able to take her innocence, but he can never prevent her from showing her guilt.

Thus Beatrice's rape, like Prometheus's torture, is, at least in theory, the fortunate fall that takes her out of herself and allows her body to express not only her passions but the passions of others. As Barbara Groseclose has noted, popular versions of the story, including the one from which Shelley worked, do not actually mention the incestuous rape. They mention Francesco Cenci's attempts to seduce his daughter, but no actual consummation. Indeed, the original story meted out a sort of bodily justice: Beatrice, the innocent, remains whole, while Count Cenci, the debauched corruptor, dies by being pierced through the eye and through the neck with nails.³ Shelley, however, reverses the story's bodily justice. Beatrice is pierced by her father, while even in death Count Cenci's body is kept whole, strangled and dumped in the garden "that there might be no blood" (4.4.45). The consummation of the rape makes Beatrice's "piercing" literal in the same way that Prometheus's piercing or Christ's piercing is literal. It brings the outside world into the inside of the body, and in some ways brings the inside of the body into the outside (as when Cenci fantasizes that Beatrice will have a child as a result of the rape), troubling the boundaries of the very medium that Beatrice would use to express herself. Beatrice's body is opened to accept the world; Cenci, even in death, closes the world out.

And indeed, this is the way that Beatrice experiences the rape. Where before she recognizes her body as composed (at least partially) of Cenci, the rape makes her body quite literally not her own:

> I see a woman weeping there
> And standing calm and motionless, whilst I
> Slide giddily as the world reels. (3.1.10–12)

The body that would have previously "clothed" her for her "impersonation" on the scene of the world is now a prison, alien to her:

> No, I am dead! These putrefying limbs
> Shut round and sepulchre the panting soul
> Which would burst forth into the wandering air! (3.1.26–28)

Even Lucretia notices "Thou art unlike thyself" (3.1.81). But what Lucretia and Beatrice only imperfectly realize is that Beatrice's body, in being alienated, has also been combined. The force that "eats into my sinews, and dissolves / My flesh into pollution, poisoning / The subtle, pure, and inmost spirit of life!" (3.1.21–23) is also the force that makes her a "[p]rodigious mixture, and confusion . . . strange / Of good and ill" (3.1.52–53), that "glues / [Her] fingers and limbs to one another" even as it "twine[s]" them "[w]ith one another" because of the "restless life / Tortured within them" (3.1.83–85).

This is the source of Shelley's fascination with Beatrice. For in Shelley's experience of her, she is never quite pure, and that lack of purity makes her as close as one can get to Shelley's combined theatrical body in the real world. Her portrait is a study in contrasts. Although there is a "fixed and pale composure upon the features," she also seems "sad and stricken down in spirit." But even her "despair" is "lightened by the patience of gentleness." She is bound—or at least "[h]er head is bound with folds of white drapery"—but "the yellow strings of her golden hair escape, and fall about her neck." Her eyes, "which we are told were remarkable for their vivacity," are "swollen with weeping and lustreless," but nonetheless "beautifully tender and serene." Indeed, her very nature, like her body, is composite: she unites "simplicity and dignity" with "loveliness and deep sorrow"; her nature is both "simple" and "profound"; she "appears to have been one of those rare persons in whom energy and gentleness dwell together without destroying one another" (242). Her "circumstances" may be the "mask and the mantle in which circumstances clothed her for impersonation on the scene of the world" (242), but her body, after the rape, is the perfect theatrical mask, which combines gentleness and profundity, "sensibility" and "imagination," containment and escape, loveliness and deep sorrow.

This is what makes hair—both "entangled" and "bound"—such a powerful symbol in the play. It is a symbol of female sexuality, but more than that, it is a part of the body that breaches the distinction between inside and outside. It can be used as an instrument, as when Cenci "sometimes hales [Beatrice] / From hall to hall by the entangled hair" (3.1.44–45) (one can imagine Cenci "haling" Beatrice either by the sleeve of her garment or by her arm—either by something unambiguously part of her or by something unambiguously separate). It can be cut without pain, separated and alienated in a way that something unambiguously a part of the body (like, say, an arm) cannot. But it is definitely a part of the body; indeed, it grows seemingly from inside to out, as if, like Minerva springing from Zeus's forehead, the mind could make itself external. Furthermore, like few other parts of the body, it can be both "entangled" and "bound"; indeed, as the image of Cenci haling Beatrice about by the "entangled" hair makes clear, the hair, like the body (in Shelley's metaphor) becomes more entangled as the body is broken in pain. Indeed, when it is freed (unbound) it is in its nature to become tangled. Hair in *The Cenci*, then, like vines in *Alastor* or gore in *Prometheus*, is the sign of the body's ability to bring its inside into the outside and to become tangled and intertwined—with itself and with others.

Shelley's sense of Beatrice as a composite entity also explains the odd sense of distance with which he treats her moral responsibility in the Preface. Shelley comes at the issue first through a general discussion of morality—"Undoubtedly, *no person* can be truly dishonoured by the act of another" (240, emphasis added)—as if the relevant point were not the morality of Beatrice's individual character (as Shelley suggests when he weighs in against the "enforcement" of "dogmas" in drama) but rather the moral truth that Beatrice herself cannot follow. But the point, in fact, is both. Through her composite nature, Beatrice can express both the "gentleness" that would make the "fit return . . . for the most enormous injuries . . . kindness and forbearance, and a resolution to convert the injurer from his dark passions by peace and love" and the "revenge, retaliation [and] atonement" that are "pernicious mistakes" (240). Beatrice is both herself, as a "tragic character" (240) who can "find . . . sympathy in [her] interest among the mass who surround[s] [her]" (240)—and note that even here, Shelley uses the plural, "finding sympathy in *their* interest among the mass who surround *them*" (240)—and the "any person" or "no person" who can illustrate Shelley's moral point.

The Cenci is a tragedy of interconnectedness. Beatrice is able to evoke sympathy because she plays on the connection that her audience must feel with her. All are tied together as family, countrymen, and fellow Catholics. Cenci's mock communion sacrament emphasizes that they are all part of the same body, "clothed" in the same flesh. But that same tie means that Beatrice cannot be totally innocent or totally good. She cannot be set apart from the world of sin she grew up in; its fear, falseness, and cruelty are a part of her that she cannot deny. If Beatrice could have stayed innocent, she might have been "wiser and better." But she would never be a tragic character. Like Prometheus and Asia, healed in the fullness of time, or the Poet's dream vision in *Alastor*, she might have slipped away into a world of bliss, beyond judgment, beyond sympathy. As it is, she exists combined, tied to her mother, her brother, her country, and church. The final gesture of Beatrice and her mother binding up each other's hair for the executioner shows that they go interwound—just as dramatic forms should be. What is left behind is the rhetorical heroism—the lone girl who can tell power to retire to its chamber, or who can mock her torturer from limbs that she knows are unclean. What room might the drama have for such a character? How might that character fit into the human race?

Demogorgon: Shelley's Immaterial Voice

Instructed by his own failure in *The Cenci*, Shelley turns to a different form of combination in the fourth act of *Prometheus Unbound*, one that allows combination but still preserves the distance that the characters need to assert themselves in their own voices. Shelley continues to rely on interpenetration: Ione describes

> How every pause is filled with under-notes,
> Clear, silver, icy, keen, awakening tones
> Which pierce the sense and live within the soul
> As the sharp stars pierce Winter's chrystal air
> And gaze upon themselves within the sea. (4.1.189–93)

And the centerpiece of Panthea and Ione's song is

> A sphere, which is as many thousand spheres,
> Solid as chrystal, yet through all its mass
> Flow, as through empty space, music and light:
> Ten thousand orbs involving and involved, . . .
> Sphere within sphere, and every space between
> Peopled with unimaginable shapes . . .
> [E]ach intertranspicuous. (4.1.238–46)

Forces interpenetrate. The Spirits of Air and of Earth meet and sing together, but although the motto of their song is "Unite!" (4.1.80), they come together only long enough to experience each other's presence, and in the end, "[b]reak the dance, and scatter the song" (4.1.159, 175). The child and the Orb in Panthea and Ione's vision remain separate—the infinite human meeting the infinite earth. In fact, as Ione points out, the infant "mocks" the Orb's harmony (4.1.269). The two figures, each an amalgam of colors, shapes, and sounds, complement each other rather than merging into one permanent and unchanging figure. And indeed, the Earth and the Moon, the final duet of the act, are linked but also separated by gravity, pulled together put prevented from ever becoming one. Each can provide the life and comfort of the bodily form, as Asia does in the previous acts of *Prometheus*, because they are together but separate. They combine, but on this mask each expression remains sufficiently delineated that there is no danger of merger into one permanent and unchanging form.

It is also notable that Shelley ends act 4, not with Prometheus or Asia, but with Demogorgon, the "mighty Darkness / ... Ungazed upon and shapeless" with "neither limb / Nor form—nor outline" (2.4.2–6). In act 2 of *Prometheus*, Demogorgon was a shapeless power, able to assert the willless will of necessity on earth but unable to make any sort of assertive answer to Asia's questions, leaving her to "gaze / On the revolving world" (2.4.117–18) and to "answer . . . / As [her] own soul would answer" (2.4.124–25). In act 4, Demogorgon still has not gained a shape; he continues to be a "mighty Power, which is as Darkness" (4.1.510), and Shelley's only references to him compare him to the wind, as in the Moon's "I hear—I am a leaf shaken by thee!" (4.1.528) and the voice's "Thy voice to us is wind among still woods" (4.1.548). But in spite of his lack of a body, Demogorgon has gained something like an individual assertive voice. He combines the voices of Earth, Moon, kings, the dead, the elemental Genii, spirits whose homes are flesh, and Man, but he is no longer an empty receptacle for those voices, a mere medium for their combination. He either quiets them—as in the kings' "Our great Republic hears ... we are blest, and bless" (4.1.533)—or obliterates them—as in the Earth's "I hear,—I am as a drop of dew that dies!" (4.1.523). Demogorgon's combination is an assertive combination that mixes the various voices and moods that make up the world around him but does not obliterate the assertive force of his individual personality.

The odd thing about Demogorgon's appearance, of course, is that he still does not have a body. One might think that the obstacle to presenting the combined body would be the combination—that it would be difficult to mold all the expressions necessary to a character into a permanent and unchanging mask. But Shelley has solved that problem through multiple voices: the Earth, Moon, kings, dead, elemental Genii, animals, and people speak in their own voices (and their own bodies) combined into chorus with Demogorgon. Instead, there seems to be something about the specifically individual voice that cannot be contained within the body, and this is why Shelley chooses Demogorgon to deliver his final speech rather than Asia or Prometheus. The individual body has the power to impress and withstand—to suffer. But only the disembodied or broken body has the power to spread information and hope. Ione and Panthea make this clear in their response to the spirits. Panthea asserts the individual:

> I rise as from a bath of sparkling water,
> A bath of azure light, among dark rocks,
> Out of the stream of sound— (4.1.503–5)

But Ione corrects her:

> Ah me, sweet sister,
> The stream of sound has ebbed away from us
> And you pretend to rise out of its wave
> Because your words fall like the clear soft dew
> Shaken from a bathing wood-nymph's limbs and hair. (4.1.505–9)

Panthea believes that the stream of sound has restored her body individually, but Ione realizes that the self only "pretends" to arise out of its wave in order to disseminate words, which fall like the "clear soft dew" of the stream she has just left. Demogorgon makes this possibility of dissemination explosive. When his "Power" rises "as Darkness," "the sky / Is showered like Night, and from within the air / Bursts, like eclipse which had been gathered up / Into the pores of sunlight" and makes "the bright Visions / Wherein the singing spirits rode and shone / Gleam like pale meteors through a watery night" (4.1.510–16). Like Panthea, Demogorgon assumes an individual voice only in order to burst, carrying that individual voice, like individual pieces of matter, into the bodies of others.

Thus Shelley abandons the power of the body he carefully constructed in *The Cenci* in order to create a new type of bodily presence. Demogorgon's body has the same sort of force as Beatrice's. It can combine, and in that combination, it has a unique rhetorical power. But the body must also be able to be broken in order to spread that power—to wield power effectively.

As I have been suggesting, the term "mask" has a different valence than it has usually been given in Shelley's criticism. Shelley's "masks" have generally been taken as coverings that diminish the force of poetry, as when "[t]he distorted notions of invisible things which Dante and his rival Milton have idealized, are merely the mask and the mantle in which these great poets walk through eternity enveloped and disguised" (498) or when "the crimes and miseries in which [Beatrice Cenci] was an actor and a sufferer are as the mask and the mantle in which circumstances clothed her for her impersonation on the scene of the world" (242). But even as they "distort," "envelop," "disguise," and enable "impersonation," the masks that poets and characters wear also enable them to combine and instantiate. They are the super bodies that make it possible for poetry to "transmute . . . all that it touches, and [change] every form moving within the radiance of its presence . . . to an incarnation of the spirit which it breathes" (505). Masks give poetry its power.

Shelley would continue to use masks in his later work, both to "mask" characters and in later "masque" forms like the "Masque of Anarchy" and the "Triumph of Life." But perhaps his most famous mask is the one that Shelley himself wears in "Adonais." There, Shelley mantles his own body in a way that both combines and bursts, that claims the power of presence even as it augments and spreads it. Shelly begins as a "frail Form / A phantom among men" (271), turned against himself, so that "his own thoughts . . . / Pursued, like raging hounds, their father and their prey" (278–79). He: a "pard-like" spirit (280) or a "herd-abandoned deer" (297) that combines human and animal, a "Love" masked in "desolation," a "Power / Girt round with weakness," a "dying lamp, a falling shower, / A breaking billow" (281–85) that combines civilization (the lamp) with nature, a wild Maenad combined with civilized and mournful elegist. Although it abandons a stable identity—Urania asks "who art thou?" (303)—it retains its power to move, as "[a]ll stood aloof, and at his partial moan / Smiled through their tears" (299). Indeed, even without identity (or perhaps because of its combined identity) it is universally known—"well knew that gentle band / Who in another's fate now wept his own" (300). Like Prometheus or Beatrice, it has the capacity to stand as a concrete symbol of oppression, as "[h]e answered not, but with a sudden hand / Made bare his branded and ensanguined brow, / Which was like Cain's or Christ's" (304–6). But like Demogorgon, it threatens to burst into pieces, spreading that power through the world—"even whilst we speak / Is it not broken?" (285).

Shelley's self-portrait also adds an additional element: withering. Unlike the full body of Demogorgon, which threatens to burst in meteors flying over space, Shelley's "falling shower" and "breaking billow" are followed by the line, "On the withering flower / The killing sun smiles brightly" (287). And this is Shelley's fear. Like Wordsworth, Shelley looks back to an imaginary time when the body conveyed an almost mystical power, and although he is at many times optimistic about his power to regain that power by rebuilding the body so that the body can combine the many expressions appropriate to it and ultimately disseminate those expressions to a waiting audience, there is also the fear that this rebuilding is necessitated by the fact that the body has "withered." Unlike the body dissolved, melted, or exploding, the withered body remains, but has the capacity to express nothing. As in the "Sensitive Plant," while all the plants of the garden can make their "breath" into their "voice and . . . instrument" (1.15–16) and "lay" the "soul of [their] beauty bare" (1.32), Shelley's own body, like the body of the sensitive plant, lacks the power to give poetic fruit. All of his body building is simply a mask, and while at some points Shelley expresses confidence in the "masks and mantles" that allow his characters to be seen in the world, the body underneath, far from being powerful, is broken and withered, an observing being rather than a rhetorical one. Only in death can the "soul of Adonais, like a star" (494) fulfill its rhetorical promise to stand as an icon of community, while Shelley's own body, in a bark, is borne "darkly, fearfully afar" (492), either to fulfill its own rhetorical promise in death or to sink into its own bodily oblivion.

5

Creative Spectacle

Hunt, Hazlitt, De Quincey

On March 24, 1811, audiences at Covent Garden were treated to a production of George Colman's *Blue Beard* performed with a company of horses galloped onstage in the play's climatic battle scene, delighting audiences and startling critics. It was a capstone to nearly half a century of amazing spectacles. Panoramas and dioramas, pantomimes with amazing transformations, naval battles staged in tanks of real water at Sadler's Wells, trained dogs, child actors, plays advertising special scenery (often painted to match actual travels) by de Loutherbourg—the stage in the Romantic period saw a boom in magnificent and astonishing spectacles.

It is fair to say that our view of these Romantic spectacles has largely been defined by William Wordsworth, Edmund Burke, and Thomas Paine. For Burke and Paine, these large, magnificent creations had the capacity to overwhelm critical judgment. For Burke, hyperbolic images of power reinforce the power of dictatorships; for Paine "the effect of those cruel spectacles exhibited to the populace, is to destroy tenderness, or excite revenge; and by the base and false idea of governing men by terror, instead of reason, they become precedents." Wordsworth is even more explicit about the spectacle's ability to diminish human creativity. The eye, that "most despotic of senses" (*Prelude* 11.171–76), can, if given too much sway, "lay . . . / The whole creative powers of man asleep" (*Prelude* 7.654–66)[1]

As Gillen D'Arcy Wood has pointed out, Wordsworth's view has come to dominate the cultural response to spectacle through the twentieth century, extending even to Baudelaire and the Frankfurt School. And while recently there have been scattered attempts to challenge this vision—Michael Gamer and Jane Moody's view that spectacular productions in the illegitimate theatre could act as countercultural force or satire, or Iain McCallman's idea that early experiments with "virtual reality" enabled their creators and participants to engage in utopian fantasy—there has not yet been a theory that catches the ingenuity and imaginativeness of the spectacles themselves.

I would like to suggest such a theory, based on three "moments" in criticism: Leigh Hunt's criticism of the hippodrama craze around 1811–1812, William Hazlitt's attempt to distinguish "art" from mere "spectacle" in "The Indian Jugglers" around 1821, and Thomas De Quincey's experience with reproductions of the Greek drama in large theatres toward the end of the "Romantic Century" in 1840.[2] What ties these moments together is not the spectacles or theatrical conditions they analyze. While most address spectacles that are broadly theatrical, their interests range from street theatre to politics, their venues from street theatre to major theatrical houses. What these critics have in common is their common interest in creating a theory of spectacle that rejects the idea that spectacle overwhelms the viewer and turns its watchers into mindless and vacuous subjects. Instead, they see spectacle as a creative force that can improve the minds of its audience and bring them together as a nation.

What motivates this theory is an audience in need of education. All three of these discussions first appeared in the popular press: Hunt's in the *Examiner*, Hazlitt's in *Table Talk*, De Quincey's in *Blackwoods* and *Tait's Magazine*. While each of these journals reached a different audience, all tried to shape discourse community out of a disparate collection of readers, and to create a vision of a literate reading public in which all citizens could, at least theoretically, participate.[3] Hunt, Hazlitt, and De Quincey not only give their readers credit as thinking subjects, able to withstand the overwhelming effects of spectacle, but also gently initiate them into modern culture. Like the magazines themselves, spectacle should shape its audience into a literate nation of thinking citizens.

The way that these critics worked their magic was by using a discourse familiar to the Romantic period: the sublime. While Michael Gamer has argued that the dominant mode of writing about one particular spectacle, the hippodrama, was satire, "that mode of writing most expected to defend tradition and expel all interlopers" (308), these middle-class, popular critics, while they often did write in the satiric mode, were much more concerned with the spectacle as a means of negotiating political and cultural power—the province *par excellence* of the sublime. Although the dominant critical tradition on the sublime emphasizes its tendency to support the terror of established power and domesticate revolutionary energy,[4] particularly the revolutionary energies of theatrical crowds,[5] more recent criticism has realized that the sublime is often a two-edged sword. While the Burkean theory of the sublime emphasized spectacle's ability to terrify, making its viewers small and helpless, the Kantian or religious sublime emphasized the mind's ability to expand in the face of an overwhelming or dangerous stimulus.[6] And as Karen Swann has pointed out, the line between the sublime and the vulgar is much closer than high-culture critics would like; both the high culture of Milton and the low energies of the crowd partake of a novelty and thirst for stimulation that makes them close cousins born of eighteenth-century popular print culture rather than the polar opposites of the sublime and the vulgar.

But like the sublime itself, Hunt, Hazlitt, and De Quincey's view of creative spectacle was not without its contradictions. How could one create a nation out of independent, thinking subjects? Does the fact that the audience is always in its senses diminish its force as a unified body? These are the questions that occupied Hunt, Hazlitt, and De Quincey as they tried to create a creative sublime.

Leigh Hunt and the Animal Sublime

Of course, it is not unusual to locate a concern for the sublime in the Romantic period. But locating it in such simple objects as horses and dogs, actors and audiences requires some explanation. After all, most objects exhibited on the Romantic stage are quite ordinary objects, quite unlike the rocky crags, infinite oceans, and obscure horizons that we generally think of as sublime. But in their capacities onstage, dogs, horses, and their more exotic counterparts fit perfectly into Romantic theories of the way that the sublime should operate. For both Burke and Kant, the essence of the sublime is the unassimilable.[7] Power, obscurity, privation, and infinity all place the viewer out of control of the object, and it is ultimately that lack of control that produces the sublime response of terror and delight. The mind confronts a body that is too large, too small, too monstrous, too magnificent, too numerous, too difficult, too powerful.

But the problem with natural objects onstage is precisely that they are outside of the illusion—outside the control of the viewer or even the stage manager. "A clock that is working," Walter Benjamin notes in "The Work of Art in the Age of Mechanical Reproduction," "will always be a disturbance on the stage . . . Even in a naturalistic play, astronomical time would clash with theatrical time" (247). The problem, as Burt States explains it, is not that such a clash would actually occur—especially in a naturalistic play where theatrical time is roughly identical to real time—but rather with our awareness that the clock is visibly obeying its own laws of behavior. And indeed, this rule seems to apply to material objects in general. We all know how distracting it can be when an actor drops a prop, or a stagehand forgets to clear a piece of scenery. For a moment, the illusion is broken—we see things obeying their own laws rather than the laws of the play.

As States explains, these principles apply with even more force when we see an animal on stage. "An animal can be trained or tranquilized, but it cannot categorically be depended upon" (32). Since the animal does not know it is in a play, "we don't get good behavior, only behavior" (32). The problem is that the animal is not acting, even when trained. It always exists outside the theatrical illusion, a spot of realness in a world of fakery. And as States points out, this realness can be used to great advantage on stage:

> What surprises us, of course, is that the dog can be used in the play, that it unknowingly cooperates in creating the illusion. And this surprise arises from our observation of the dog as a dog-in-itself. Questions like this might occur: Isn't it interesting that the dog will submit to being on stage? Then, of course, the answer: It isn't submitting, it is simply being itself. What if it barks? Urinates? Obviously, even these natural acts . . . would contribute to further comedy. So the illusion has suddenly become a field of play, of "what if?" The illusion has introduced something into itself to demonstrate its tolerance of things. It is not the world that has invaded the illusion; the illusion has stolen something from the world in order to display its own power . . . The theater has, so to speak, met its match: the dog is blissfully above, or beneath, the business of playing, and we find ourselves cheering its performance precisely because it isn't one. (33–34)

The sublime, then, is the process of confronting an unrepresentable body, a body that is too solid to ignore but yet too strange to fit into the categories of the mind's understanding. And for the Romantics—at least those Romantics who wrote about the stage— the animal onstage proved to be the archetypal unassimilable body. Too animate to be mechanical, too natural to be actors, too trained to be fully natural, too impressive to be ignored, horses, dogs, and elephants onstage represented a challenge to traditional notions of stagecraft, a challenge that could only be addressed by saying what the animals were not.

Thus the dominant trope in the critique of realistic spectacles, especially spectacles like the hippodrama that used objects from everyday life, is their unrepresentability. Leigh Hunt calls George Colman's *Blue Beard* (Covent Garden 1811) "unworthy of criticism" (45); the *Morning Chronicle*'s review of *Timour the Tartar* laments, "Amidst the clattering of hoofs, the clangor of swords and spears, and the shouts of an enraptured audience, it is scarcely possible . . . for criticism to speak" (qtd. in Gamer, 317). Hunt's review of Colman's *Blue Beard* is typical. Although, as Michael Gamer has observed, the tone of the review is light—a gentle making fun of equestrian stagecraft rather than an all-out polemic against it—the review exhibits the confusion of pleasure and terror, and the horror at an object that has become unassimilable and inexpressible, that we have come to associate with the sublime. The play, Hunt tells us, is "one of those wretched compounds of pun and parade, which serve to amuse the great babies of this town and to frighten the less" (45)—unclassifiable in both its genre and its effect. But the horses onstage would seem to be the frightening part of the spectacle. Hunt tells us that "[t]hese prepossessing palfreys appear to be about twenty in number, and come prancing on the Stage into rank and file with as much orderliness as their brethren at the Horse Guards, facing directly to the spectators . . . so that when the riders draw their swords, the appearance is not a little formidable, and seems to threaten a charge into the pit" (46). And as if twenty horses were not enough, the horses gallop repeatedly over mound and bridge, "till every steed has reappeared often enough to represent ten or a dozen others" (47), they become "interestingly entangled in a crowd," so that one almost cannot tell which horse is which, and finally they scale a drawbridge "by three or four at a gallop," which "calls down the thunder of the galleries," so that both onstage and in battle, "Blue Beard and his myrmidons [are] utterly eclipsed" (47).

But the horses' physical presence is not the only thing frightening about these horse-actors. What seems to be more relevant, at least for Hunt, is the inability to tell whether these horses are actors, and the way that their horsey acting calls into question the distinction between man and beast, actor and nonactor, so that one almost cannot tell whether the spectacle is of human design. "That actors should make beasts of themselves is no new thing," Hunt opines, "but the gravis Esopus of our Stage, Mr. Kemble, must turn beasts into actors; and accordingly, after having had dog actors at Drury-Lane, and jack-ass actors (emblematic wags!) at Sadler's Wells, we are now presented with horse actors at 'classical' Covent Garden" (45). Making actors of horses automatically makes horses of actors, and even horses of managers, as if the spectacle of presenting the animal onstage lowers the human actors to the level of animals. And the confusion whether animals onstage have turned actors into horses is nothing compared to the confusion of whether horses can actually become actors. Hunt's experience of the horses onstage appears, on the one hand, terrifyingly natural: the horses lined up "with as much orderliness as their brethren at the Horse Guards" and "threaten[ing] a charge into the pit" (46) are acting exactly like horses act in real life. In fact, there is a fear that the horses onstage might act too much like real horses and charge in spite of themselves. But at the same time, Hunt defends against the assault of the real horses by making them into bad actors. Their galloping "exhibit[s] a manifest constraint and timidity," so that "when they pretend to come in at full speed, [they] have a jumping motion resembling that of rabbits" (48). The "excessive politeness" of the mounted combatants, "and the delicate attention they pay to each other's convenience, reminds one of the celebrated battle of Fontenoy, where the officers of the French and English guards, coming together, pulled off their hats to each other and mutually insisted upon giving up the honour of the first fire" (46).

All of this is good fun, of course, but Hunt has a very serious problem in mind: the decline of public taste. The truly shocking thing about the sublimity of the horses onstage is that, as Karen Swann suggests, their sublime threatens to turn into the vulgar. Where the sublime produces the intensity of pleasure combined with terror—"delight," to use Burke's word—the horses onstage produce another sort of confusion—the intensity of terror combined with amusement. Indeed, terror and amusement split the subject, as in Hunt's remark that the spectacle of *Blue Beard* serves to "amuse the great babies of this town and to frighten the less" (45), as if terror and amusement could not exist within a single subject at the same time. And indeed, they cannot. Terror implies that the subject takes the spectacle somewhat seriously—that the subject might actually be frightened by the materiality of the object, like the horses that seem to be threatening a charge into the pit. But "amusement" implies precisely that the audience does not take the spectacle seriously, that they know all the time that the horses are simply a human production, "acting" for their benefit. Hunt puts the matter more succinctly in his review of *Quadrupeds*: large spectacles "inevitably lead to the substitution of shew for sense" (50). They take what should be serious and make it amusing, take what should be dangerous and make it no danger at all. Burke's sense of the sublime as an escape from danger, then, becomes the sense of an inevitable escape. Far from bringing a sense of relief, a sense of danger narrowly averted, they bring a sense of danger inevitably averted. The natural has been completely subsumed into spectacle; "shew" has supplanted "sense." In the terror of the sublime, the mind recognizes the object as an object. It sees the object's difference, as manifested in its physicality, and it recognizes that object as unassimilable into the self. In amusement, as States's analysis would suggest, the illusion has stolen from the world to confirm its own power; it has brought the horses under its dominion.

For Hunt, the political states of this confusion are high, for if the audience views the spectacle as mere entertainment, it risks confusing the reality of objects in everyday life. Hunt launches two critiques of the production. First, he criticizes the spectacle for being too literal: "With the jokes about troopers trooping off, and persons unable to keep a secret because their teeth chatter, the reader is no doubt well acquainted, and quite willing, I trust, to have no further acquaintance" (45). But then he criticizes the spectacle for being not literal enough: "In one of the songs a Turkish girl is made to talk of her lover's 'ringlets,' [when] . . . said lover . . . is represented on the stage with a turban and no hair at all" (45), and there are paintings onstage when "the introduction of paintings in a room is contrary to the religion as well as customs of the Mahometans" (45). And in the same vein, Hunt cannot tell whether the horses onstage are too literal or not literal enough. Hunt praises the realism of using actual horses onstage: "Joking apart, it is no doubt interesting to see of what so noble an animal as the horse is capable; and it is still more agreeable to be relieved from those miserable imitations of him, which come beating time on the Stage with human feet, and with their hind knees the wrong way . . . for if men, and not puppets, act men, there seems to be no dramatic reason why horses should not act horses" (47). But in almost the same breath, he argues that their equine acting is exactly the thing that deprives the horses of their true animality. One of the objections Hunt raises to the horses onstage, in addition to their degradation of the public taste, is the cruelty to the horses themselves: "A sprightly horse has a profusion of graceful and active movements; and it is his nature perhaps to be fond of a certain kind of exertion. He delights, when in health and vigour, in scouring the fields; and feels, we are told, an emulous ardour in the race ... [T]he fields and the raceground are proper places for him; the turf incites him to activity, and the open air breathes health and pleasure into his veins" (48). The stage deprives the horse of his horsiness: "The closeness of the stage, the running round and round, the bending of knees, the driving up steep boards, and above all, the mimicry of absolute death ... give the animal considerable pain, and have ... cost a hundred times as much in the training" (48). The very thing that makes the horses onstage "real," the thing that gives them both their fright and their amusement, is exactly what blinds the audience to their actual condition as horses, the falseness of placing horses in the illusion, and the cruelty that must have been practiced to persuade the horses to perform the feats of amusement and terror that secured their place on the Romantic stage.

But it is in this literalness that hope lies. For even as Hunt realizes that the confusion of the sublime often slides into mere amusement, he also recognizes that the very impenetrability of the spectacle holds out the hope that spectator can finally learn to look around the amusement and see the reality behind it. The motto of *Blue Beard* is *Panduntur Portae*—"having opened the sacred door"—and the audience, like the play's Fatima, might have prematurely opened the door to "too powerful a stimulus to the senses of the common order of spectators" (47). But just as *Blue Beard*'s Fatima is saved, ironically, by horses, the common spectator might be saved by them as well. During the course of the review, the terms that Hunt uses to describe the public audience progress, from the "great babies" (and lesser) (45) of the opening line, to the "infant spectator" (45), "the common order of spectators" (47), and finally to the "rational spectator" (48). And in the same way Hunt's own tone progresses during the course of the review, from satire to respect and finally to social critique. By the end of the review, what had begun as simple ridicule has ended up being a plea for "humanity"—both on the part of theatrical managers and on the part of the audience itself. It is as if the realistic spectacles, perhaps "too powerful a stimulus" for some, lead the others to progress.

Thus Hunt's review of *Quadrupeds, or The Manager's Last Kick*, one of the burlesques that capitalized on *Blue Beard*'s popularity, is an impassioned plea for audience choice. Hunt is quite adamant that the "vitiated state of public taste" is not the fault of the public, but the fault of the managers: "It is in vain therefore that [the Managers] effect . . . to throw the blame of their spectacles and hippodramas upon the vitiated state of the public taste. It was the vitiated state of their own wants that induced them to grasp at profit in this manner" (50). The "rational" spectators of *Blue Beard* are fully equipped to choose between pantomime and Shakespeare, and, if they are not allowed to see Shakespeare in his proper ("natural") setting, they at least know well enough to shun the extreme spectacles available to them. Strangely enough, it is the bad things that might shock spectators into a taste for the good.

De Quincey and the Political Sublime

Hunt does not explain how the sublime can affect some of his "babies" differently than others. But for Thomas De Quincey, unifying the audience is the point. Although, as Charles Rzepka has pointed out, the evidence that De Quincey ever attended the magnificent spectacles of London or Bath is somewhat spotty,[8] De Quincey's *The English Mail-Coach* is shot through with images from spectacle and pantomime, images that seem to draw the crowd together in a powerful political imaginary. Like pantomime, the mail-coach focuses the attention of crowds on powerful visual effects as it rides through the country on its "awful political mission," spreading news of the English victories at Talavera, Badajoz, Salamanca, and Waterloo: "The gatherings of gazers about a mail-coach had one centre, and acknowledged only one interest" (qtd. in Rzepka, "Bang Up!" 85). And even though De Quincey takes the minor pantomime role of "clown" in the political spectacle, he still shares the glory of English victory: "Five years of life it was worth paying down for the privilege of an outside place on a mail-coach, when carrying down the first tidings of any such event" (qtd. in Rzepka, "Bang Up!" 76).

But the real place that De Quincey's political analysis of spectacle plays itself out is not *The English Mail-Coach*, but his analysis of Greek drama. Although self-consciously removed from the contemporary British theatre, De Quincey's "Theory of Greek Tragedy," written for *Blackwood's* in 1840, echoes the complaints that his contemporaries had about the modern British spectacle: the theatres had grown too large, the spectators could no longer see and hear, it was difficult to see the actor's faces and hear the subtleties of dialogue. Indeed, in a review of Sophocles's *Antigone* written for *Tait's Magazine* six years later, De Quincey compares the Greek tragedy to the Italian Opera in its use of heightened diction, its recitative, its use of music and dance, and above all, the grandeur of its spectacle. And even the "Theory of Greek Tragedy" speaks of "passion which advanced and precipitated itself through such rapid harlequin changes would at best impress us with the feeling proper to a hasty melodrama, or perhaps serious pantomime" (348).

So, not surprisingly, the distinction De Quincey draws between the Greek drama and the "English"—by which he seems to mean Shakespeare—is that the Greek theatrical experience draws its audience together through the compelling force of the sublime. The Greek tragedy represents a theatre "ultra-human and Titanic" (346). The large size of its theatres makes it impossible to see the human face: "The person must be aggrandized, the countenance must be idealized . . . the unassisted human figure would have been lost; the unexaggerated human features would have been seen as in a remote perspective, and, besides, have had their expression lost; the unreverberated human voice would have been undistinguishable from the surrounding murmurs of the audience" (346). Even the stories are frozen back in time: "a life more awful and still, amongst men so far removed that they had become invested with a patriarchal, or even an antediluvian, mistiness of antiquity, and often into the rank of demigods" (349). The English drama, he writes, is a drama of character: "Shakespeare—that is, English Tragedy—postulates the intense life of flesh and blood, of animal sensibility, of man and woman—breathing, waking, stirring, palpitating with the pulses of hope and fear" (348). But as De Quincey writes in his review of *Antigone*, Greek tragedy is "awful rather than impassioned" (374). It is "a breathing from the world of painting . . . We read there the abstraction of a life that reposes, the sublimity of a life that aspires, the solemnity of a life that is thrown to an infinite distance . . . it is the sleep of a life sequestrated, solemn, liberated from the bonds of space and time, and (as to both alike) thrown (I repeat the words) to a distance which is infinite" (374–75).

This type of drama produces an entirely different response in the audience. The English tragedy tempts the audience to identify with its characters as they are tossed about by the vicissitudes of the action: "it is like a midnight of shipwreck, from which up to the last, and till the final ruin comes, there still survives the sort of hope that clings to human energies" (375). The Greek, by contrast, throws the audience into inevitable terror: "we see a breathless waiting for a doom that cannot be evaded—a waiting, as it were, for the last shock of an earthquake, or the inexorable rising of a deluge" (375). The audience does not merely follow the vicissitudes of the characters—after all, there are no vicissitudes to be followed—nor is it right to say that they partake in the characters' suffering, since the Greek tragedy is "a life removed by a great gulf from the ordinary human life even of kings and heroes" (347). The audience experiences its own terror—the terror of a life on a different scale, the terror of the human face and figure aggrandized and made strange. And it also experiences a type of privation, the privation of life, of action, of hope. "That kind of feeling which broods over the Grecian Tragedy, and to court which feeling the tragic poets of Greece naturally spread all their canvas, was more nearly allied to the atmosphere of death than that of life" (374), De Quincy writes in his review of *Antigone*, "It affects us profoundly, but not by agitation" (375). In the Greek tragedy, the audience feels the stillness of shared terror. It experiences the sensation of being dwarfed by the catastrophe. And above all, it feels the sensation of being presented with something absolutely outside itself, absolutely other, that nonetheless affects it profoundly.

The loss of this experience is, of course, a profound aesthetic loss, but for De Quincey, it is a political loss as well. For De Quincey, the experience of the sublime in Greek tragedy is an inherently communal experience: "Every citizen was entitled to a place at the public scenical representations . . . He was present, by possibility and by legal fiction, at every performance: therefore room must be prepared for him" (346); "Every citizen had a right to accommodation" (375). Where the English tragedy individualizes each member of the audience as they separately identify with individual characters, the Greek tragedy unites the audience in a common experience of terror. This democratic focus makes possible a powerful communal experience: an "impressive picture" that "of itself appeal[s] to every one of thirty thousand hearts" and "challenge[s] universal attention" (355). Certainly this communal spirit could be used for patriotic purposes—De Quincey notes the way that the very situation of the *Heracleidae* involves a "compliment to Athens" that the Athenian audience could not fail to appreciate (356). But overt political commentary is not the way that the Greek drama works its political magic. De Quincey even speculates that the *Charles I* of Banks, a restoration tragedy since lost, was coldly received "not because it [was] too modern," or too political, but because the questions it involved were "too *notorious* and too domineering," so that they "eclipse . . . and dwarf . . . any separate or private interest of an individual prince, though otherwise and by his personal character, in the very highest degree, an object of tragic sympathy" (353). The play might be political or not, but the real political force lies in the way that the spectacle unifies the audience, joins them together in the experience of a grandeur beyond themselves, and puts them into the presence of another world.

De Quincey's stated political use for these spectacles is specifically to galvanize a new, middle-class reading audience. His writings, he says, are not for an audience of experts or antiquarians, but for a new reading public: one not classically educated but eager to be marshaled. "I am not addressing those already familiar with the Greek Drama," he writes in his review of *Antigone*, "but those who frankly confess, and (according to their conjectural appreciation of it) who regret, their non-familiarity with that Drama" (365). De Quincey sees these new readers quite distinctly in terms of class:

> The aristocracy of the land have always been, in a moderate degree, literary ... But a class of readers prodigiously more extensive has formed itself within the commercial orders of our great cities and manufacturing districts. These orders range through a large scale. The highest classes amongst them were always literary. But the interest of literature has now swept downwards through a vast compass of descents: and this large body, though the busiest in the nation, yet, by having under their undisturbed command such leisure times as they have *at all* under their command, are eventually able to read more than those even who seem to have nothing else but leisure. (366)

Ironically, these readers are not the most isolated classes, but the most involved: "it should be remembered that their stations in society, and their wealth, their territorial duties, and their various public duties in London—as at court, at public meetings, in Parliament, &c.—bring crowded claims upon their time; whilst even sacrifices of time to the graceful courtesies of life are, in reference to *their* stations, a sort of secondary duties" (366). Nonetheless, De Quincey reiterates, "from their immense numbers, they are becoming effectually the body that will more and more impress upon the moving literature its main impulse and direction" (366). De Quincey's efforts to educate the public on the Greek tragedy, then, are self-consciously an effort to perform the function that the Greek tragedy once performed: to bring all classes, the aristocracy, the wealthy tradesmen, and the emerging business class, together into one society, and to have that society be the one that creates both the political and cultural life of England.

Thus De Quincey's project with spectacle is similar to the one that Cian Duffy has observed in De Quincey's writing about the novel: to bring an unruly new reading public under the great umbrella of the sublime. But theatrical spectacle offers De Quincey a possibility that the novel does not. Like Hunt, De Quincey has dreams of taking the unity provided by the sublime one step further: to bind his audience together under a political reality that is unquestionably "real." Thus De Quincey insists at the end of his review of the Edinburg production of *Antigone* that the audience has seen not a production, but the literal Antigone herself:

> To have seen a Grecian play is a great remembrance. To have seen Miss Helen Faucit's Antigone, were *that* all, with her bust . . . and her uplifted arm "pleading against unjust tribunals," is worth—what is it worth? Worth the money? How mean a thought! To see *Helen*, to see Helen of Greece, was the chief prayer of Marlowe's Dr. Faustus—the chief gift which he exacted from the fiend. To see Helen of Greece? Dr. Faustus, we *have* seen her: Mr. Murray is the Mephistopheles that showed her to us. It was cheap at the price of a journey to Siberia, and is the next best thing to having seen Waterloo at sunset on the 18th of June 1815. (387)

De Quincey's rhapsody slides seamlessly from Miss Faucit to Antigone to Helen of Greece and finally to Waterloo at sunset; the audience that could make the jump from Miss Faucit to Antigone, it seems, is also an audience that could be unified under a more contemporary type of political spectacle. And in fact, as De Quincey no doubt knows, the Mephistpheles Mr. Murray and all the other Mephistopholean managers had been trying a similar feat. As Gillian Russell, Richard Altick, and David Mayer have all argued, political spectacles were the order of the day through the Napoleonic war and into the Victorian period, with the theatres often acting as *de facto* news agencies, presenting panoramas and spectacles of England's latest victories. And while Peter Otto has argued that the panorama, through its focus on simulation, drew attention to the constructed nature of the real, its pretense of surrounding the viewer with the scene of battle did create an appearance, however contingent, of being there. Thus, in De Quincey's eyes, through their magic the public not only received the glorious news, as it did in the *English Mail-Coach*. It could actually be present at the victory.

But as fantastic as De Quincey's visions of the real are, he always knows that they are fantastic. It takes not only the sublime but also the audience's imagination to transform Miss Faucit into Antigone, or transport the theatre onto the battlefield of Waterloo. As Rzepka observes, "theatrical spectacle has become a species of hallucination, and the symbolic space of modern tragedy has collapsed into the unmediated, pure Imaginary" ("Dark Problem" 115). Indeed, Rzepka continues, "The state of mind in which, according to De Quincey, we view Greek tragedy resembles hypnogogic states of dream-waking that are typical of the opium hallucinations described in the *Confessions of an English Opium-Eater*" (115). There is, in De Quincey's analogy with Helen of Troy, a suggestion of a cheat—Mephistopheles is giving Faust a dream when he has asked for a reality. Just as Antigone gains literal substance from Waterloo, Waterloo suddenly becomes a land of dreams by association, as easily conjured (and as easily conjurable) as a stage reproduction of Helen of Troy. At the moment of his own vision of Helen, De Quincey is struck not only with Hunt's speechlessness—the "what-is-it" that comes from an object that resists interpretation—but finally with the very aesthetic vocabulary that the literal is supposed to avoid:

> Then suddenly—O heavens! what a revelation of beauty!—forth stepped, walking in brightness, the most faultless of Grecian marbles, Miss Helen Faucit as Antigone. What perfection of Athenian sculpture! The noble figure, the lovely arms, the fluent drapery! What an unveiling of the ideal statuesque! Is it Hebe? is it Auroura? Perfect she is in form, perfect in attitude,—
> "Beautiful exceedingly
> Like a ladie from a far countrie." (382)

The opium-eater's Antigone is not only an object that is undeniably aesthetic, an actress playing a statue playing Antigone, but furthermore, an actress whose fullest expression is lines of poetry—lines of poetry that are neither De Quincey's nor Antigone's. The nearer the physical object becomes, the farther away it seems. Although the moment unifies the audience—it is at this moment that the critics "all at one moment unanimously fell in love with Miss Faucit" (382)—the audience is unified by a dream.

In fact, even De Quincey's vision of audience unity might also be a construct of his imagination. When De Quincey arrives uncharacteristically early at the Edinburg performance of *Antigone*, he finds himself strangely in the position of the unified public: "I was the audience; I was the public!" (381). But De Quincey's description vacillates between the glory of finding himself—surprisingly—in the position of the unified crowd and the lonely fact that he is only one: "Was there an echo raised? it was from my own steps. Did anybody cough? it was too evidently myself ... And, if any accident happened to the theatre, such as being burned down, Mr. Murray would certainly lay the blame upon me!" (381). Even as De Quincey wants to glorify the unanimity of the crowd's reaction—"We critics, dispersed through the house, in the very teeth of duty and conscience, all at one moment unanimously fell in love with Miss Faucit" (382)—he is happy to see the crowd's diversity—"I was not sorry when an audience, by mustering in strength through all parts of the house, began to divide my responsibility as to burning down the building" (381).

But for De Quincey, there is a virtue in being well deceived. The audience has been so taken with aesthetic distance—so corrupted by a world where even murder can be considered one of the fine arts—that it needs the experience of the real, even if that experience is only a cheat. Indeed, audience unity may be for De Quincey a cheat as well. While Hunt envisions the unified audience as a fundamentally political body—a body with the power to assert its wishes over structures of power within the political world—De Quincey seems to envision the unified audience as an experience, an experience that may be just as simple (and as illusory) as De Quincey's own experience as a public of one.

Hazlitt and the Creative Sublime

At best, De Quincey's vision of audience unity is one that requires audience creativity, a collective exercise of the imagination that creates the literal object as much as it perceives it. But few Romantic critics go further with the idea that spectacle sets off a creative chain reaction in its spectators than William Hazlitt in "On the Indian Jugglers." At first Hazlitt's essay seems to rehearse the familiar Romantic commonplace on the value of spectacle—"mechanical" excellence might amaze and delight, but works of genius, which seek to copy "the face of nature or 'human face divine'" (132), will ultimately stand the test of time. But what is strange about the essay is the way that actor and spectator seem to change places, so that the work of one almost seems to be the work of the other. The reader is at once placed in the shoes of the artist—"Coming forward and seating himself on the ground in his white dress and tightened turban, the chief of the Indian Jugglers begins with tossing up two brass balls, which is what any of us could do, and concludes with keeping up four at the same time, which is what none of us could do to save our lives, not if we were to take the whole of our lives to do it in" (128)—and then, with a flick of the pen, in the shoes of the admiring spectator—"To conceive of this effort of extraordinary dexterity distracts the imagination and makes admiration breathless... You are in pain for the result, and glad when the experiment is over" (128–29). Likewise, Hazlitt himself shifts roles—he imagines himself as a spectator in the Parliament, at the jugglers, at the rope-dancers at the same time that he talks about his writing. He talks about being a spectator of the rope-dancer at the same time that he is an artist copying a picture of Reynolds. Indeed, we might say that the essay makes Hazlitt a spectator of his own practice—a writer watching himself write as a spectator would watch a politician or a rope-dancer.

Even the spectacles that Hazlitt chooses reinforce this feeling of actor becoming spectator. Great surgeons mix with great actresses; painters, rope-dancers, politicians, and fives[9] players all come under Hazlitt's eyes as practitioners of art, subject, perhaps, to the admiring gaze of the viewers. The very example with which he concludes, John Cavanagh, the great fives player, reinforces the thin line between actor and spectator. It is a game that everyone can play, and everyone can watch.

The reason that Hazlitt needs to make this extraordinary effort is that for him, the very unity that De Quincey seeks is something terrible, a deprivation of individuality and creativity that impoverishes the nation even as it unifies it. For Hazlitt, the depersonalized mass brought about by the sublime press of great national events is precisely the problem:

> The cause of the evil complained of, like the root of so many other grievances and complaints, lies in the French Revolution. That event has riveted all eyes, and distracted all hearts; and, like people staring at a comet, in the panic and confusion in which we have been huddled together, we have not had time to laugh at one another's defects, or to condole over one another's misfortunes. We have become a nation of politicians and newsmongers; our inquiries in the streets are no less than after the health of Europe; and in men's faces, we may see strange matters written—the rise of stocks, the loss of battles, the fall of kingdoms, and the death of kings. (109)

This broad focus, while conducive to the sublime, is poison to the drama: "Our attention has been turned, by the current of events, to the general nature of men and things; and we cannot call it heartily back to individual caprices, or head-strong passions, which are the nerves and sinews of Comedy and Tragedy" (109–10). The essence of the drama is the individual character, not the social whole, and anything that acts to blur distinction destroys the dramatic interest of a piece.

For Hazlitt, the failure of the drama hurts more than just drama. The presence of the staggering events of the time, and the absence of the drama as a model for the class of individual characters, has served to alienate people from themselves. "In a word," Hazlitt writes, "literature and civilization have abstracted man from himself so far, that his existence is no longer *dramatic*" (110). He is even more explicit in his essay on comedy: "Our peculiarities have become insipid sameness; our eccentricity servile imitation; our wit, wisdom at second-hand; our prejudices indifference; our feelings not our own; our distinguishing characteristic the want of all character" (101). This insipid sameness, according to Hazlitt, is directly related to the decline of the stage and the rise of print:

> We are become a nation of authors and readers, and even this distinction is confounded by the mediation of the reviewers. We all follow the same profession, which is criticism, each individual is every thing but himself, not one but all mankind's epitome, and the gradations of vice and virtue, of sense and folly, of refinement and grossness of character, seem lost in a kind of intellectual *hermaphroditism* ... [This] change of manners, produced partly by the stage itself, and the total disappearance of the characters which before formed the very life and soul of Comedy, might have something to do with the decline of the Stage. (101–2)

The world of print has turned readers into *hermaphrodites*: they are neither readers nor writers, actors nor spectators. They see themselves writing when they are actually reading, acting when they are actually spectating; as Colin Campbell would have it, they are caught in a culture of simulation where the pleasure of daydream substitutes for actual experience and creates the continually renewed stimulation needed for the consumer culture. But for Hazlitt, the problem is not so much the simulation as the lack of individual character. A reader who identifies so thoroughly with a character that he neglects his own personality, a spectator who puts himself so thoroughly in the place of an actor that he forgets that he is not acting—both forget themselves, and in the process, they cut off the raw material that the drama needs to renew itself: new men, individual characters, persons who are not watchers of this great drama but actors in it, or persons who know that they are not actors but watchers. Politics and the drama, then, feed on each other. The great events that confront men tend to take them out of themselves and make them characters unfit for the drama; the drama then suffers from a lack of personality, and authors are forced to "startle the audience, in lieu of more legitimate methods of exciting their sympathy" and to write dramas that "strike ... and stagger ... the mind" (116). The very force that, for De Quincey, made the audience more able to come into the presence of real characters flattens character for Hazlitt; the force that unifies the audience into a nation threatens to destroy the personality of the characters in it.

Hazlitt's burden, then, is to preserve one sort of the sublime, the sublime that "shew[s] the man" (137), against a mechanical sublime that dwarfs human agency. Both are sublime—the Indian jugglers "distract ... the imagination and make ... admiration breathless ... You are in pain for the result, and glad when the experiment is over" (128–29); in true art "we enter upon that enchanted ground that the human mind begins to droop and flag as in a strange road, or in a thick mist, benighted and making little way with many attempts and many failures" (134). So it is not surprising that Hazlitt describes the activity of the man of genius in the same way he describes the activity of the audience at a spectacle: the Indian juggler "distracts the imagination and makes admiration breathless" (128); the artist creating a work of pure genius finds that "the human mind begins to droop and flag as in a strange road, or in a thick mist, benighted and making little way with many attempts and many failures" (134). Both the literal work of art and the literal fact of human nature (which the work of true genius always copies) challenge the artist/audience. Their impenetrability spurs creativity. A spectator confronted with the spectacular fact of the Indian juggler must not only wonder about its source (as with Hunt); he must also create a story. He puts himself into the juggler's shoes ("which is what any of us could do ... which is what none of us could do to save our lives" [128]); he extrapolates the practice to his own artistic creativity ("I can make a very bad antithesis without cutting my fingers" [131]); he imagines the material conditions that created the spectacle ("you improve by perpetual practice, and you do so infallibly" [131]; "You can put a child apprentice to a tumbler or rope-dancer with a comfortable prospect of success" [135]); he speculates on its value ("Ingenuity is genius in trifles, greatness is genius in undertakings of much pith and moment" [135]). For Hazlitt, a distracted and breathless imagination is not necessarily a silenced one; it is the imagination on its first step toward speaking.

For this reason, Hazlitt has the most difficult time judging the greatness of activities that require spectators. He has almost talked himself out of allowing acting into the canon of genius—"No act terminating in itself constitutes greatness" (137)—when he stops himself—"Is not an actor then a great man, because 'he dies and leaves the world no copy?' I must make an exception for Mrs. Siddons, or else give up my definition of greatness for her sake" (137). And he ends his essay with an encomium to John Cavanagh, the great fives player, who, while "a singular instance of manual dexterity" (135) deserves about 1,500 words of praise (quoted from the *Examiner*). What both professions have in common that chess players, naval commanders, chemists, and even politicians do not share is a cadre of admiring spectators—Cavanagh's eulogy mentions a group of "by-standers drinking the cider, and laughing all the time" (140) in addition to the admiring writer for the *Examiner* and his readers. Although Hazlitt does not make the reasons for his hesitation explicit, the presence of spectators implies that the acts of Cavanagh and Mrs. Siddons do not "terminate in [them]selves." They spark creative acts of spectatorship—acts that might better fit the artistic mind for its own confrontations with the sublime. It is for this reason that Hazlitt cannot condemn the Indian jugglers, even though their acts might be inferior to great works of genius. They are part of an economy that promotes and circulates works of genius wherever they might be found.

But Hazlitt is only partially successful in reclaiming the sublime for the realm of the human. For even though Hazlitt's sublime is created by man, about man, in order to expand men's minds and allow them to see the man, it still comes from a realm outside of human control. The "eternal principle . . . must be taught by nature and genius, not by rules of study" (133); "Talent differs from genius, as voluntary differs from involuntary power" (135). Both artist and audience become involuntary spectators to a power that is beyond them both. In attempting to create a sublime that is beyond the simply material, beyond human skill, Hazlitt has, in his own way, created a sublime as inhuman as that which he sought to avoid.

The problem of horses, dogs, and elephants onstage, and of the extravagant scenery that accompanied them, then, is a problem of what to do with the sublime in that most concrete of audience situations—the situation in which the audience is not removed from the terrifying object by the medium of paint or print, but is rather confronted with the sublime object in all its terrifying concreteness.

They speculate that the very closeness of the sublime might prove Burke's principle that "[w]hen the danger or pain press too nearly, they are incapable of giving any delight, and are simply terrible" (71); if the distance is not built in through the medium, the audience might create its own distance by dismissing what is meant to be sublime as merely amusing, and thus miss the combination of pleasure and pain that is the essence of the sublime. But, at the same time, the closeness of the danger, and its concreteness, raises the possibility that the audience might be unified by its shared terror, and its very unassimilibility raises the possibility that somehow the audience might somehow be shaken out of its tendency to remake the illusion in its own image, and might finally be compelled to recognize the other for what it is in itself, rather than what the audience wants to make it to be through the magic of theatrical illusion. This dynamic explains the contradictory push and pull that Romantic audiences and theatre managers seem to feel toward the horses, dogs, and elephants that occupy their stage: on the one hand an amazing attraction; on the other a figure of ridicule to be poked fun at in prologues, epilogues, and satirical afterpieces. Everyone involved seemed to recognize that real objects—horses, dogs, elephants, spectacular scenery, and acts of mechanical excellence—threatened to change the nature of the theatrical experience: to amaze, dazzle, and distract, to heighten doubt even as they heightened realism, and perhaps even to throw the effect of the actor's body itself into question. Animals threatened to make the theatre less human, not because they were not human themselves, but because they threw the nature of the physical body into question and opened up the question of the audience's response to it. By presenting an illusion that was not assimilable solely as an illusion, a body that the mind could not absorb, those onstage animals changed the entire nature of Romantic illusion, and with it, the entire notion of the Romantic theatre.

Conclusion

Reaching a Mass Audience Face to Face

The Ancient Mariner reaches a mass audience one person at a time. He holds each one with his skinny hand and glittering eye. Each thrills to mast-high ice cliffs, the sun bloody and red, the skeletal ghost ship, and the water snakes flashing golden fire while simultaneously tracking the flow of emotion on the Mariner's ancient face. Each listens like a three years' child. The next morning, each rises a sadder and a wiser man.

It is a fantasy of the author-audience relationship we see over and over again in the Romantic period. The audience can experience the most grandiose tales, seek strange truths, confront the distant and impenetrable, but do so with a human companion. Authors can reach the world but do so without losing their humanity. Even as authors confront an audience wider, more fragmented and more diverse,[1] the authorial voice becomes more intimate and more personal, as if the way to handle a mass public is to address each one individually.

In claiming that this voice evolved from the theatre, I hope to show how closely related print and theatre were in the chaotic early development of mass culture. Of course it is widely recognized that theatre and print were part of the same social scene. Writing about plays and performers, theatregoing, and theatre buildings formed a major part of the periodical and newspaper press, and printed play texts, playbills, prologues, epilogues, and critical essays attracted a significant reading audience. But such obvious and banal observations do not come close to assessing the impact that theatre had on developing the textual voice that we have come to know as Romantic, or exploring the relationship between them. In fact, the relationship between theatre and the growing forms of print was much more like an Oedipal rivalry than peaceful commercial coexistence.

Poets envied theatre's reach, its embodiment, its political and cultural importance. They projected onto it their own fears about being unable to reach a mass audience. They derided its crowds, its spectacle, and its disgusting embodiment even as they tried to reproduce those things themselves.

This, I would submit, is the way that media and genres work in a time of technological change. As Walter Benjamin observed in "Art in the Age of Mechanical Reproduction," new artistic technologies always change the forms of art that come before them. Old technologies do not go away as new ones come in. They change and adapt, developing new forms and functions, creating new niches for themselves that the newer forms might enhance. Even forms that stay the same are read differently in light of the new technologies that occupy their cultural scene—for example, when reading the novel has a cultural capital superior to watching the film version. And just as old technologies adapt to the new, newer technologies take their form from the old. Computer screens made to look like "desktops," the electronic communications we call "mail," and engineered composite building materials made to look like natural wood or stone all show that new technologies do not enter the world fully formed. The new always takes its shape from what is known, making itself familiar by taking on elements of what it replaced. As Jay David Bolter and Richard Grusin have shown, new and old media function in a complex dialectic of mutual influence, interacting in complex ways that change both old and new.

In this case, the interaction between theatre and mass print produced a unique poetic voice that we have come to call "Romantic." Like the actors at the major houses, authors tried to simulate close personal contact. The poet speaks in his own voice, often in a situation where he is surrounded by one or more listeners. Sometimes those listeners are real (as in Coleridge's "Eolian Harp"); sometimes they are imagined (as in Coleridge's "This Lime-Tree Bower"). Often, too, they take these listeners on a grand journey, into spectacular scenes or the world of the mind, combining the intimacy of the old theatres with the spectacle of the new. This is why often listeners are distant enough that they seem almost imaginary. Coleridge's "pensive Sara" in the "Eeolian Harp," Dorothy in Wordsworth's "Tintern Abbey," the absent Charles in Coleridge's "This Lime-Tree Bower My Prison," the present-but-absent lover in Byron's "So We'll Go No More A-Roving"—all strike a compromise between being there and being gone.

Theatre gives us a historical context for this odd movement. It explains why Romantic authors so compulsively assemble audiences and why those audiences always seem to be disappearing. And in this regard, poetry—and especially canonical Romantic poetry—is not alone. Popular dramatic forms like the pantomime, popular print forms like the review, and less canonical dramas also exhibit an anxiety about the audience and a phantasmatic desire to accommodate closeness and distance. Joanna Baillie's *Count Basil*, for example, begins with an audience gathered to watch a magnificent procession. But while Baillie has her citizens rhapsodize about the princess's treasure, they are reprimanded by an old veteran, who has come only to see if the princess has the same heart-kindling smile as her mother: "I came not for the show" (1.1.18). Romantic poetry and drama is full of moments where authors anxiously reach for their audience, only to find that the audience is more distant, more recalcitrant or more illusory than they had hoped.

I began this book as a project on embodiment in the theatre as a way of looking at the boundary between performed and closet drama. But I found very quickly that bodies had a way of shifting and disappearing, even in arts like the pantomime and the hippodrama that seem most embodied. The body could signal the closeness of an older organic world, where (in Colley Cibber's terms) the voice was in the center of the house.[2] But the body could also be large, impenetrable and frightening, like the massy black entablatures on the set of *Harlequin and Humpo* or the houses that imprison Mme. Tricastin and Sardanapalus. The theatre's corporeality gave authors a concrete way to imagine how they might relate to a mass audience, but even when that imagination was made physical in sets and costumes, painted flats and stages, and the very real and concrete bodies of actors and audiences, it proved malleable, as subject to the whim of the imagination as words themselves. Spectacle served Romanticism as its technological "other"—magnificent, overwhelming, sublime—but in most Romantic analyses, it was incorporated into the human, whether by alternating between intimacy and distance (as in the pantomime) or by reinvigorating the human audience that consumed it (as in the criticism of Hunt, Hazlitt, and De Quincey). Often, as in Shelley, the body must be present but torn apart and mixed together, so that it retains its humanity but accommodates the humanity of others. Romantic authors in both print and theatre might long for the security and comfort of the body, but they found the body most useful to them when they could import that body into the more fluid and imaginative world of text.

What is left of the theatre is the voice. It is the vestige of the human face and body that remains on the page, and it was an important part of the Romantic project to keep it. Wordsworth's vision of the poet as a "man speaking to men" testifies to the importance the Romantics placed on preserving the speaking body in the poetry they considered of the best quality, and it is an element of the Romantic project that haunts analyses of literature to the present day. If we accept the theatre as a foundational context for the Romantic voice—and if we see the bodily and performed dimension of the text that this history brings forth—we have a way of seeing literature that both emphasizes the isolation of the Romantic voice and recognizes its social longings. I want to emphasize that this is a much different vision of the literary project than the one presented by scholars like Alvin Kernan, Clifford Siskin, and Paul Keen, who envision the concept of "literature" as one largely created by mass print. This history is certainly true, and is an important part of the imaginative construct we have inherited. But even as print pushes imaginative literature toward the abstract, solitary, and universal, there is an undercurrent of theatre lurking beneath that pushes toward the particular, embodied, and social. We can see elements of this idea of literature in Jeff Cox's idea of Romanticism taking place in avant-garde groups, or in the essays in Alexander Dick and Angela Esterhammer's collection on Romanticism and the performative. Taking the voice seriously as an acting voice means situating literature within its particular time, place, and authorial context. But it also implies reaching out to an imagined social world that might be larger than the author's realistic reading public.

Indeed, I would like to end with a modern metaphor taken from Louis Menand's essay on the voice that introduces the 2004 collection of *The Best American Essays*. As editor of the annual essay collection, Menand faced a difficult task. Unlike the editors of the annual *Best American Short Story* and *Best American Poetry* collections, the editor of the essay volume not only has to define "quality" in a climate skeptical of aesthetic values (as all editors do), but he is also forced to pull out an aesthetic category, "the essay," which is notoriously close to journalism, history, and other sorts of professional writing that are not traditionally considered to have literary or aesthetic value. The very term "creative nonfiction"—a term often used to describe the type of essays generally included in the annual essay volume—is troubled by its relationship to (presumably) non-creative nonfiction: that vast mass of journalism, memoir, biography, blog posts, scholarship, reports, and other prose that populates our professional, information-age culture. The very premise of *Best American Essays*, in other words, enacts the division between professional writing and "literature" that Kernan and Siskin have identified as a development of advanced print culture.

When the time came to choose the essays that would qualify for the collection, then, Menand, a cultural critic at Harvard whose early work analyzed T. S. Eliot's redefinition of literature, falls back on that old literary standby—voice. In fact, he uses the quality of "voice" to define all good writing: "One of the most mysterious of writing's immaterial properties is what people call its 'voice.' Editors sometimes refer to it, in a phrase that underscores the paradox at the heart of the idea, as the 'voice on the page.' Many editors think that a voice is what makes great writing great. Most writers do, too" (xiv). As the foregoing indicates, Menand is somewhat embarrassed about using "voice" as a criterion for choosing the essays in his volume. "You cannot taste a work of prose," he writes: "It has no color and it makes no sound. Its shape is without significance. When people talk about writing, though, they often use adjectives borrowed from activities whose products make a more direct appeal to the senses—painting, sculpture, music, cuisine. People say, 'The writing is colorful,' or 'pungent,' or 'shapeless,' or 'lyrical,' and no one asks them where, exactly, they perceive these qualities" (xiv). It is not exactly the same as personality: "There are writers read and loved for their humor who are not especially funny people, and writers read and loved for their eloquence who, in conversation, swallow their words or can't seem to finish a sentence" (xv). But it is not free from personality either: "Writing is personal; it feels personal" (xvii). Somehow the personality it conveys is not exactly the individual's. Menand is sometimes inclined to get mystical about this mysterious voice. It is an "immaterial property" (xiv), "a phantom" (xv), "a neural kink or the grace of God" (xvii), "something inside you [that comes] up with the words" (xvii).

The voice that Menand chooses, however, is not a speaking voice, and certainly not a conversational voice—something he characterizes as "yakking away to yourself all the time" (xv). Instead, the "voice" that Menand finds in literature is a performance voice, and specifically a *singing* voice. The opera singer, the chanteuse, the lonely singer-songwriter: all are better analogues for the written voice than the orator or conversationalist. And singing is an interesting choice. Singing is an art that prizes the singer's relationship to his or her audience. Except for opera and musicals—and sometimes even then—here is no "fourth wall" between the singer and her audience. Even in the largest opera hall or stadium, even over the radio or on a recording, audience members can feel like the singer is singing directly to them. And singing is a cooperative art. Although some singers will sing all alone and *a capella*, most are accompanied by other instruments. A good number perform songs composed by other composers. And all but the most solitary sing for an audience. In fact, singing is one of the most interactive of the performing arts.

If we understand theatre's influence on the development of literature, we can see that Menand's "phantom" is actually the remnant of the actor's voice in the modern world of reproducible type. We value literature's "taste," "smell," "shape," and "voice" because we remember a time when literature was close and interactive, when its voice was public, when an audience responded. The voice can recall lost worlds because it is part of the world. It is not an individual voice but a social voice. As Colly Cibber would say, the voice is once again in the center of the house.

If we are redefining Romanticism away from a collection of solitary, politically isolated speakers, we could do worse than to embrace the idea of voice. For voice is not just the remnant of a coterie oral culture, a vestige of aristocratic patronage that we are well rid of. Instead, it is the vestige of a public, cooperative effort. The "voice" that was eventually incorporated into literature is print's attempt to maintain a public voice in a medium designed for individual consumption. While part of the creation of literature institutionalizes the private reading and writing of imaginative, politically neutral works, literature always has, at its very heart, the vision of a man onstage speaking to an interactive crowd—"a man," as Wordsworth says, "speaking to men." It is a way for a writer to believe that she is speaking to, and for a reader to believe that he is a member of, an imaginary "public."

The Romantic poetic voice is always a compromise. It takes the physicality of actor and audience and moves that physicality into the realm of print. There, it can pan and zoom, moving closer and farther away, borrowing the theatre's concreteness without being trapped by it. It can be individual, organic, and social while adapting to the wondrous, the technological, and the mass. In its fantasy it is like the Ancient Mariner, reaching a mass audience face to face.

Notes

Introduction

1. George Colman the Younger, "[On the Size of the Theatres]," quoted in Richard Brinsley Peake, *Memoirs of the Colman Family*, 224–25.
2. Mayer, *Harlequin in His Element*, 22.
3. Lest this reading seem like a stretch, the Haymarket had a reputation for passing pleasant afternoons. One might recall Samuel Foote's ruse to get around the Licensing Act in 1747, when he invited his "friends" for a "dish of Chocolate," with the play provided "*gratis*" afterwards. There is a particularly humorous account of this incident in Forster, *Oliver Cromwell, Daniel DeFoe*, 358–359.
4. Bronson, "Strange Relations," 302.
5. Klancher, *The Making of English Reading Audiences*, 14.
6. Ibid., 14.
7. Much good work has been done in this area, though I am thinking particularly of Cox, *Poetry and Politics*, and Murphy, "Impersonation and Authorship." For a good recent summary, see Clery, *Authorship, Commerce and the Public*.
8. Nicoll, *History of English Drama*, 3:32.
9. Although there are many excellent sources for the "illegitimate" stage, including Richard Altick's *The Shows of London*, the best remains Jane Moody's *Illegitimate Theatre in London, 1770–1840* (Cambridge: Cambridge University Press, 2000).
10. Leacroft, *Development of the English Playhouse*, 91.
11. Ibid., 170.
12. Nicoll, *The Garrick Stage*, 20–21.
13. *Edinburgh Weekly Journal*, Wednesday, Feb. 28, 1827, quoted in Nicoll, *History of English Drama*, 4:25.
14. Leigh Hunt, *Dramatic Criticism*, 259.
15. Mayer, *Harlequin in His Element*, 22.
16. F. G. Tomlins, *A Brief View of the English Drama, from the Earliest Period to the Present Time: With Suggestions for Elevating the Present Condition of the Art, and of Its Professors* (1840), quoted in Nicoll, *History of English Drama*, 4:24–25.
17. Leacroft, *Development of the English Playhouse*, 155.
18. Ibid., 170.
19. Baillie, *Plays on the Passions*, 70.

Chapter 1

1. *The Thespian,* as quoted in Cox and Gamer 356.
2. Hunt, as quoted in Cox and Gamer 336–37.
3. See Jameson's *Political Unconscious.*
4. St. Clair, *The Reading Nation,* 1–19.
5. John O'Brien offers a compelling account of the eighteenth-century pantomime's role in shaping an "entertainment" culture in *Harlequin Britain.* For a glimpse of the British pantomime's history in communal fairs and festivals, see also Marilyn Gaull, "Pantomime as Satire."
6. Mayer, *Harlequin in his Element,* 22–23.
7. De Quincey, *Collected Writings,* 10:97.
8. Both "Pantomime as Satire" and *Harlequin Britain* have excellent descriptions on the state of the documentary evidence still available.
9. McKee, *Scenarios of the Commedia dell'Arte,* xiii.
10. Hunt, *Dramatic Criticism,* 144.
11. De Quincey, *Collected Writings,* 10:97.
12. Moody, *Illegitimate Theatre,* 210.
13. Frederick Burwick has an excellent discussion of these debates in *Illusion and the Drama,* 153–60.
14. Dibdin, *Remininiscences of Thomas Dibdin,* quoted in Cox and Gamer 205.
15. Adolphus, *Memoirs of John Bannister,* 2:203.
16. There is some dispute over the size of Holland's 1794 Drury Lane. According to Leacroft, it was originally intended for the theatre to hold 3,919, though the capacity varied according to the renovations made between 1794 and 1809. The figure varies between 2,000 and 3,919. See Leacroft, *Development of the English Playhouse,* 155 and n36.
17. All citations to *Harlequin and Humpo* and its reviews are to Cox and Gamer, *The Broadview Anthology.*

Chapter 2

1. Byron, *Don Juan,* 11.441–42.
2. Baillie, "To the Reader," extracted in Cox and Gamer, *The Broadview Anthology,* 373.
3. Wordsworth, *The Borderers,* 3–6.
4. Thomas Crochunis, "Joanna Baillie's Ambivalent Dramaturgy," 169.
5. Reviews of Joana Baillie's *Plays on the Passions* are included in Baillie, *Plays on the Passions,* 52–53.
6. Keats, *Letters,* 2:234.
7. Crochunis, "Ambivalent Dramaturgy," 169.
8. It is tempting to put Lamb's antitheatricality down to the failure of his farce *Mr. H* at Drury Lane. But in fact, Lamb's involvement with the drama is long and sustained. He wrote a dramatic sketch, *The Witches,* in 1798; a tragedy,

John Woodvil, in 1802; and another farce, *The Pawnbroker's Daughter*, in 1825. Lamb's argument that in staging the tragedies of Shakespeare "instead of realising an idea, we have only materialised and brought down a fine vision to the standard of flesh and blood" can be found in "On the Tragedies of Shakespeare Considered with Reference to their Fitness for Stage Representation" (1811).

9. The two most significant early voices in this debate were Samuel Chew, *The Relation of Lord Byron to the Drama of the Romantic Period*, and David Erdman, "Byron's Stage Fright," but the debate continues in the work of Alan Richardson, Michael Simpson, and others.
10. Two recent biographies by Annibel Jenkins and Roger Minvell give fuller descriptions of Inchbald's life and career.
11. Lord Byron, preface to *Marino Faliero: Doge of Venice*.
12. See Paula Backscheider and Ellen Donkin. As Backscheider points out, there was one other play, *A Case of Conscience*, which was not staged in Inchbald's lifetime. However, this play was written specifically for John Philip Kemble, and the only reason that it was not staged was because Kemble was touring the continent at the time.
13. The reason that I single out *Marino Faliero* and *Sardanapalus* as his most stageable is their stage history. Although Erdman argues that Byron thought about staging as early as his first drama, *Manfred*, *Marino* was the first play that his publishers and managers picked up for the stage. Robert William Elliston staged the play for Drury Lane in 1821, and T. J. Dibdin planned to produce a melodrama on the same subject. Byron vehemently protested and had his friends obtain an injunction against the plays; Elliston's went forward despite the injunction and closed after two nights. The entire story is told in colorful detail in Boleslaw Taborski's *Byron and the Theatre*, 157–65. I include *Sardanapalus* not only because it was written around the same time (as was *The Two Foscari*) but also because it remains the most staged of Byron's dramas, with 186 performances in London as of 1972. *Manfred* is second with 165—doubtless because of its early canonicity—Werner is third with 139, and *Marino* is fourth with 52 (Taborski 154–55). For an excellent description of the saga surrounding *Marino*'s performance, see Boleslaw Taborski.
14. The quote comes from Elizabeth Inchbald, "Advertisement" to *The Massacre*.
15. Charles Lamb, "On the Tragedies of Shakespeare Considered with Regard to Their Fitness for Stage Representation."
16. Nielsen, "A Tragic Farce," 265–74.
17. Quoted in Roger Manvell, *Elizabeth Inchbald*, 94–95.
18. Byron first used the phrase in a letter to Samuel Rogers in 1814, attributing the phrase to Mirabeau. L. E. Marshall, who wrote an excellent article tracing the relationship between the phrase and Horne Tooke's theories of language, could not find the saying in the writings of Mirabeau (Marshall 804–5).
19. Paul West actually uses the term "puppet." See also McGann, Christensen, and Jewett.
20. Bill Brown, *Thing Theory*, 5n15, quoted in Potkay, *Ethics of Things*, 393.
21. Potkay, *Ethics of Things*, 401.

22. I should note here that I disagree with Lansdown's idea that the plebeians' interpretation of what they are seeing is incorrect. In my view, Marino's sympathies with the people are quite well founded—he betrays his class and his duties to enter into a revolutionary conspiracy that is at least ostensibly for the benefit of the people—and the thread of armed revolution in the play seems to be quite serious—for the Doge, if not for Byron. My views are much closer to Michael Simpson's here—Byron wants to exercise some type of power over his audience—but we cannot leave the dramatic nature of this fantasy unexplored even as we examine *Marino* as a closet drama.
23. See Melynda Nuss, "'The Gory Head Rolls Down the Giants' Steps!'"
24. Actually, *Marino*'s run, while short, was normal for a new tragedy. See Taborski, Cox, and Gamer.
25. Jerome Christensen's *Lord Byron's Strength* and Susan Wolfson's wonderful "A Problem Few Dare Imitate" explore Byron's discourse on effeminacy.

Chapter 3

1. All citations to *The Prelude* are to the 1805 version unless otherwise noted.
2. Wordsworth wrote to Matthews, "You inquired after the name of one of my poetical bantlings, children of this species ought to be named after their characters, and here I am at a loss, as my offspring seems to have no character at all" (Johnston 348). Here Wordsworth seems to recognize not only the uncertain genre of his poem—he calls it a "poetical bantling"—but also the fact that his poem does not properly fit as a narrative or as a character sketch, as "children of this species ought to be named after their characters," and his poem has "no character at all."
3. Nicoll, *History of English Drama*, 4:23–24.
4. Mona Ozouf and Lynn Hunt have written the pioneering work on the festivals of the French Revolution.
5. Jewett, *Fatal Autonomy*, 399. Kenneth Johnston has made a convincing case for the biographical elements in both Mortimer and Rivers (*Poet, Lover, Rebel, Spy* 500–504).
6. Citations to *The Borderers* are from the text of the earlier version.
7. *The Borderers* is famous for its references to Shakespeare, and Reeve Parker has noted specific references to Ducis's *Othello* in "Reading Wordsworth's Power," 300–304.
8. Parker, "Reading Wordsworth's Power," 299–300.
9. Reeve Parker has already noted the way that verbal power is used to enchant and enthrall in *The Borderers*, and the way that *The Borderers* denies its hero the sort of rhetorical heroism that was so powerful in the French Revolution ("In Some Sort Seeing with My Proper Eyes" 371–90).
10. Parker, "Reading Wordsworth's Power," 310–12.
11. Parker, "In Some Sort Seeing," 322.
12. I am taking my text from the earlier version that Wordsworth wrote as a stand alone poem in 1798 except where otherwise indicated.

13. Lewis Carroll, *Upon the Lonely Moor* (1856), quoted in Jonathan Wordsworth 417.
14. Susan Wolfson makes the excellent point that the solitary's questions are meant to evoke a heroic argument from the soldier—exactly the sort of "gross and violent stimulant" that Wordsworth deplored on the stage—but his questions receive only a "calm" and "concise" answer—not at all what the young man might have hoped for or expected. Wolfson, *The Questioning Presence*, 141.
15. Wordsworth, Note to "The Thorn," in *Wordsworth's Poetry*, 688.
16. Ford T. Swetnam has also noted this similarity in "Satiric Voices of *The Prelude*," 102.
17. Wordsworth, *Lyrical Ballads*, 156.
18. Jonathan Wordsworth's discussion of the composition history of book 7 and Wordsworth's plans for *The Prelude* can be found at the beginning of chapter 9 of *William Wordsworth: The Borders of Vision*, 279–82.
19. Robert Adam's decorations for the 1778 renovation of Drury Lane were so magnificent that patrons claimed that the richness of the decoration distracted from the play. The decorations were toned down in 1783, but even into the early nineteenth century, Lamb and Hunt remarked on the lushness of the interior decoration at the major theatres. *See* Leacroft, *Development of the English Playhouse*, 127; Lamb, "My First Play"; and Hunt, "Covent Garden Redecorated."
20. Moody, "Fine Word, Legitimate!," 223–44.
21. For an excellent discussion of Wordsworth's earlier radicalism and book 7 of *The Prelude*, especially Wordsworth's problematic relationship with Burke, see Mary Jacobus, "That Great Stage Where Senators Perform."
22. William Galperin has also noticed Wordsworth's similarity to the panoramic artist (*Return of the Visible* 54–55).
23. Mary Jacobus's "Splitting the Race of Man in Twain" and Betsy Bolton's *Women, Nationalism and the Romantic Stage* both argue that the mother and her babe are a manifestation of Wordsworth's condemnation of the theatre, and with it, his condemnation of women. I do not wish to argue with their points about women. However, I do believe that there is something more interesting going on with theatricality than their readings would suggest.
24. Of course, as Jacobus and Bolton have shown, the association between prostitutes and actresses was well established, despite Sarah Siddons's efforts to the contrary.
25. It is interesting how often Wordsworth uses physical metaphors to describe his experience as an audience member. In book 7, he is "wrought upon by tragic sufferings" (501), just as the baby in "The Thorn" "wrought about" its mother's heart to bring her senses back again, and of course, in a common metaphor for spectacles, he was most passionately "moved" (504).

Chapter 4

1. Cox, *Poetry and Politics*, 142.
2. Michael Simpson, *Closet Performances*, 166.
3. Groseclose, "The Incest Motif," 224.

Chapter 5

1. This and all subsequent citations are to the 1805 version. For a discussion of the way that Romantic visual culture—both theatrical and otherwise—has shaped our present-day discussion of realistic media, see Gillen D'Arcy Wood.
2. For the "Romantic Century" concept, I am indebted to Susan Wolfson.
3. The most complete study of popular journals is Jon Klancher's *The Making of English Reading Audiences, 1790-1832*. As Klancher points out, journals tried to create a public sphere out of a deeply divided nation. Their analysis of spectacle continued the project by envisioning spectacle as a force that could unify the public body at the same time that it created independent, thinking citizens.
4. Ronald Paulson, W. J. T. Mitchell, and Daniella Mallinick all note the way that Edmund Burke's theory of the sublime mirrors his support of established monarchical and patriarchal power; the essays in a 1987 *Studies in Romanticism* forum on the sublime emphasize the containment of revolutionary energy, including Arac, Hays, and Simpson.
5. Jonathan Arac and Michael Hays have argued the Romantic period's preference for closet reading and avoidance of comedy are both ways to avoid the loud crowds and social world that the theatre entails.
6. Daniella Mallinick has recently used the distinction between the Burkean and Kantian sublime to analyze the use of the sublime in feminist writers like Mary Wollstonecraft, who use the Kantian sublime to criticize the Burkean version.
7. Indeed, this is the portion of the sublime that has made it through to twentieth-century criticism. For Lyotard, for example, the sublime is the thrill of the present moment, "the occurrence, the *Ereignis*, has nothing to do with the *petit frisson*, the cheap thrill, the profitable pathos, that accompanies an innovation" (106).
8. Rzepka's "Bang Up!" provides an excellent discussion of De Quincey's experience with the theatre. Although De Quincey "rarely mentions actual attendance at the playhouse," he does mention the English Opera House in his *Confessions*, and there is some evidence that he attended the theatre as early as age 14, and of course he did review the Edinburg production of *Antigone* for *Tait's Magazine*. Rzepka makes a convincing case that De Quincey uses pantomimic imagery and techniques in *The English Mail Coach*, and even suggests a particular performance that could have been the basis for some of De Quincey's writing.
9. The City Fives Association website, http://www.playfives.co.uk, describes fives as "a version of handball . . . in which players compete by hitting a ball with their hands against a wall . . . The rules are similar to squash."

Conclusion

1. Klancher, *The Making of English Reading Audiences.*
2. Leacroft, *Development of the English Playhouse*, 91.

Works Cited

Abrams, M. H. *Natural Supernaturalism: Tradition and Revolution in Romantic Literature*. New York: Norton, 1971.
Adolphus, John. *Memoirs of John Bannister, Commedian*. 2 vols. London: Richard Bentley, 1839.
Aeschylus. *Prometheus Bound*. Trans. David Grene. *Aeschylus I: Agamemnon, The Libation Bearers, The Eumenides, Prometheus Bound*. Ed. David Grene and Richmond Lattimore. New York: Modern Library, 1942.
Allen, Danielle S. *The World of Prometheus: The Politics of Punishing in Democratic Athens*. Princeton: Princeton UP, 2000.
Altick, Richard. *The Shows of London*. Cambridge: Belknap, 1978.
Anderson, Emily Hodgson. *Eighteenth-Century Authorship and the Play of Fiction: Novels and the Theater, Haywood to Austen*. New York: Routledge, 2009.
Arac, Jonathan. "The Media of Sublimity: Johnson and Lamb on *King Lear*." *Studies in Romanticism* 26.2 (Summer 1987): 209–20.
Aristotle. *Aristotle's Treatise on Poetry*. Ed. and trans. Thomas Twining. London: Payne and Son, 1789; rpt. New York: Garland, 1971.
Auslander, Philip. *Liveness: Performance in a Mediatized Culture*. London: Routledge, 1999.
Backscheider, Paula, ed. *The Plays of Elizabeth Inchbald*. New York: Garland, 1980.
Baer, Marc. *Theatre and Disorder in Late Georgian London*. Oxford: Clarendon Press, 1992.
Baillie, Joanna. *Plays on the Passions*. Ed. Peter Duthie. Peterborough: Broadview, 2001.
Benjamin, Walter. "The Work of Art in the Age of Mechanical Reproduction." *Illuminations*. Ed. and with an introduction by Hannah Arendt. Trans. Harry Zohn. New York: Schocken Books, 1968.
Bialostosky, Don H., and Lawrence D. Needham, eds. Introduction. *Rhetorical Traditions and British Romantic Literature*. Bloomington: Indiana UP, 1995.
Biggs, Murray. "Staging *The Borderers*: Dragging Romantic Drama Out of the Closet." *Studies in Romanticism* 27.3 (Fall 1988): 411–18.

Blake, William. *Milton. The Complete Poetry and Prose of William Blake*. Ed. David V. Erdman. Berkeley: U of California P, 1982.
Bloom, Harold. *Shelley's Mythmaking*. Ithaca: Cornell UP, 1959.
Boaden, James. *Memoirs of the Life of John Philip Kemble, Esq., Including a History of the Stage, From the Time of Garrick to the Present Period*. Philadelphia: Robert H. Small, 1825.
Bolter, J. David, and Richard Grusin. *Remediation: Understanding New Media*. Cambridge: MIT Press, 2000.
Bolton, Betsy. *Women, Nationalism and the Romantic Stage: Theatre and Politics in Britain, 1780–1800*. Cambridge: Cambridge UP, 2001.
Booth, Michael R. *Theatre in the Victorian Age*. Cambridge: Cambridge UP, 1991.
Bronfen, Elisabeth. *Over Her Dead Body: Death, Femininity and the Aesthetic*. New York: Routledge, 1992.
Bronson, Bertrand H. "Strange Relations: The Author and His Audience." In *Facets of the Enlightenment, Studies in English Literature and Its Contexts*. Berkeley: U California P, 1968. 298–325.
Burke, Edmund. *Reflections on the Revolution in France and on the Proceedings in Certain Societies in London Relative to that Event*. Ed. with an introduction by Conor Cruise O'Brien. New York: Penguin, 1982.
———. "The Sublime and Beautiful." *Contextualizing Aesthetics: From Plato to Lyotard*. Ed. H. Gene Blocker and Jennifer M. Jeffers. Belmont: Wadsworth, 1999.
Burroughs, Catherine B. *Closet Stages: Joanna Baille and the Theater Theory of British Romantic Women Writers*. Philadelphia: U Pennsylvania P, 1997.
Burwick, Frederick. *Illusion and the Drama: Critical Theory of the Enlightenment and Romantic Era*. University Park: Pennsylvania State UP, 1991.
———. *Mimesis and Its Romantic Reflections*. University Park: Pennsylvania State UP, 2001.
———. *Playing to the Crowd: London Popular Theatre, 1780–1830*. Basingstoke: Palgrave, 2011.
———. *Romantic Drama: Acting and Reacting*. Cambridge: Cambridge UP, 2011.
Byron, George Gordon, Lord. *Byron's Letters and Journals*. Ed. Leslie A. Marchand. Cambridge: Harvard UP, 1977.
———. *The Complete Poetical Works*. Ed. Jerome J. McGann. 7 vols. Oxford: Clarendon Press, 1980–1993.
———. *Miscellanies*. 3 vols. London: John Murray, 1837.
Campbell, Colin. *The Romantic Ethic and the Spirit of Modern Consumerism*. Oxford: Basil Blackwell, 1987.

Carlson, Julie A. "Forever Young: Master Betty and the Queer Stage of Youth in English Romanticism." *South Atlantic Quarterly* 95.3 (Summer 1996): 575–602.

———. *In the Theater of Romanticism: Coleridge, Nationalism, Women.* Cambridge: Cambridge UP, 1994.

———. "A New Stage for Romantic Drama." *Studies in Romanticism* 27.3 (Fall 1988): 419–27.

Cavell, Stanley. *The Claim of Reason: Wittgenstein, Skepticism, Morality, and Tragedy.* New York: Oxford UP, 1979.

Chew, Samuel C. *The Relation of Lord Byron to the Drama of the Romantic Period.* Baltimore: Johns Hopkins UP, 1914.

Christensen, Jerome. *Lord Byron's Strength: Romantic Writing and Commercial Society.* Baltimore: Johns Hopkins UP, 1993.

Clery, E. J., Caroline Franklin, and Peter Garside, eds. *Authorship, Commerce and the Public: Scenes of Writing, 1750–1850.* Basingstoke: Palgrave, 2002.

Coleridge, Samuel Taylor. *The Portable Coleridge.* Ed. I. A. Richards. New York: Viking Press, 1950.

Cooke, Michael G., and Alan Bewell. "Introduction." *Studies in Romanticism* 27.3 (Fall 1988): 353–54.

Cox, Jeffrey N. *Poetry and Politics in the Cockney School: Keats, Shelley, Hunt and their Circle.* Cambridge: Cambridge UP, 1998.

———. "Spots of Time: The Structure of the Dramatic Evening in the Theater of Romanticism." *Texas Studies in Language and Literature* 41 (1999): 403–25.

Cox, Jeffrey N., and Michael Gamer, eds. *The Broadview Anthology of Romantic Drama.* Peterborough: Broadview, 2003.

Crary, Jonathan. *Techniques of the Observer: On Vision and Modernity in the Nineteenth Century.* Cambridge: MIT Press, 1998.

Crochunis, Thomas C. "Authorial Performances in the Criticism and Theory of Romantic Women Playwrights." *Women in British Romantic Theatre: Drama, Performance and Society 1790–1840.* Ed. Catherine Burroughs. Cambridge: Cambridge UP, 2000. 223–56.

———. "Joanna Baillie's Ambivalent Dramaturgy." *Joanna Baillie, Romantic Dramatist: Critical Essays.* Ed. Thomas C. Crochunis. London: Routledge, 2004.

Curran, Stuart. "The Political Prometheus." *Studies in Romanticism* 25.3 (Fall 1986): 429–55.

De Quincey, Thomas. *The Collected Writings of Thomas De Quincey.* Ed. David Masson. London: A. and C. Black, 1897.

Dick, Alex, and Angela Esterhammer. *Spheres of Action: Speech and Performance in Romantic Culture.* Toronto: U of Toronto P, 2009.

Donkin, Ellen. *Getting Into the Act: Women Playwrights in London 1776–1821*. New York: Routledge, 1995.
Duffy, Cian. "'His *Canaille* of an Audience': Thomas De Quincey and the Revolution in Reading." *Studies in Romanticism* 44.1 (2005): 7–22.
Emeljanow, Victor. *Reflecting the Audience: London Theatregoing 1840–1880*. Iowa City: U of Iowa P, 2001.
Erdman, David V. "Byron's Stage Fright: The History of His Ambition and Fear of Writing for the Stage." *English Literary History* 6.3 (1939): 219–43.
Forster, John. *Oliver Cromwell, Daniel DeFoe, Sir Richard Steele, Charles Churchill, Samuel Foote: Biographical Essays*. London: John Murray, 1860.
Galperin, William H. *The Return of the Visible in British Romanticism*. Baltimore: Johns Hopkins UP, 1993.
Gamer, Michael. "A Matter of Turf: Romanticism, Hippodrama, and Legitimate Satire." *Nineteenth-Century Contexts* 28.4 (2006): 305–44.
Garber, Frederick. *Wordsworth and the Poetry of Encounter*. Urbana: U Illinois P, 1971.
Gaull, Marilyn. "Pantomime as Satire: Mocking a Broken Charm." *The Satiric Eye: Forms of Satire in the Romantic Period*. Ed. Steven E. Jones. Basingstoke: Palgrave, 2003. 207–24.
Groseclose, Barbara. "The Incest Motif in Shelley's *The Cenci*." *Comparative Drama* 19.3 (Fall 1985): 222–39.
Harrison, Margot. "No Way for a Victim to Act?: Beatrice Cenci and the Dilemma of Romantic Performance." *Studies in Romanticism* 39 (Summer 2000): 187–211.
Hartman, Geoffrey. *Wordsworth's Poetry 1787–1814*. Cambridge: Harvard UP, 1987.
Hays, Michael. "Comedy as Being/Idea." *Studies in Romanticism* 26.2 (1987): 221–30.
Haywood, Ian. *Bloody Romanticism: Spectacular Violence and the Politics of Representation, 1776–1832*. New York: Palgrave, 2006.
Haywood, Ian, and John Haliwell. "Romantic Spectacle—An Introduction." *Romanticism on the Net* 46 (May 2007): n. pag. Web. 17 December 2008.
Hazlitt, William. *William Hazlitt: Selected Writings*. Ed. and with an introduction by Jon Cook. Oxford: Oxford UP, 1991.
Heffernan, James A. W. "Wordsworth's London: The Imperial Monster." *Studies in Romanticism* 37 (Fall 1998): 421–43.
Hertz, Neil. "The Notion of Blockage in the Literature of the Sublime." *The End of the Line: Essays on Psychoanalysis and the Sublime*. New York: Columbia UP, 1985.
Hoagwood, Terence. "Elizabeth Inchbald, Joanna Baillie and Revolutionary Representation in the 'Romantic' Period." *Rebellious Hearts: Women*

Writers and the French Revolution. Ed. Adriana Craciun and Kari E. Lokke. Albany, NY: State U of New York P, 2001. 293.316.

Hogle, Jerrold E. *Shelley's Process: Radical Transference and the Development of His Major Works.* New York: Oxford UP, 1988.

Hughes, Leo. *The Drama's Patrons: A Study of the Eighteenth-Century London Audience.* Austin: U of Texas P, 1971.

Hunt, Leigh. *Leigh Hunt's Dramatic Criticism, 1808–1831.* Ed. Lawrence Huston Houtchens and Carolyn Washburn Houtchens. New York: Columbia UP, 1949.

Hunt, Lynn. *The Family Romance of the French Revolution.* Berkeley: U of California P, 1992.

Inchbald, Elizabeth. *The Massacre.* Ed. with an introduction by Paula R. Backscheider. 2 vols. New York: Garland, 1980.

Jacobus, Mary. *Romanticism, Writing, and Sexual Difference.* Oxford: Clarendon Press, 1989.

Jameson, Fredric. *Political Unconscious.* Ithaca: Cornell UP, 1982.

Jenkins, Annibel. *I'll Tell You What: The Life of Elizabeth Inchbald.* Lexingon: U of Kentucky P, 2003.

Jewett, William. *Fatal Autonomy: Romantic Drama and the Rhetoric of Agency.* Ithaca: Cornell UP, 1997.

Johnston, Kenneth R. *The Hidden Wordsworth: Poet, Lover, Rebel, Spy.* New York: Norton, 1998.

Kant, Immanuel. *The Critique of Judgment. Contextualizing Aesthetics: From Plato to Lyotard.* Ed. H. Gene Blocker and Jennifer M. Jeffers. Belmont: Wadsworth, 1999.

Keats, John. *Letters of John Keats.* Ed. Hyder Rollins. 2 vols. Cambridge: Harvard UP, 1958.

Keen, Paul. *The Crisis of Literature in the 1790s: Print Culture and the Public Sphere.* New York: Cambridge UP, 1999.

Kernan, Alvin. *Printing Technology, Letters and Samuel Johnson.* Princeton: Princeton UP, 1987.

Klancher, Jon. *The Making of English Reading Audiences, 1790–1832.* Madison: U of Wisconsin P, 1987.

Knapp, Stephen. *Personification and the Sublime: Milton to Coleridge.* Cambridge: Harvard UP, 1985.

Lamb, Charles. *The Complete Works and Letters of Charles Lamb.* New York: Bennett A. Cerf, 1935.

Lansdown, Richard. *Byron's Historical Dramas.* Oxford: Clarendon Press, 1992.

Leacroft, Richard. *The Development of the English Playhouse.* Ithaca: Cornell UP, 1973.

Liu, Alan. *Wordsworth: The Sense of History.* Stanford: Stanford UP, 1989.

Lockridge, Laurence. "Justice in *The Cenci*." *Wordsworth Circle* 19.2 (1988): 95–98.
Lyotard, Jean-François. "The Sublime and the Avant-Garde." *Contextualizing Aesthetics: From Plato to Lyotard*. Ed. H. Gene Blocker and Jennifer M. Jeffers. Belmont: Wadsworth, 1999.
Mallinick, Daniella. "Sublime Heroism and *The Wrongs of Women*: Passion, Reason, Agency." *European Romantic Review* 18.1 (2007): 1–27.
Manning, Peter J. "Reading Wordsworth's Revisions: *Othello* and the Drowned Man." *Reading Romantics: Text and Context*. Oxford: Oxford UP, 1990.
Manvell, Roger. *Elizabeth Inchbald: A Biographical Study*. Lanham: UP of America, 1972.
Marshall, David. "The Eye-Witnesses of *The Borderers*." *Studies in Romanticism* 27.3 (Fall 1988): 391–98.
———. *The Figure of Theater: Shaftesbury, Defoe, Adam Smith and George Eliot*. New York: Columbia UP, 1986.
Marshall, L. E. "'Words Are Things': Byron and the Prophetic Efficacy of Language." *Studies in English Literature, 1500–1900* 25.4 (Autumn 1985): 801–22.
Mayer, David, III. *Harlequin in his Element: The English Pantomime 1806–1836*. Cambridge: Harvard UP, 1969.
McCalman, Iain. "The Virtual Infernal: Philippe de Loutherbourg, William Beckford and the Spectacle of the Sublime." *Romanticism on the Net* 46 (May 2007): n. pag.17 December 2008.
McKee, Kenneth. "Foreword." *Scenarios of the Commedia dell'Arte: Flaminio Scala's Il teatro delle favole rappresentative*. Ed. and trans. Henry F. Salerno. New York: New York UP, 1967.
Meisenhelder, Susan E. *Wordsworth's Informed Reader: Structures of Experience in his Poetry*. Nashville: Vanderbilt UP, 1988.
Menand, Louis. "Introduction." *The Best American Essays 2004*. Boston: Houghton Mifflin, 2004. xiv–xviii.
Moody, Jane. "'Fine Word, Legitimate!': Toward a Theatrical History of Romanticism." *Texas Studies in Literature and Language* 38.3–4 (1996): 223–44.
———. *Illegitimate Theatre in London, 1770–1840*. Cambridge: Cambridge UP, 2000.
Mulrooney, Jonathan. "Keats in the Company of Kean." *Studies in Romanticism* 42.2 (Summer 2003): 227–50.
———. "Reading Theatre: 1730–1830." *The Cambridge Companion to British Theatre 1730–1830*. Ed. Jane Moody and Daniel O'Quinn. Cambridge: Cambridge UP, 2007.

Murphy, Peter T. "Impersonation and Authorship in Romantic Britain." *English Literary History* 59.3 (1992): 625–49.

Nicoll, Alardyce. *The Garrick Stage.* Athens: U of Georgia P, 1980.

———. *A History of English Drama 1660–1900.* 5 vols. Cambridge: Cambridge UP, 1930–37.

Nielsen, Wendy C. "A Tragic Farce: Revolutionary Women in Elizabeth Inchbald's *The Massacre* and European Drama." *European Romantic Review* 17.3 (July 2006): 265–74.

Nuss, Melynda. "'The Gory Head Rolls Down the Giants' Steps!': The Return of the Physical in Byron's *Marino Faliero.*" *European Romantic Review* 12.2 (Spring 2001): 226–36.

O'Brien, John. *Harlequin Britain: Pantomime and Entertainment, 1690–1760.* Baltimore: Johns Hopkins UP, 2004.

———. "Pantomime." *The Cambridge Companion to British Theatre 1730–1830.* Ed. Jane Moody and Daniel O'Quinn. Cambridge: Cambridge UP, 2007.

O'Quinn, Daniel J. "Elizabeth Inchbald's *The Massacre*: Tragedy, Violence and the Network of Political Fantasy." *British Women Playwrights around 1800.* 1 June 1999. 8 pars. http://www.etang.umontreal.ca/bwp1800/essays/oquinn_massacre.html.

———. "Scissors and Needles: Inchbald's *Wives as They Were, Maids as They Are* and the Governance of Sexual Exchange." *Theatre Journal* 51 (1999): 105–25.

———. *Staging Governance: Theatrical Imperialism in London, 1770–1800.* Baltimore: Johns Hopkins UP, 2005.

Otto, Peter. "Between the Virtual and the Actual: Robert Barker's Panorama of London and the Multiplication of the Real in Late Eighteenth-Century London." *Romanticism on the Net* 46 (May 2007): n. pag. 22 December 2008.

Ozouf, Mona. *Festivals and the French Revolution.* Trans. Alan Sheridan. Cambridge: Harvard UP, 1988.

Paine, Thomas. *The Policital Works of Thomas Paine.* Chicago: Belford, Clarke and Co., 1887.

Parker, Reeve. "In Some Sort Seeing with My Proper Eyes': Wordsworth and the Spectacles of Paris." *Studies in Romanticism* 27.3 (Fall 1988): 369–90.

———. "Reading Wordsworth's Power: Narrative and Usurpation in *The Borderers.*" *English Literary History* 54 (1987): 299–331.

Pascoe, Judith. *Romantic Theatricality: Gender, Poetry, and Spectatorship.* Ithaca: Cornell UP, 1997.

Paulson, Ronald. *Representations of Revolution.* New Haven: Yale UP, 1983.

Peake, Richard Brinsley. *Memoirs of the Colman Family, including their Correspondence with the Most Distinguished Personages of their Time.* 2 vols. London: T. Brettell, 1841.
Phelan, Peggy. *Unmarked: The Politics of Performance.* London: Routledge, 1993.
Potkay, Adam. "Wordsworth and the Ethics of Things." *Publications of the Modern Language Association* 123.2 (March 2008): 390–404.
Purinton, Marjean. *Romantic Ideology Unmasked: The Mentally Constructed Tyrannies in Dramas of William Wordsworth, Lord Byron, Percy Shelley, and Joanna Baille.* Newark: U of Delaware P, 1994.
———. "Theatricalized Bodies and Spirits: Gothic as Performance in Romantic Drama." *Gothic Studies: An International Journal of Criticism, Theory, History, and Cultural Studies* 3/2 (August 2001): 134–55.
———. "Women's Sovereignty on Trial: Joanna Baillie's Comedy 'The Tryal' as Metatheatrics." *Women in British Romantic Theatre: Drama, Performance and Society 1790–1840.* Ed. Catherine Burroughs. Cambridge: Cambridge UP, 2000. 132–60.
Richardson, Alan. *A Mental Theater: Poetic Drama and Consciousness in the Romantic Age.* University Park: Pennsylvania State UP, 1988.
———. "A Neural Theatre." *Joanna Baillie, Romantic Dramatist: Critical Essays.* Ed. Thomas C. Crochunis. London: Routledge, 2004. 130–45.
Russell, Gillian. *The Theatres of War: Performance, Politics and Society, 1793–1815.* Oxford: Clarendon Press, 1995.
Rzepka, Charles J. "*Bang-Up!* Theatricality and the 'Diphrelatic Art' in De Quincey's *English Mail-Coach.*" *Nineteenth-Century Prose* 28.1 (2001): 75–101.
———. "The 'Dark Problem' of Greek Tragedy: Sublimated Violence in De Quincey." *The Wordsworth Circle* 29.2 (1998): 114–20.
Scarry, Elaine. *The Body in Pain: The Making and Unmaking of the World.* New York: Oxford UP, 1985.
Schiller, Friedrich. *The Robbers and Wallenstein.* Trans. F. J. Lamport. London: Penguin Classics, 1979.
Scott, Sir Walter. *Periodical Criticism by Sir Walter Scott.* Edinburgh: Robert Cadell, 1835.
Sedgwick, Eve Kosofsky. *Epistemology of the Closet.* Berkeley: U of California P, 1990.
Shakespeare, William. *Othello.* Ed. M. R. Ridley. London: Routledge, 1958.
Shelley, Percy Bysshe. *Shelley's Poetry and Prose.* Ed. Donald H. Reiman and Neil Fraistat. New York: Norton, 2002.
Silverman, Kaja. *Male Subjectivity at the Margins.* New York: Routledge, 1992.
Simpson, Erik. *Literary Minstrelsy, 1770–1830.* Basingstoke: Palgrave, 2008.

Simpson, Michael. *Closet Performances: Political Exhibition and Prohibition in the Dramas of Byron and Shelley*. Stanford: Stanford UP, 1998.
Siskin, Clifford. "VR Machine: Romanticism and the Physical." *European Romantic Review* 12.2 (Spring 2001): 158–64.
———. *The Work of Writing: Literature and Social Change in Britain 1700–1830*. Baltimore: Johns Hopkins UP, 1998.
Stafford, Barbara. *Body Criticism: Imaging the Unseen in Enlightenment Art and Medicine*. Cambridge: MIT Press, 1991.
States, Bert O. *Great Reckonings in Little Rooms: On the Phenomenology of Theater*. Berkeley: U of California P, 1985.
St. Clair, William. *The Reading Nation in the Romantic Period*. Cambridge: Cambridge UP, 2004.
Stewart, Susan. *On Longing: Narratives of the Miniature, the Gigantic, the Souvenir, the Collection*. Durham: Duke UP, 1993.
Strand, Ginger, and Sarah Zimmerman. "Finding an Audience: Beatrice Cenci, Percy Shelley, and the Stage." *European Romantic Review* 6.2 (Winter 1996): 246–68.
Swann, Karen. "The Sublime and the Vulgar." *College English* 52.1 (1990): 7–20.
Swetnam, Ford T., Jr. "The Satiric Voices of *The Prelude*." *Bicentenary Wordsworth Studies in Memory of John Alban Finch*. Ed. Jonathan Wordsworth, Ephim Fogel, and Beth Darlington. Ithaca: Cornell UP, 1970.
Taborski, Boleslaw. *Byron and the Theatre*. Salzburg: Institut Fur Englische Sprache und Literatur, 1972.
Watkins, Daniel P. *A Materialist Critique of English Romantic Drama*. Gainesville: U of Florida P, 1993.
Whitaker, Thomas R. "Reading the Unreadable, Acting the Unactable." *Studies in Romanticism* 27.3 (Fall 1988): 355–68.
Wolfson, Susan. "'A Problem Few Dare Imitate': Sardanapalus and 'Effeminate Character.'" *English Literary History* 58.4 (Winter 1991): 867–902.
———. *The Questioning Presence: Wordsworth, Keats, and the Interrogative Mode in Romantic Poetry*. Ithaca: Cornell UP, 1986.
Wood, Gillen D'Arcy. *The Shock of the Real: Romanticism and Visual Culture, 1760–1860*. New York: Palgrave, 2001.
Wordsworth, Jonathan. *William Wordsworth: The Borders of Vision*. Oxford: Clarendon Press, 1982.
Wordsworth, William. *The Borderers*. Ed. Robert Osborn. Ithaca: Cornell UP, 1982.
———. *The Prelude: 1799, 1808, 1850*. Ed. Jonathan Wordsworth, M. H. Abrams, and Stephen Gill. New York: Norton, 1979.
———. *William Wordsworth*. Ed. Stephen Gill. Oxford: Oxford UP, 1984.
Wordsworth, William, and Samuel Taylor Coleridge. *Lyrical Ballads*. 2nd ed. Ed. W. J. B. Owen. Oxford: Oxford UP, 1969.

Index

Adelphi, the, 6
Aeschylus, 6
    Prometheus Bound, 129–31
Anderson, Emily Hodgson, 5
animal performers, 1–2, 6, 32, 151, 153–59, 169–70
    in pantomime, 18
Arnold, Samuel, 8
Astley's, 6
Austen, Jane, 2

Backscheider, Paula, 36, 37
Baillie, Joanna, 9, 33–34
    Count Basil, 173
    introduction to *Plays on the Passions*, 9, 33–34
    reputation, 33–34
Bannister, John, 24
Benjamin, Walter, 154, 172
Betty, William Henry West. *See* infant Roscius
Bewell, Alan, 64, 67
Blackwoods, 5
Blake, William, 87
Bolter, Jay David, 172
Bolton, Betsy, 3, 36–37
Broadview Anthology of Romantic Drama, 23
Bronfen, Elisabeth, 42
Bronson, Bertrand, 5
Burke, Edmund, 75, 103–7, 151–57, 170, 181n21, 182n4, 182n6
Burney, Frances, 5

Burroughs, Catherine, 36
Burwick, Frederick, 17, 178n13
Byron, George Gordon, Lord, 8, 10–11, 33–36, 44–58, 179n13
    Childe Harold's Pilgrimage, 44
    Don Juan, 8, 33, 44–46
    Drury Lane Theatre, managing board, 35
    Marino Faliero, Doge of Venice, 33–36, 44, 46–52, 53, 54
    "mental theatre," 34, 37
    opening address, 1812 reopening of Drury Lane, 24, 45
    Prophecy of Dante, 44
    Sardanapalus, 48, 53–58, 173
    "So We'll Go No More A-Roving," 172
    theories of language, 44–46

Carlson, Julie, 140
Carroll, Lewis, 89
Cavanagh, John, 166, 169
censorship, 36, 42–43, 50
Christensen, Jerome, 45, 46–47, 49, 50, 55, 179n19, 180n25
Cibber, Colley, 7, 9, 173, 176
closet drama, 3, 4, 9–11, 13, 15, 33–58, 137, 173–74, 180n22, 182n5
clown, 16–21, 26–31, 101, 159
    See also pantomime
Coburg, the, 6

Coleridge, Samuel Taylor, 2, 4, 5, 34, 78, 101, 106, 172
  conversation poems, 2
  "Eolian Harp," 172
  lectures on Shakespeare, 78
  "This Lime-Tree Bower My Prison," 2, 172
  Remorse, 4
  Rime of the Ancient Mariner, 171, 176
Colman, George
  Blue Beard, 151, 155, 156–59
comedy, 13, 14, 36, 80, 101, 154, 166–67
Cooke, Michael G., 64, 67
Covent Garden Theatre, 1, 6–7, 57, 151, 181n19
  animal acts, 18, 151, 153–59, 170
  Dibdin, Thomas, 23
  pantomimes at, 16, 17, 18, 20, 22, 23
  Wordsworth, William, rejection of *The Borderers*, 11, 61, 66, 84, 86, 87
Cox, Jeffrey N., 23, 129, 174
Crochunis, Thomas, 33, 44

De Loutherbourg, Philip James, 151
De Quincey, Thomas, 11, 151–53, 159–65, 166, 168, 173
  Antigone, review of, 159–64
  English Mail-Coach, 159, 163
  rhetoric, 14, 15
  and pantomime, 14, 15, 159
  "Theory of Greek Tragedy," 159–64
Dibdin, Thomas, 13–14, 18, 23–32, 179n13
  Harlequin and Humpo, 13–14, 23–32
Dick, Alexander, 174

Dickens, 20
Diderot, Denis, 140
distance, 1–7, 9–10, 11, 14, 17, 21, 25, 30, 50, 59, 87–89, 93, 105, 113, 125, 129, 143, 145, 161, 165, 173
Drury Lane Theatre, 1, 6–7, 29, 178n8, 179n13, 181n19
  animals at, 156
  Byron on the managing board, 35
  Dibdin, Thomas, 23
  1812 reopening, 23–24, 35, 45, 50, 56–57
  pantomimes at, 16, 17, 20, 23, 25
  Shakespeare Jubilee, 23
  size, 24, 178n16
Duffy, Cian, 163

Edgeworth, Maria, 5
Eliot, T. S., 175
Esterhammer, Angela, 174
farce, 15, 23, 36–37, 39, 42, 80
Female Spectator, The, 60
French Revolution, 36, 42, 68, 79, 104–5, 107, 166
  performances and festivals, 60, 66, 104–5, 180n4

Galperin, William, 102–3, 109, 181n22
Gamer, Michael, 23, 151, 152, 155
Garber, Frederick, 98
Garrick, David, 6–7, 13, 24
Gaull, Marilyn, 15
Godwin, William, 35–36, 39, 43–44, 72–73, 75
Grimaldi, Joseph, 18, 19, 20
Groseclose, Barbara, 141
Grusin, Richard, 172
Gulliver, Lemuel, 21

Harlequin, 14–17, 26–31, 101
  harlequinade, 17–19, 22, 25–26, 30–32, 160, 173
  De Quincey and, 14, 15, 160
  shift from frame story to harliquinade, 17
  See also pantomime
Harlequin and Humpo, 13–14, 23–32, 173
Harrison, Margot, 140
Hartman, Geoffrey, 93–94, 97
Haymarket Theatre, 1–3, 6–7, 8, 9, 177n3
Haywood, Eliza, 5
Hazlitt, William, 11, 151–53, 165–69, 173
  "On Dramatic Poetry," 166–67
  "On the Indian Jugglers," 165–70
  "On Modern Comedy," 167
Heffernan, James A. W., 106, 108
Hoagwood, Terence, 36
Hogle, Jerrold, 120, 140–41
Holcroft, 35–36
Hunt, Leigh, 7, 11, 151–59, 163–65, 168, 173
  circle, 129
  and pantomime, 13, 15–16, 19

Inchbald, Elizabeth, 5, 10, 34–44, 58
infant Roscius, 107

Jewett, William, 46
Johnson, Samuel, 46, 60
Johnston, Kenneth, 59, 65, 69, 75, 100

Kant, Immanuel, 151–55
Kean, Edmund, 57
  and Keats, 5
Keats, John, 59
  and drama, 5, 34

Eve of St. Agnes, 2
  and Kean, 5
Keen, Paul, 174
Kemble, John Philip, 8, 24, 156, 179n12
Kernan, Alvin, 174–75
Klancher, Jon, 5
Knapp, Stephen, 96, 98

Lamb, Charles, 34, 37, 42, 178–79n8, 181n19
Lawrence, W. J., 8
"legitimate" theatre, 1–3, 6, 9, 13–14, 20, 23–24, 29–30, 102, 151–52, 168
Lewis, Matthew G.
  Timour the Tartar, 155
"literature," 3–5, 85, 162, 167, 174–76
Liu, Alan, 74, 114

Manning, Peter, 78
Marshall, David, 81
Marshall, L. E., 44–45, 179n18
Mayer, David, 15, 163
McCallman, Iain, 152
Meisenhelder, Susan Edwards, 61–62
melodrama, 15, 23, 101, 129, 160
Menand Louis, 174–76
Moody, Jane, 3, 16, 18, 21, 22, 29, 102, 151
Mulrooney, Jonathan, 5

Napoleon, 19, 21
Nicoll, Alardyce, 7
Nielsen, Wendy, 42

O'Brien, John, 14, 15, 27, 178n5
Olympic, the, 6
O'Quinn, Daniel, 36, 39, 40, 42
Otto, Peter, 163

Paine, Thomas, 151–52
panoramas and dioramas, 9, 16, 64, 99–105, 111–12, 114, 151, 163
pantomime, 10, 13–32, 112–13, 129, 151, 173
 animals in, 18
 "big heads," 20
 clown, 18, 19, 21, 26, 27–31
 and 1812 reopening of Drury Lane, 24
 exoticism, 16, 18
 relationship to fairs and festivals, 15
 scenery, 16, 27–32
 shift from frame story to harliquinade, 17
 social class in, 27
 transformations, 26, 28–30
 See also clown; Harlequin; harlequinade
Parker, Reeve, 64, 65, 68, 70, 72, 80–81
Pascoe, Judith, 36–37, 99
Potkay, Adam, 45, 51
Price, Richard, 104–5
provincial theatres, 6, 13
Purinton, Marjean, 36

Richardson, Alan, 33
Romanticism, 4, 14, 116, 171–76
Rzepka, Charles, 159, 164

Sadler's Wells, 6, 101–3, 151, 156
 Dibdin, Thomas, 23
 pantomimes in, 16, 18, 21
Scarry, Elaine, 132–33
Schiller, Friedrich
 Die Rauber, 77, 80
Schlegel, A. W., 16, 17
Scott, Sir Walter, 4, 7
Sedgwick, Eve Kosofsky, 62

Shakespeare, 1, 2, 6, 13, 23, 34, 37, 78, 159, 160, 178–9n8
 King Lear, 122
 Macbeth, 64
 Othello (and *Borderers*), 64, 67–68, 70–71, 78, 124, 180n7
Shelley, Percy, 5, 11, 34, 76, 119–49, 173
 "Adonais," 148–49
 Alastor, 120–29, 133, 137, 143, 144
 The Cenci, 34, 120, 138–45, 147
 Defence of Poetry, 120–29, 137
 Julian and Maddalo, 131
 "Masque of Anarchy," 148
 Prometheus Unbound, 5, 34, 76, 119–20, 129–39, 141, 142, 144, 145–48
 "Sensitive Plant, The" 119–20, 148–49
 "Triumph of Life," 148
Siddons, Sarah, 24, 169
Silverman, Kaja, 131, 135
Simpson, Michael, 45, 131
singing, 175–76
Siskin, Clifford, 174–75
Southey, Robert, 44
spectacle, 3, 10, 11, 20, 22, 25–32, 35, 40–42, 51, 56–57, 60, 66, 85–86, 98–99, 102–5, 109, 111–12, 114–15, 120, 151–70, 173
 panoramas and dioramas, 16, 102–3, 111–12, 151
Spectator, The, 60
spectatorship, 40–43, 57, 59–60, 62–64, 66, 79, 81–82, 84–89, 94–95, 98–115, 129–30, 133, 137, 155, 158–59, 165–70
States, Burt, 153–57
St. Clair, William, 14
Stendahl, 16

Stewart, Susan, 21
Strand Opera House, 8–9
sublime, 11, 59, 122, 153–70, 173
Surrey, the, 6, 23
Swann, Karen, 153, 156

telegraphs, 1–2
theatre
  architectural layout, 7, 24, 66, 102
  fairs, 15, 105
  and literary tradition, 6–7
  "minor" theatres, 23
  and physicality, 6–7, 37–44, 103, 171–76
  scenery, 16, 22, 28–32
  size, 7, 24, 66
  and social class, 6–7, 27, 153, 162–63
  street theatre, 9, 15, 25, 28–30
  unity of time, place and action, 16–17
  variety of types, 9, 14, 25
Tomlins, F. G.
  A Brief View of the English Drama, 8, 66
Tooke, Horne, 44–45, 179n18
tragedy, 14, 36, 40, 74, 122, 129, 138, 139, 144, 159–64, 166

Walpole, Horace, 40
Wolfson, Susan, 87, 93
women in theatre, 5, 36–37, 107–8

Wood, Gillen D'Arcy, 151
Wordsworth, Jonathan, 98, 100
Wordsworth, William, 2, 4, 5, 8, 11, 33–34, 59–117, 151, 172, 174, 176
  attitude towards drama, 4, 33–34, 61–117, 151
  The Borderers, 60, 61–85, 86, 87, 115
  "Composed Upon Westminster Bridge," 113–16
  Descriptive Sketches, 61, 100
  "Discharged Soldier, The," 60, 86, 87–90, 95
  early career, 61
  "An Evening Walk," 61, 100
  "Expostulation and Reply," 59
  "I Wandered Lonely," 59, 113
  "Ode: Intimations of Immortality," 59
  Peter Bell, 96
  preface to *Lyrical Ballads*, 8, 59, 85–87, 116, 174
  Prelude, 59, 79, 85–86, 87–90, 98–115
  "Ruined Cottage, The," 65
  "Salisbury Plain," 61
  "Simon Lee," 86
  "Solitary Reaper, The," 59, 113
  "Tables Turned, The," 86
  "Thorn, The," 60, 86, 90–98
  Tintern Abbey, 2, 59, 60, 65, 172
  "We Are Seven," 86

GPSR Compliance

The European Union's (EU) General Product Safety Regulation (GPSR) is a set of rules that requires consumer products to be safe and our obligations to ensure this.

If you have any concerns about our products, you can contact us on

ProductSafety@springernature.com

In case Publisher is established outside the EU, the EU authorized representative is:

Springer Nature Customer Service Center GmbH
Europaplatz 3
69115 Heidelberg, Germany

www.ingramcontent.com/pod-product-compliance
Lightning Source LLC
LaVergne TN
LVHW051912060526
838200LV00004B/103